Flash Developm
Android Cookbook

ver 90 recipes to build exciting Android applications with
ash, Flex, and AIR

Joseph Labrecque

PUBLISHING

BIRMINGHAM - MUMBAI

Flash Development for Android Cookbook

First published: June 2011

Production Reference: 1100611

Published by Packt Publishing Ltd.
32 Lincoln Road
Olton
Birmingham, B27 6PA, UK.

ISBN 978-1-849691-42-0

www.packtpub.com

Cover Image by Ed Maclean (edmaclean@gmail.com)

Credits

Author
Joseph Labrecque

Reviewers
Fabio Biondi

Sean Moore

Leonardo Risuleo

Acquisition Editor
Wilson D'souza

Development Editor
Neha Mallik

Technical Editors
Shreerang Deshpande

Merwine Machado

Project Coordinator
Jovita Pinto

Proofreader
Aaron Nash

Indexer
Monica Ajmera

Production Coordinator
Alwin Roy

Cover Work
Alwin Roy

Foreword

Mobile is as HOT as a Habanero Chili!

It's taken a few years, but mobile and devices are finally hot. How hot? Like biting into a freshly ripe, raw, Habanero chili kind-a-HOT. Can you taste the virtual heat on your virtual tongue yet?

Yowza! The point I'm trying to get across is this. The broader mobile and device industry has finally gone mainstream. Why else would you be reading this right now? Intellectual curiosity? Well, maybe, but I'm wagering much more likely, because you want to learn about the amazing and wonderful world of mobile, today!

Yes, folks, I think you'll agree almost 100 percent that mobile is finally hip, cool, sleek, and dare I say it: **glitzy**. Unless you been living in some proverbial cave for the last few years, you know this for a fact! Like it or not, our modern societies now operate in a world dominated with internet connected small-screen pocket-sized Smartphone, e-readers, mid-screen sized Tablets, and large screen digital TVs, and countless other gadgets and gizmos in all their bountiful and lavish form factors. In fact, with all these devices and platforms, recently, it occurs to me as if we're all at some gigantic virtual party, and there's one huge smorgasbord on the dinner table for developers to dig into. Of course, I'm sure you'll agree the Android dish is one of the main courses you are eyeing to gobble down, first, right?

As an early adopter to the mobile industry, and one of the brave souls who pioneered work with Flash and other early mobile technologies on various mobile and device platforms over the years, it gives me great satisfaction to see what I had been advocating has finally come to fruition. Yes! That proverbial egg timer has finally rung, and the apps are flying out of the oven. Careful, boy are they RED HOT!

It strikes me that with all the excitement in developer kitchen these days, it feels a bit like the explosive growth of the early days of the World Wide Web back in the 90's. There are some changes now, though. One of the big changes now, is that we now have all these form factors with various screens instead of those clunky desktop PCs and CRTs!

Smart phones and other devices have turned our cell phones into our pocket sized computers. Yes, I said computers! Like it or not, for much of the modern world, our personal computers of today, now fit in our pockets, and they are part of our daily lives and routines as we move through the world.

Mmmmmm...Yummy! Pocket-sized Android device treats for desert, anyone?!

Android with a dash of Flash

So, how does Adobe fit into all this? Well, Adobe has been hard at work over the past few years refining their suite of tools and products to help with the growing challenge of allowing designers and developers to design, develop, and deploy compelling mobile and device experiences, faster, better, and easier. There is no shortage of exciting and compelling stream of news and innovations coming from Adobe's Engineering 'kitchen' these days as I write this passage!

Adobe Flash, Flex, and AIR have been retooled, retrofitted, and enhanced to make it significantly easier for existing Flash and Flex professionals to start leveraging Adobe Creative Suite and other tools to target not only Android but also OS, BlackBerry Tablet OS, and other mobile and device platforms soon to come. To me, the Flash Platform is like a fork utensil. When it's appropriate, by all means use it to your advantage, especially when trying to get food into your mouth!

The general idea of write once, tweak, and deploy to as many supported targets as possible is a very real; and attainable goal when you look at what Adobe can provide these days. Whether you're a long-time Flash veteran new to the mobile aspects developing for Android, or whether you're a seasoned native Android developer curious about the Flash Platform; you'll find recipes to help quench your thirst and fill your belly. All you have to do is give it a try and see the results!

This book will help you do that! So "What's Cooking" in this Book?

As a famous chef might say in his famous cooking shows in the US, "BAM"!

In this title, Joseph takes you through some recipes on how to leverage your existing Flash and ActionScript skills to build for Android Platform. I have gotten the unique pleasure of seeing some of the early material. Strap on your coding apron and get ready to bake some code recipes very soon, my fellow readers!

In this title, Joseph will explain more than one hundred examples about how to dealing with things like multi-touch and gesture input, accessing GPS and location features, leveraging the accelerometer, as well as tying into audio and visual inputs such as camera and microphone on mobile devices. He'll also cover working with media such as images, video and audio, and handling device layout and scaling, plus more tasty morsels of mobile development goodness using ActionScript for AIR using Flash and Flex based mobile applications on the Android Platform. Although this 'cookbook' assumes you know at least some ActionScript and Flash basics, most will be able to pick up much of the code and start running with it, given it's in a nice, juicy, step by step, recipe style format. You should be able to apply these code snacks to your favorite designer or developer workflow whether you're using Flash Builder, Flash IDE, or any other piece of popular Flash authoring environment out there.

Well, are you hungry yet? Yes? Good! Well, time to get your inner-baker on, and cook some flashy applications! After all, you have all those millions of hungry Android consumers to feed with your tasty, finger licking good, creations. The oven is pre-heated, now. Joseph's waiting for you in his coding kitchen. He's got lots of little snacks for you to try out. Let's meet him in his kitchen and start cooking up some Android based recipes using ActionScript, shall we?

P.S. Sorry if I made you physically hungry or thirsty while reading this foreword. Why not grab a beer, or a red bull.

Also, why not put in that phone order in for pizza delivery? Now's the perfect time before you dig in!

Bon Appétit and happy coding!

Scott Janousek,
Mobile and Device Technologist,
Gadget Geek and CEO/Founder of Hooken Mobile

About the Author

Joseph Labrecque is primarily employed by the University of Denver as a senior interactive software developer specializing in the Adobe Flash Platform, where he produces innovative academic toolsets for both traditional desktop environments and emerging mobile spaces. Alongside this principal role, he often serves as adjunct faculty, communicating upon a variety of Flash Platform solutions and general web design and development subjects.

In addition to his accomplishments in higher education, Joseph is the proprietor of Fractured Vision Media, LLC; a digital media production company, technical consultancy, and distribution vehicle for his creative works. He is founder and sole abiding member of the dark ambient recording project 'An Early Morning Letter, Displaced' whose releases have received international award nominations and underground acclaim.

Joseph has contributed to a number of respected community publications as an article writer and video tutorialist. He regularly speaks at user group meetings and industry conferences such as Adobe MAX, FITC, and D2WC. In 2010, he received an Adobe Impact Award in recognition of his outstanding contribution to the education community. He has served as an Adobe Education Leader since 2008 and is also a 2011 Adobe Community Professional.

Visit him on the web at `http://memoryspiral.com/`.

Special thanks to my wife Leslie, and to our daughters; Paige and Lily, for bearing with me during the production of this work.

About the Reviewers

Fabio Biondi is a freelancer living in the north east of Italy. Since 2003 he deals almost exclusively with the Adobe Flash Platform technologies.

He is an Adobe Certified Instructor (ACI) in Flex, AIR, Flash Professional, Flash Catalyst, and FlashLite (ACE) and lately he has devoted time and resources to the development of mobile and social networking applications.

Fabio runs a blog (`www.fabiobiondi.com/blog`) and a YouTube Channel (`http://www.youtube.com/user/BiondiFabio`) where he provides free tutorials, scripts, and news about the latest Adobe Flash Platform technologies.

I would like to thank my girlfriend Lisa, for always supporting and encouraging me, and the Packt Publishing guys, Jovita and Wilson, for the opportunity they have given to me.

Sean Moore has been developing web applications since 1998. He's been passionate about Flash and ActionScript development for over eight years and working with Flex for over four years. He was chosen to be a Flex Developer Community Champion and an Adobe Community Professional by Adobe for his hard work and dedication to the Flash Platform Community. Sean is a certified Flash developer and also a certified Flex developer. Sean specializes in the development of Adobe AIR applications. He is the creator of the ActionScript Cheatsheets. Sean has provided development and consulting services for 2Advanced, Adobe Consulting, and Universal Mind. He's also worked with many small businesses on Flash, Flex, and AIR applications. Sean has written Flex and AIR articles for Adobe, O'Reilly, and Flash Magazine. He's provided technical authoring for Manning Publications, Addison Wesley and O'Reilly. Sean has also given presentations at various user groups on best practices for Flex development. Sean is also very interested in BCI technology and Arduino development.

I'd like to thank the author for doing such a great job and also asking me to be a technical reviewer.

Leonardo Risuleo is a designer and developer with several years experience in mobile, new media and user experience. He's a highly dedicated professional and passionate about what he does. He started back in 2003 and during these years he worked on a variety of different mobile and embedded platforms for a number of well known brands. Leo designs, prototypes, and develops mobile applications, games, widgets, and websites.

Apart from being a Flash Platform enthusiast, Leo also contributes to the Flash and mobile community as an author and blogger, and he's co-founder of the Italian 'Mobile & Devices Adobe User Group'. From 2008 to 2010, Leo had the honor to be Forum Nokia Champion—a recognition and reward program for top mobile developer worldwide.

In 2010 he formally founded Small Screen Design, a design and development studio focused on mobile design and user experience.

www.PacktPub.com

Support files, eBooks, discount offers and more

You might want to visit www.PacktPub.com for support files and downloads related to your book.

Did you know that Packt offers eBook versions of every book published, with PDF and ePub files available? You can upgrade to the eBook version at www.PacktPub.com and as a print book customer, you are entitled to a discount on the eBook copy. Get in touch with us at service@packtpub.com for more details.

At www.PacktPub.com, you can also read a collection of free technical articles, sign up for a range of free newsletters and receive exclusive discounts and offers on Packt books and eBooks.

http://PacktLib.PacktPub.com

Do you need instant solutions to your IT questions? PacktLib is Packt's online digital book library. Here, you can access, read and search across Packt's entire library of books.

Why Subscribe?

- ▶ Fully searchable across every book published by Packt
- ▶ Copy and paste, print and bookmark content
- ▶ On demand and accessible via web browser

Free Access for Packt account holders

If you have an account with Packt at www.PacktPub.com, you can use this to access PacktLib today and view nine entirely free books. Simply use your login credentials for immediate access.

Instant Updates on New Packt Books

Get notified! Find out when new books are published by following @PacktEnterprise on Twitter, or the *Packt Enterprise* Facebook page.

Table of Contents

Preface

With the ongoing explosion of the mobile Android operating system and proliferation of Android powered devices in the smart phone and tablet computing markets, this is the perfect time to explore the world of Android development using the Flash Platform. Adobe recently released statistics announcing that by the end of 2011, it is projected that more than 200 million smartphones and tablets will support Adobe AIR applications. For 2011, the company expects the mobile Flash Player to be supported on more than 132 million units worldwide. This book provides a variety of fundamental recipes exploring common needs of the mobile Android developer when utilizing these Flash Platform runtimes.

Many existing Flash application developers are excited with the prospect of building mobile applications for Android devices, but where to begin? Expand your reach into mobile application development by using this text as a guide. When possible, the recipes in this book are written using pure ActionScript 3, allowing the reader to work through each example in the tool of their choice. In some instances, we demonstrate the power and flexibility of the mobile Flex framework when dealing with specific layout and structural needs. Jump-start your experience with mobile Android through the step-by-step examples found within.

Flash Development for Android Cookbook will demonstrate a wide variety of mobile-specific examples specifically conceived to be direct and useful in the development of applications for Android devices. Everything you need to get started is included along with suggestions to further your experience with Flash, Flex, and AIR when developing mobile Android applications.

Topics covered within this book include development environment configuration, mobile project creation and conversion, the use of touch and gestures, responding to changes in location and device movement in 3D space, the capture, generation, and manipulation of images, video and audio, application layout and structure, tapping into native processes and hardware, and the manipulation of the file system and managing local application databases. The book will also cover things such as Android-specific device permissions, application optimization techniques, and the packaging and distribution options available on the mobile Android platform.

What this book covers

Chapter 1, Getting Ready to Work with Android: *Development Environment and Project Setup*, demonstrates the configuration of a number of development environments and tools which can be used in developing Flash content for mobile Android.

Chapter 2, Interaction Experience: *Multitouch, Gestures, and Other Input*, informs the reader with a variety of unique touch and gesture interactions that can be used across Flash Platform runtimes.

Chapter 3, Movement through Space: *Accelerometer and Geolocation Sensors*, empowers your applications with the ability to pinpoint a user's precise geographic location and even determine local changes in device shift and tilt through the on-board accelerometer.

Chapter 4, Visual and Audio Input: *Camera and Microphone Access*, discusses how to capture still images, video, and audio from integrated device hardware through both Flash based capture methods and while employing native camera applications.

Chapter 5, Rich Media Presentation: *Working with Images, Video, and Audio*, takes a look at a variety of media presentation mechanisms available to us on the Flash Platform including playback of progressive and streaming video, the use of Pixel Bender shaders, and even audio generation.

Chapter 6, Structural Adaptation: *Handling Device Layout and Scaling*, discusses a variety of methods we can use to gain detailed information regarding device displays, and the usage of this data when sizing and positioning visual elements along with structured layout through the mobile Flex framework.

Chapter 7, Native Interaction: *Stage WebView and URI Handlers*, demonstrates methods of utilizing native applications such as the Web browser, e-mail, SMS, Telephone, and Maps as extensions of our Flash based experience.

Chapter 8, Abundant Access: *File System and Local Database*, provides the readers with details of the steps necessary to access, open and write to file streams on the device storage, create and manage local SQLite databases, and preserve application state upon application interruption.

Chapter 9, Manifest Assurance: *Security and Android Permissions*, demonstrates the various Android Manifest permissions and provides examples of Market filtering, encrypted database support, and other security-minded techniques.

Chapter 10, Avoiding Problems: *Debugging and Resource Considerations*, looks at ways in which a developer can streamline the efficiency of an application by tapping into the device GPU, handling user interaction in responsible ways, and memory management techniques.

Chapter 11, Final Considerations: *Application Compilation and Distribution*, advises the reader on project preparation, code signing, release compilation, and distribution through the global Android Market.

What you need for this book

To make use of the recipes included in this book, you need access to software for developing Android applications with the Flash Platform. We recommend using Adobe Flash Builder 4.5, Adobe Flash Professional CS5.5, or PowerFlasher FDT 4.2 and above. These Integrated Development Environments are preferred because of their specific support of a mobile Android workflow, but you may actually use any application you prefer to write code that will be compiled for AIR for Android and deployed to mobile devices.

You will, however, need access to the following (if not using these particular IDEs):

▶ Adobe AIR SDK – for compiling your Flash applications to .APK for Android

▶ Flex 4.5 SDK – if you want to take advantage of the mobile Flex framework

The Adobe AIR SDK is included with both Flash Professional CS5.5 and Flash Builder 4.5. The Flex 4.5 SDK is included with Flash Builder 4.5. If using alternative software to develop Flash based Android applications, these SDKs can be downloaded freely from the Adobe open source website.

You will also want to be sure to have access to a device running Android 2.2 or above with AIR for Android 2.5 or above installed for demonstrating the recipes, and testing your own applications.

Who this book is for

This book contains recipes covering a variety of topics from the very simple, to those which are more advanced. If you are a seasoned Flash developer, this book will get you quickly up to speed with what is possible with Android. For those who are new to Flash, welcome to the world of visual rich, rapid application development for mobile Android devices! If you have any interest in Flash development for Android, this book has you covered.

Conventions

In this book, you will find a number of styles of text that distinguish between different kinds of information. Here are some examples of these styles, and an explanation of their meaning.

Code words in text are shown as follows: "Create a new file called `recipe1.py` to put all of this recipe's code."

A block of code is set as follows:

```
streamClient = new Object();
    streamClient.onBWDone = onTextData;
    streamClient.onTextData = onTextData;
    streamClient.onMetaData = onMetaData;
    streamClient.onCuePoint = onCuePoint;
```

New terms and important words are shown in bold. Words that you see on the screen, in menus or dialog boxes for example, appear in the text like this: "There are many choices of **IDE (Integrated Development Environment)** for developing Flash platform projects for Android devices".

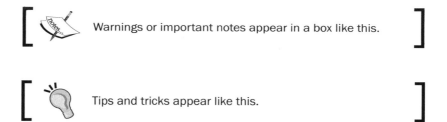

Warnings or important notes appear in a box like this.

Tips and tricks appear like this.

Reader feedback

Feedback from our readers is always welcome. Let us know what you think about this book—what you liked or may have disliked. Reader feedback is important for us to develop titles that you really get the most out of.

To send us general feedback, simply send an e-mail to `feedback@packtpub.com`, and mention the book title via the subject of your message.

If there is a book that you need and would like to see us publish, please send us a note in the **SUGGEST A TITLE** form on `www.packtpub.com` or e-mail `suggest@packtpub.com`.

If there is a topic that you have expertise in and you are interested in either writing or contributing to a book, see our author guide on `www.packtpub.com/authors`.

Customer support

Now that you are the proud owner of a Packt book, we have a number of things to help you to get the most from your purchase.

Downloading the example code

You can download the example code files for all Packt books you have purchased from your account at `http://www.PacktPub.com`. If you purchased this book elsewhere, you can visit `http://www.PacktPub.com/support` and register to have the files e-mailed directly to you.

Errata

Although we have taken every care to ensure the accuracy of our content, mistakes do happen. If you find a mistake in one of our books—maybe a mistake in the text or the code—we would be grateful if you would report this to us. By doing so, you can save other readers from frustration and help us improve subsequent versions of this book. If you find any errata, please report them by visiting `http://www.packtpub.com/support`, selecting your book, clicking on the **errata submission form** link, and entering the details of your errata. Once your errata are verified, your submission will be accepted and the errata will be uploaded on our website, or added to any list of existing errata, under the Errata section of that title. Any existing errata can be viewed by selecting your title from `http://www.packtpub.com/support`.

Piracy

Piracy of copyright material on the Internet is an ongoing problem across all media. At Packt, we take the protection of our copyright and licenses very seriously. If you come across any illegal copies of our works, in any form, on the Internet, please provide us with the location address or website name immediately so that we can pursue a remedy.

Please contact us at `copyright@packtpub.com` with a link to the suspected pirated material.

We appreciate your help in protecting our authors, and our ability to bring you valuable content.

Questions

You can contact us at `questions@packtpub.com` if you are having a problem with any aspect of the book, and we will do our best to address it.

1
Getting Ready to Work with Android: Development Environment and Project Setup

This chapter will cover the following recipes:

- ► Using Flash Professional CS5.5 to develop Android applications
- ► Targeting AIR for Android with Flash Professional CS5.5
- ► Using Flash Builder 4.5 to develop Android applications
- ► Enabling Flash Builder 4 or Flex Builder to access Flex Mobile SDKs
- ► Using Flash Builder 4 and below to develop Android applications
- ► Using Powerflasher FDT 4.2 to develop Android applications
- ► Enabling Powerflasher FDT 4.1 to access Flex Mobile SDKs
- ► Using Powerflasher FDT 4.1 and below to develop Android applications
- ► Converting a Standard Flex project to a Flex Mobile project
- ► Configuring the AIR SDK to Package AIR for Android applications on Windows
- ► Configuring the AIR SDK to Package AIR for Android Applications on Linux or Mac OS

Introduction

There are many choices of **IDE** (**Integrated Development Environment**) for developing Flash platform projects for Android devices. We will focus on a few of the most popular: Adobe Flash Professional, Adobe Flash Builder, and Powerflasher FDT. This chapter will include recipes geared to getting a new Android project started in each IDE, and making the most of what is available with regard to workflow and toolsets. You will learn how to configure each environment in order to develop for the Android operating system.

Flash Builder and FDT, along with the Flex framework have the most to offer for Android development as there is a streamlined workflow, set of controls, and containers available especially for the development of mobile Android projects using Adobe AIR for Android as a development platform.

Flash Professional provides some workflow tools, but the main benefit lies in potential familiarity with the environment, and the generation of projects not tied to the Flex framework. This IDE is often used for game development because of its open nature.

For the purists or users of alternative IDEs, it is also possible to generate Android applications through a command line interface using the free AIR SDK tools.

Using Flash Professional CS5.5 to develop Android applications

Flash Professional is a good choice for building Android applications that are more lightweight than their Flex-based counterparts. There is not as robust a workflow in the case of Flash Professional when compared to what is included with an IDE such as Flash Builder, but depending upon the application being developed, it may be the better tool for the job.

Flash Professional CS5.5 includes everything needed to target Android already baked in!

How to do it...

Setting up an AIR for Android project in Flash Professional CS5.5 is very direct:

1. We will first create a new project by choosing **AIR for Android** under the **Create New** section of the **Flash Professional** welcome screen:

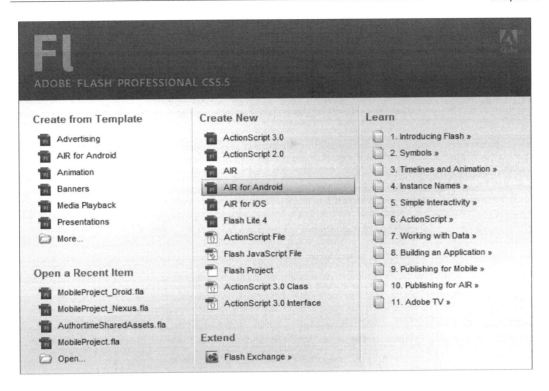

2. We can then verify that we are targeting AIR for Android by taking a look at the document properties under the **Properties** panel:

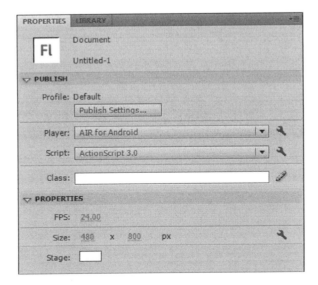

3. We can also modify existing Flash documents to target Android by selecting **AIR for Android** as the **Player** option.

4. Now, simply build your Flash project as you normally would. Adobe has made the process of targeting Android with Flash Professional CS5.5 absolutely painless.

How it works...

With Flash Professional CS5.5, we have more compiler options available to us than ever before. Taking the steps outlined in the preceding section will ensure that your project is capable of targeting AIR for Android in place of the desktop Flash Player or AIR for desktop by adding a number of Android-specific compiler options to our publish settings.

There's more...

If developing for the mobile Flash Player for Android, we will not need to configure anything for the AIR runtime. To target Flash Player, we must simply keep in mind the limitations and differences inherent to mobile Android devices.

Targeting AIR for Android with Flash Professional CS5.5

Flash Professional is a good choice for building Android applications that are more lightweight than their Flex-based counterparts. There is not as robust a workflow in the case of Flash Professional when compared to what is included with an IDE such as Flash Builder, but depending upon the application being developed; it may be the better tool for the job.

How to do it...

There are two ways of targeting AIR for Android with Flash Professional:

1. Firstly, create a new project by choosing **AIR for Android** under the **Create from Template** section of the Flash Professional welcome screen:

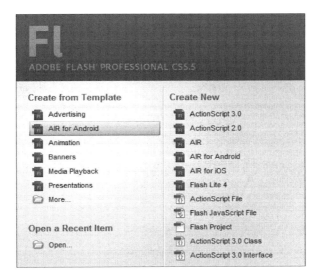

2. This will present a choice of several templates targeting **AIR for Android**. Choose the appropriate template for your device:

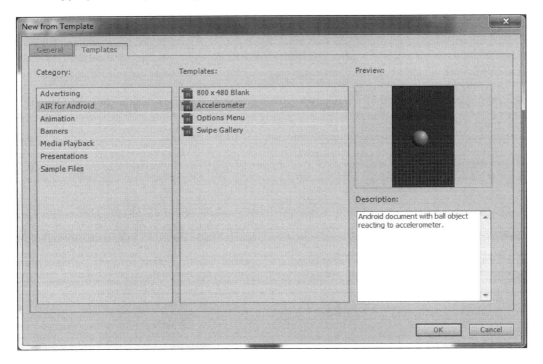

3. Alternatively, create a new ActionScript 3.0 project and open your publish settings by going to **File | Publish Settings.**

4. This will open a dialog allowing you to choose your target platform. In this case, we want to select **AIR Android** as the appropriate **Player**:

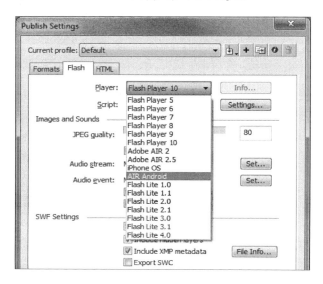

5. Now you will be able to adjust **Application** and **Installer Settings** targeting Android, and compile projects into `.apk` files.

How it works...

With recent versions of Flash Professional, we have more compiler options available to us than ever before. Taking the stepsoutlined abovewill ensure that your project is capable of targeting AIR for Android in place of the desktop Flash Player or AIR for desktop by adding a number of Android-specific compiler options to our publish settings.

There's more...

If developing for the mobile Flash Player for Android, we will not need to configure anything for the AIR runtime. To target Flash Player, we must simply keep in mind the limitations and differences inherent to mobile Android devices.

See also...

For more information about compiling AIR for Android applications with Flash Professional, you will want to refer to *Chapter 11, Final Considerations: Application Compilation and Distribution*

Using Flash Builder 4.5 to develop Android applications

Flash Builder 4.5 already comes equipped with everything, we need to begin developing mobile applications using either ActionScript or the mobile Flex Framework. For those unfamiliar with the differences between ActionScript and Flex, basically, the Flex framework provides a set of components, layouts, and data control that is preconfigured for building Flash applications, whereas when using ActionScript by itself, everything must be written from scratch. Flex 4.5 includes mobile features such as optimized component skins to run very well on devices, a new `ViewNavigator` application type, which is tailored to the mobile experience, and includes support for touch and gestures across the mobile-optimized component set.

How to do it...

In place of a normal ActionScript project or Flex project, we must specifically create either an ActionScript Mobile project or Flex Mobile project:

1. In the Flash Builder **Package Explorer**, right-click on some empty space and choose **New | Flex Mobile Project** or **New | ActionScript Mobile Project**:

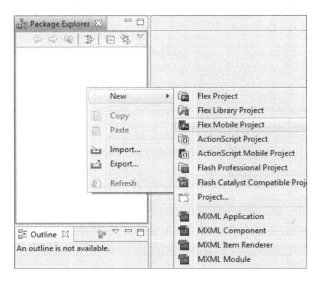

2. We will then provide the mobile project with a name and choose where Flash Builder should store the project files on the local machine.

3. The next step allows us to choose the target platform, in this case, **Google Android**, and define which application template to use (if you are making use of the mobile Flex framework). We can also set the default `View` name on this screen through the **Initial view title** input..

4. Additionally, we will choose whether or not the application will reorient based upon device tilt with the **Automatically reorient** option. We can select to display the application at full screen by selecting the **Full screen** checkbox.

5. One last selection to make on this screen is whether we would like to use density aware skins in our mobile components by selecting the **Automatically scale application for different screen densities** checkbox and selecting the appropriate Application DPI setting.

6. The rest of the project setup is really the same as any other project in Flash Builder.

How it works...

The choices we make when setting up a new project in Flash Builder determine which libraries are imported, and used in an application. Defining a mobile application will not only include specific component skins targeted to mobile, but will also restrict us from using components, which are inappropriate for such use. We will also have full access to mobile-specific application structures such as the mobile `ViewNavigator`, `ActionBar`, or `TabBar`. These additions to the mobile Flex framework can be used to greatly speed up the development of stateful mobile Android applications, as they deal with application structure, navigation controls, and layout.

See also...

You can actually use previous versions of Flash Builder to compile AIR for Android applications. Check out the next recipe, *Enabling Flash Builder 4 or Flex Builder to access Flex Mobile SDKs* for an example of this.

Enabling Flash Builder 4 or Flex Builder to access Flex Mobile SDKs

You don't necessarily need to have the latest version of Flash Builder to write applications for Android. This recipe will demonstrate how to integrate the latest Flex SDK into an older version of Flash Builder (or even Flex Builder) to take advantage of the mobile framework improvements.

Even though we will be able to use the new component sets and streamlined structure for Android, many of the workflow enhancements such as support for a new mobile application view structure, optimized component skins with touch and gesture support, and other niceties found in newer versions of Flash Builder simply will not exist and we will have to compile the application for distribution using the AIR SDK and command line tools.

How to do it...

The following steps are used for getting an older version of Flash Builder configured for Android development:

1. Visit the Adobe Open Source website at `http://opensource.adobe.com/` and locate the latest build of the Flex SDK.

2. Download a ZIP file of the latest Adobe Flex SDK and extract it to a hard drive to a location you will remember. For instance, C:\SDKs\Flex.

3. Launch Flash Builder and go to **Window | Preferences**.

4. Scroll down the **Flash Builder** menu item and select **Installed Flex SDKs**. You will now see a list of each of the SDKs currently available in your copy of Flash Builder:

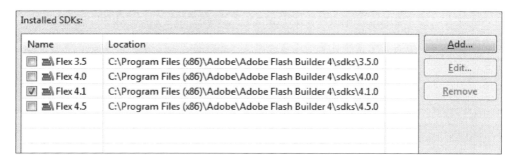

5. Click the button labeled **Add...** and browse to the location of the Flex SDK you recently downloaded.

6. Provide the dialog with a meaningful name and click **OK**. For example, Flex 4.5. If we want to be very specific, we can always name it the full build name, such as: Flex 4.5.0.16076.

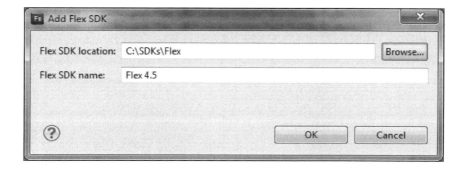

7. The Flex 4.5 SDK will now be available for use in your application. To use it in a project, simply select this SDK when creating a new project or when modifying the **Flex Compiler** properties in an existing project.

How it works...

Using a more recent version of the Flex SDK within Flash Builder allows us access to the mobile theming options and other specific APIs not available in previous SDK releases. This will also expose mobile classes to code hinting and other IDE workflow constructs.

There's more...

If changing the Flex SDK version to be used in a project, we may receive a number of warnings or errors due to changes in the framework from version to version. Simply go through the project files and correct each warning or error that appears within the **Problems** panel to correct any issues.

If developing projects that target Flash Player on Android, you simply need to be mindful of device and operating system constraints.

See also...

It is important to note that versions of Flash Builder prior to Flash Builder 4.5 will not include the ability to compile projects to .APK (the Android application file extension) and you will need to compile your project using the freely available AIR SDK. See *Chapter 11,* for information on how to do this.

It is also worth a mention that while you can develop your applications for Android using older versions of Flash Builder, you will not receive many of the benefits provided by a newer release, such as code completion.

Using Flash Builder 4 and below to develop Android applications

To develop mobile Android application in Flash Builder 4, we will need to configure Flash Builder to enable access to a mobile Flex SDK. See the previous recipe if you have not yet configured Flash Builder or Flex Builder in this manner.

How to do it...

There is no specific mobile workflow or tooling built into versions of Flash Builder prior to Flash Builder 4.5. By taking the following steps, we can ensure that our project will be mobile-compatible:

1. In Flash Builder, right-click in the **Package Explorer** panel and choose **New | Flex Project**. Alternatively, we can choose **ActionScript Project**, but this will not include any mobile benefits, as the actual Flex SDK components will not be employed. However, it is useful to note that ActionScript projects will generally perform better than their Flex counterparts simply due to the fact that they do not rely on such a heavy framework.

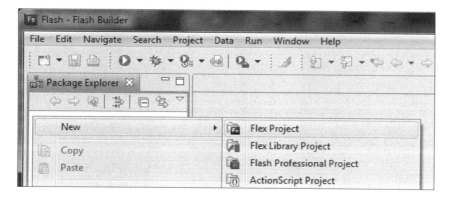

2. The **New Flex Project** dialog will appear in which you must provide a **Project name**, and select whether to create the project targeting **Web** or **Desktop**. If this project will be compiled for AIR for Android, we will want to make sure to choose **Desktop**, as this application type will target the Adobe AIR runtime. If creating a project targeting Flash Player in the browser, we will choose **Web**.

3. When choosing **Desktop**, we will also want to be sure to choose a mobile-enhanced version of the Flex SDK for our Android project. Flex 4.5 and above include everything we need to begin developing robust Android applications.

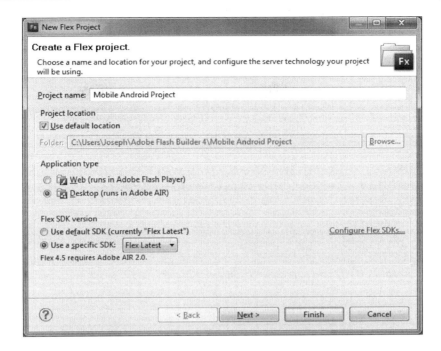

4. The last thing we must do is make sure that the mobile-enabled Flex SWCs are going to be used in our project. In order to declare `<s:ViewNavigatorApplication>` or `<s:TabbedViewNavigatorApplication>` for the main container of our project, these specific SWCs must be accessible, else Flash Builder will report errors.

5. The final section of the **New Flex Project** dialog allows us to be sure the mobile SWCs are included. You will notice that `mobilecomponents.swc` is not included in our project. Select the tab labeled **Library path** and click on the button labeled **Add SWC...:**

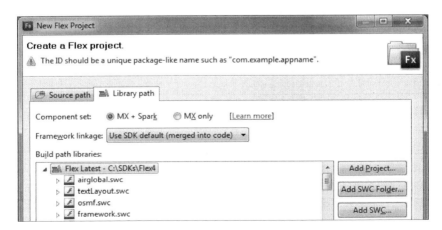

6. When the **Add SWC** dialog appears, browse to the location of the selected Flex SDK. Assuming we unpackaged the SDK to `C:\SDKs\Flex4` we will now browse to `C:\SDKs\Flex\frameworks\libs\mobile` select the `mobilecomponents.swc` file, and click on **Open**. This will add support for the mobile components to our application.

7. Complete the project setup. We are now able to use mobile specific containers and controls without receiving errors from Flash Builder, but we must make a few more adjustments in order to correctly compile our application.

8. Locate the AIR descriptor file in your project. It is normally named something like `{MyProject}-app.xml` and resides at the project root. Open this file and change the `<visible>` attribute to **true**. It may be necessary to uncomment this node, if it has been commented out.

9. Right-click on your project in the **Package Explorer** and select **Properties.**

10. Select the **Flex Compiler** menu option and add the following to the **Additional compiler arguments:** `theme=C:\{SDK Location}\frameworks\themes\Mobile\mobile.swc`

11. Finally, switch the root node of your main application file from `<s:Application>` to `<s:ViewNavigatorApplication>`. We can now author and compile applications using the mobile flex framework components.

How it works...

When specifying which type of project we want to create in Flash Builder, the IDE automatically makes available certain portions of the Flex framework so that we can work with all the components necessary for our project. Flash Builder 4 and earlier do not ship with any mobile-enabled Flex SDK and do not provide a workflow for Android projects. Because of this, we must explicitly tell Flash Builder to make use of these extra framework components.

The application descriptor file mentioned in the steps in the preceding section is used to configure an AIR application in various ways: setting the initial window properties, chrome attributes, and even system icons.

See also...

It is important to note that versions of Flash Builder prior to Flash Builder 4.5 will not include the ability to compile projects to .APK (the Android application file extension) and you will need to compile your project using the freely available AIR SDK. See *Chapter 11* for information on how to do this.

It is also worth a mention that while you can develop your applications for Android using older versions of Flash Builder, you will not receive many of the benefits provided by a newer release, such as code completion.

Enabling Powerflasher FDT 4.1 to access Flex Mobile SDKs

Powerflasher FDT is an increasingly popular development environment for authoring projects for the Flash Platform. FDT 4 comes equipped with everything you'd expect to begin developing ActionScript and Flex applications, but FDT 4.1 and below do not support any mobile workflow or ship with the mobile-enabled Flex SDK.

How to do it...

There are only a few steps to getting Powerflasher FDT 4 configured for Android development:

1. Visit the Adobe Open Source website at `http://opensource.adobe.com/` and locate the latest build of the Flex SDK.

2. Download a `ZIP` file of the latest Adobe Flex SDK and extract it to a hard drive to a location you will remember. For instance, `C:\SDKs\Flex`.

3. Launch **FDT** and go to **Window | Preferences**.

4. Scroll down the **FDT** menu item and select **Installed SDKs**. You will now see a list of each of the SDKs currently available in your copy of FD:

5. Click on the button labeled **Add** and browse to the location of the Flex SDK you recently downloaded.

6. Provide the dialog with a meaningful name and click **OK**. For example, `Flex 4.5`:

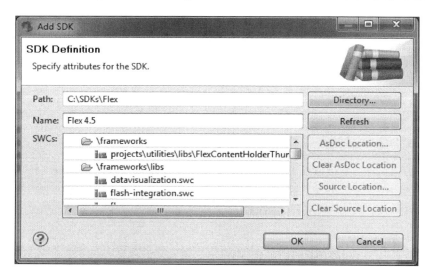

7. The `Flex 4.5` SDK will now be available for use in your application. To use it in a project, simply select this SDK when creating a new project or when modifying the **Flex Compiler** properties in an existing project:

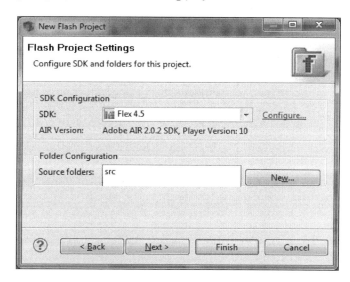

How it works...

Powerflasher FDT 4 is an Eclipse-based IDE (just like Flash Builder) and employs many of the same methods of extending the application and adding SDK packages. Using a more recent version of the Flex SDK within FDT allows us access to the mobile theming options and other specific APIs not available in previous SDK releases.

See also...

It is important to note that versions of Flash Builder prior to Flash Builder 4.5 will not include the ability to compile projects to .APK (the Android application file extension) and you will need to compile your project using the freely available AIR SDK. See *Chapter 11* for information on how to do this.

It is also worth a mention that while you can develop your applications for Android using older versions of Flash Builder, you will not receive many of the benefits provided by a newer release, such as code completion.

Using Powerflasher FDT 4.1 and below to develop Android applications

To develop mobile Android application in FDT 4.1, we will need to configure FDT to enable access to a mobile Flex SDK. See the previous recipe if you have not yet configured FDT in this manner.

How to do it...

There is no specific mobile workflow or tooling built into versions of FDT prior to FDT 4.2. By taking the following steps, we can ensure that our project will be mobile-compatible:

1. In FDT, right-click in the **Flash Explorer** panel and choose **NEW | New Flash Project**:

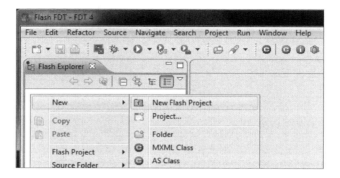

2. The **New Flash Project** dialog will appear in which you must provide a **Project name**, and select whether to create the project using **ActionScript 3** or **Flex**. We need to make sure to choose **Flex 4**, as this will include Spark components, which can be mobile-friendly if using a proper version of the Flex SDK.

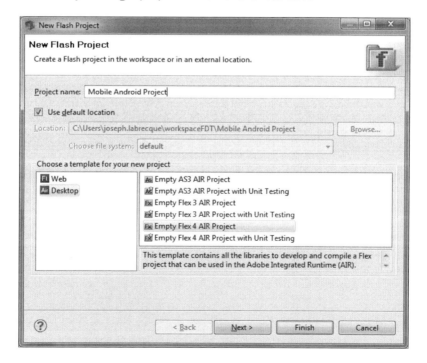

3. The next section will allow us to choose a specific Flex SDK to use in our project. We should choose a mobile-enhanced version of the Flex SDK for our Android project. Flex 4.5 and above include everything we need to begin developing robust Android applications.

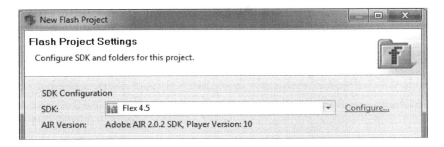

4. The last thing we must do is make sure that the mobile-enabled Flex SWCs are going to be used in our project. In order to declare `<s:ViewNavigatorApplication>` or `<s:TabbedViewNavigatorApplication>` for the main container of our project, these specific SWCs must be accessible, else FDT will report errors.

5. The next section allows us to be sure the mobile SWCs are included. Select the tab labeled **SDK Library** and click on the button labeled **Select SWCs...**

6. You will notice that `mobile\mobilecomponents.swc` is not included in our project. Select the checkbox next to this SWC and press the **OK** button to continue:

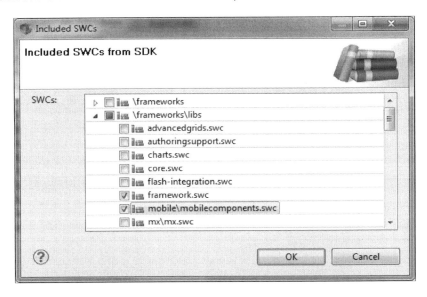

7. Now we will be able to use mobile specific containers and controls without receiving errors from FDT.

How it works...

When specifying which type of project we want to create in FDT, the program automatically makes available certain portions of the Flex Framework, so that we can work with all the components necessary for our project. FDT 4.1 and earlier do not ship with any mobile-enabled Flex SDK and do not provide a workflow for Android projects. Because of this, we must explicitly tell FDT to make use of the following extra framework components:

- ▶ **ViewNavigatorApplication**: This includes a `ViewNavigator` stack structure, in which we can push and pop different views to the top of a stack, exposing the topmost view to the user.

- ▶ **TabbedViewNavigatorApplication**: This includes the ability to have multiple `ViewNavigator` stacks within an application, controlled through a `TabBar` user interface element.

See also...

It is important to note that versions of Flash Builder prior to Flash Builder 4.5 will not include the ability to compile projects to `.APK` (the Android application file extension) and you will need to compile your project using the freely available AIR SDK. See *Chapter 11* for information on how to do this.

It is also worth a mention that while you can develop your applications for Android using older versions of Flash Builder, you will not receive many of the benefits provided by a newer release, such as code completion.

Converting a standard Flex project to a Flex Mobile project

There is currently no workflow within Flash Builder (or FDT) to convert an existing application to a mobile Android application. Depending upon the complexity of the application being converted and the version of Flex, it may be undergoing conversion from this task can range from the very simple to one that is inordinately complex. In this recipe, we will demonstrate a simpler example using basic Flex structures.

How to do it...

Create a new mobile project and copy all of the necessary files into it, retaining those portions of code which are used for mobile projects and modifying any unsupported components.

For this example, we'll use a simple Flex project targeting AIR for desktop consisting of nothing but a button component at this stage:

```xml
<?xml version="1.0" encoding="utf-8"?>
<s:WindowedApplication xmlns:fx="http://ns.adobe.com/mxml/2009"
   xmlns:s="library://ns.adobe.com/flex/spark"
   xmlns:mx="library://ns.adobe.com/flex/mx">
   <s:Button x="10" y="10" width="300" height="200" label="Button"/>
</s:WindowedApplication>
```

To convert this to a new Flex Mobile project, take the following steps:

1. Go to the menu and choose **File | New | Flex Mobile Project**.

2. Provide the project setup dialog with information about the new mobile project.

 The project cannot have the same name as any existing project within your environment.

3. Copy all of your files from the project folder in your original project into this new mobile project excluding your project descriptor file (`{myApp }.xml`) and `Default Application` files.

4. Now, copy everything within your old `Default Application` file and paste it into the `Default Application` file that was created along with your mobile project. Once everything has been copied over, right-click on the main application file and choose **Set as Default Application**.

5. Change all instances of `<s:WindowedApplication>` to `<s:ViewNavigatorApplication>` (alternatively, `<s:TabbedViewNavigatorApplication>`).

 Just as with a standard AIR `<s:WindowedApplication>`, only one instance of `<s:ViewNavigatorApplication>` or `<s:TabbedViewNavigatorApplication>` can exist within a project.

6. Look within your **Problems** panel to see whether or not any further modifications need to be made.

7. If you are not using any of the old Halo components (mx namespace) it is a good idea to remove the namespace declaration for your opening `<s:ViewNavigatorApplication>` tag.

8. Add a `firstView` attribute to the `<s:ViewNavigatorApplication>` tag. This should point to the `View` automatically created when you set up the mobile project.

9. Since visual UI elements cannot reside directly within a <s:ViewNavigatorApplication /> node, we must wrap the <s:Button /> instance within a <fx:Declarations> </fx:Declarations> tag set, or move it to a specific View.

Your `Default Application` file should now read as follows:

```xml
<?xml version="1.0" encoding="utf-8"?>
<s:ViewNavigatorApplication xmlns:fx="http://ns.adobe.com/mxml/2009"
    xmlns:s="library://ns.adobe.com/flex/spark"
    firstView="views.MobileFlexProjectHomeView">
    <fx:Declarations>
    <s:Button x="10" y="10" width="447" height="106" label="Button"/>
    </fx:Declarations>
</s:ViewNavigatorApplication>
```

Additionally, a view for this application could appear as such:

```xml
<?xml version="1.0" encoding="utf-8"?>
<s:View xmlns:fx="http://ns.adobe.com/mxml/2009"
    xmlns:s="library://ns.adobe.com/flex/spark"
    title="MobileFlexProjectHomeView ">
</s:View>
```

For more information about how Flex Mobile projects are structured, have a look at the following resource: `http://opensource.adobe.com/wiki/display/flexsdk/Developer+Documentation`.

How it works...

When using Flex, the root tag of your application determines largely what APIs and structures are available to you throughout the project. Making sure that we choose the correct root tag is very important in regard to the target platform and capabilities of our project. For AIR on Android, we will want to use either `ViewNavigatorApplication` or `TabbedViewNavigatorApplication`. Desktop applications would use the Application or `WindowedApplication` tags. Chances are, if you are building Flash content with Flex that is to be deployed to Flash Player in the browser, on both mobile and desktop you will use a straight `Application` tag for your project.

There's more...

If you don't want to deal with a lot of conversion, and are just starting out with a new project that will share the same codebase across desktop and mobile, you might consider using a Flex Library project to allow different projects to share the same underlying codebase.

Read the documentation on Flex 4 Library usage at: `http://help.adobe.com/en_US/ flashbuilder/using/WS6f97d7caa66ef6eb1e63e3d11b6c4d0d21-7fe6.html`.

Configuring the AIR SDK to package AIR for Android applications on Windows

If we are using the open source AIR **SDK** (**Software Development Kit**) with another IDE or even editing our project in a simple text editor, we can still compile applications for distribution on Android through command line tools.

How to do it...

If you do not already have the Adobe AIR SDK, you must first download it from `http://www. adobe.com/products/air/sdk/` and extract the files into a directory on your hard drive, `C:\SDKs\AIR`, for example. You must also set a `PATH` variable in your operating system pointing to the `bin` directory underneath the AIR SDK.

If you are using a Windows system, set the environment variable through the following steps:

1. Open the **System Properties** dialog. You can reach this dialog in many ways, the most direct being a right-click on **My Computer**. Then select **Properties**.

2. Choose **Advanced system settings** from the left hand menu.

3. Click on the button at the bottom of this window that says **Environment Variables...**

4. Click upon the **PATH** variable in this window and select **Edit**:

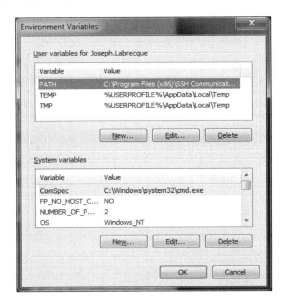

5. Now, simply add the location of your `bin` directory into the set of variables: If the last item in your variable value list has not been terminated with a semicolon, you must add one before every new item. For example: `C:\SDKs\AIR\bin`.

6. That should do it. Hit **OK** a few times and bring up the command prompt to verify that we've set this up correctly. Type in `adt -version` and hit **Enter**. If all is well, ADT will spit back a version string that looks something like `adt version "2.5.0.00000"`.

How it works...

Setting a `PATH` variable on the operating system allows us to be able to invoke the AIR Android compiler, ADT, from anywhere in our system without having to traverse file directories and specify long path names.

See also...

If using a Linux or Mac operating system, you can also set specific environment variables from within the Terminal. See the next recipe Configuring the AIR SDK to Package AIR for Android Applications on Linux or MacOS for an example of this.

Configuring the AIR SDK to package AIR for Android applications on Linux or Mac OS

If we are using the open source AIR SDK with another IDE or even editing our project in a simple text editor, we can still compile applications for distribution on Android through command line tools.

How to do it...

If you do not already have the Adobe AIR SDK, you must first download it from `http://www.adobe.com/products/air/sdk/` and extract the files into a directory on your hard drive: `/home/joseph/SDKs/AIR`, for example. You must also set a `PATH` variable in your operating system start up script pointing to the `bin` directory underneath the AIR SDK.

We will set the environment variable through the following steps:

1. Open the **Terminal**.

2. Now we must create the shell configuration profile. Enter the following into the Terminal window: cat >> .bash_profile on a Mac or cat >> .bashrc for Ubuntu (each Linux distribution may have its own particular naming convention for the startup script).

3. Next, enter export PATH=$PATH:/home/joseph/SDKs/AIR/bin to set the PATH variable pointing to the AIR development tools bin directory. Hit *Enter*.

4. Enter *Ctrl+Shift*+D to end this process.

5. Now we will check to be sure everything was added appropriately. Type cat .bashrc into the **Terminal** and hit *Enter*. You should see the PATH command spit back at you:

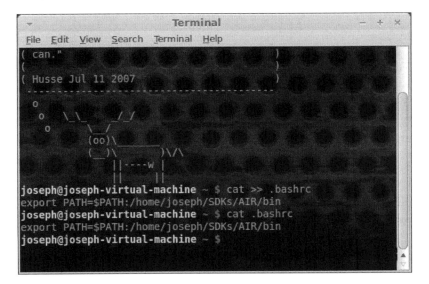

6. You may need to log out of your profile and then log back in for the new environment variable to be picked up by the system.

7. Bring up the **Terminal** again, after logging back into your profile.

8. Type echo $PATH into the Terminal and hit *Enter*. This should display everything that is included in the PATH variable including the location of our AIR bin directory.

9. That should do it. We will now verify that we've set the AIR SDK up correctly. Type in `adt -version` and hit *Enter*. If all is well, ADT will spit back a version string that looks something like `adt version "2.5.0.00000"`:

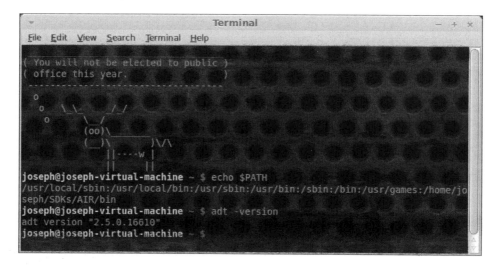

How it works...

Setting a PATH variable on the operating system allows us to be able to invoke the AIR Android compiler, ADT, from anywhere in our system without having to traverse file directories and specify long path names.

See also...

Note that you may have to log out of your session and then log back in for the new PATH variables to take effect. If using a Windows operating system, you can also set specific environment variables. See the previous recipe, *Configuring the AIR SDK to package AIR for Android applications on Windows* for an example of this.

2
Interaction Experience: Multitouch, Gestures, and Other Input

This chapter will cover the following recipes:

- ► Detecting supported device input types
- ► Detecting whether or not a device supports multitouch
- ► Verifying specific gesture support for common interactions
- ► Using gestures to zoom a display object
- ► Using gestures to pan a display object
- ► Using gestures to swipe a display object
- ► Using gestures to rotate a display object
- ► Accessing raw touchpoint data
- ► Creating a custom gesture based upon touchpoint data
- ► Emulating the Android long-press interaction
- ► Invoking the virtual keyboard programmatically
- ► Responding to Android soft-key interactions
- ► Responding to trackball and D-Pad events

Introduction

The ability to interface with a device through touch and gestures is one of the stand-out features of mobile computing and the Flash platform has full support for both multitouch and gestures on Android. This chapter will cover different ways of intercepting and reacting to user interaction whether it be through simple touch points or complex gestures, along with more traditional physical and virtual keyboard input. Making good use of this is essential to a smooth experience on mobile Android devices.

All of the recipes in this chapter are represented as pure ActionScript 3 classes and are not dependent upon external libraries or the Flex framework. Therefore, we will be able to use these examples in any IDE we wish.

Detecting supported device input types

A variety of input types are available across Android devices and depending upon the project we are working on, we may need to verify that any particular device supports the intended modes of user interaction. Fortunately, there are a number of ActionScript classes to assist us in discovering device capabilities in regard to user input.

How to do it...

We will need to use internal classes to detect whether or not multitouch is supported:

1. First, import the following classes into your project in order to check various input types across devices:
   ```
   import flash.display.Sprite;
   import flash.display.Stage;
   import flash.display.StageAlign;
   import flash.display.StageScaleMode;
   import flash.system.Capabilities;
   import flash.system.TouchscreenType;
   import flash.text.TextField;
   import flash.text.TextFormat;
   import flash.ui.Keyboard;
   import flash.ui.KeyboardType;
   import flash.ui.Mouse;
   ```

2. Declare a `TextField` and `TextFormat` object to allow visible output upon the device:
   ```
   private var traceField:TextField;
   private var traceFormat:TextFormat;
   ```

3. We will now set up our `TextField`, apply a `TextFormat`, and add it to the `DisplayList`. Here, we create a method to perform all of these actions for us:

```
protected function setupTextField():void {
  traceFormat = new TextFormat();
  traceFormat.bold = true;
  traceFormat.font = "_sans";
  traceFormat.size = 32;
  traceFormat.align = "center";
  traceFormat.color = 0x333333;
  traceField = new TextField();
  traceField.defaultTextFormat = traceFormat;
  traceField.selectable = false;
  traceField.mouseEnabled = false;
  traceField.width = stage.stageWidth;
  traceField.height = stage.stageHeight;
  addChild(traceField);
}
```

4. Now, we will simply go through and check the data returned from invoking a number of properties off of these classes. In the case of the following example, we are performing this within the following method:

```
protected function checkInputTypes():void {
  traceField.appendText("Touch Screen Type: " +
      flash.system.Capabilities.touchscreenType + "\n");
  traceField.appendText("Mouse Cursor: " + flash.ui.Mouse.
      supportsCursor + "\n");
  traceField.appendText("Physical Keyboard Type: " + flash.
      ui.Keyboard.physicalKeyboardType + "\n");
  traceField.appendText("Virtual Keyboard: " + flash.ui.Keyboard.
      hasVirtualKeyboard + "\n");
}
```

5. The result will appear similar to the following:

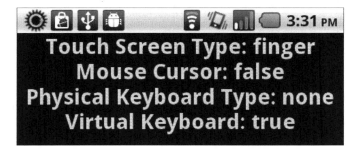

How it works...

The Flash platform runtimes are able to report certain device capabilities when invoked. The data reported will allow us to tailor the user experience, based upon what sort of input types are detected by the runtime.

Here follows a basic rundown of the four input types that can be reported upon:

`flash.system.Capabilities.touchscreenType`

Invoking this method will return a `String` constant of `FINGER`, `STYLUS`, or `NONE`. It informs us whether some sort of direct screen interaction is available on the device, and if so, what sort. In the case of Android devices, this will always return `FINGER`.

`flash.ui.Mouse.supportsCursor`

Invoking this method will return a `Boolean` of `true` or `false`. It simply informs us whether a persistent mouse cursor is available on the device. In the case of Android devices, this will most likely always return `false`.

`flash.ui.Keyboard.physicalKeyboardType`

Invoking this method will return a `String` constant of `ALPHANUMERIC`, `KEYPAD`, or `NONE`. It informs us whether some sort of dedicated physical keyboard is available on the device, and if so, what sort. In the case of Android devices, this will most likely always return `NONE`, even though certain Android models do have a physical keyboard.

`flash.ui.Keyboard.hasVirtualKeyboard`

Invoking this method will return a `Boolean` of `true` or `false`. It simply informs us whether a virtual (software) keyboard is available on the device. In the case of Android devices, this will most likely always return `true`.

Detecting whether or not a device supports multitouch

When developing projects which target the Android operating system, it is always a good idea to make sure that multitouch is actually supported on the device. In the case of an Android phone, this will probably always be the case, but what about a Google TV or AIR for TV device? Many of these are also Android-based yet most televisions do not have any touch control whatsoever. Never assume the capabilities of any device.

How to do it...

We will need to use internal classes to detect whether or not multitouch is supported:

1. First, import the following classes into your project:

```
import flash.display.StageScaleMode;
import flash.display.StageAlign;
import flash.display.Stage;
import flash.display.Sprite;
import flash.text.TextField;
import flash.text.TextFormat;
import flash.ui.Multitouch;
```

2. Declare a `TextField` and `TextFormat` object to allow visible output upon the device:

```
private var traceField:TextField;
private var traceFormat:TextFormat;
```

3. We will now set up our `TextField`, apply a `TextFormat`, and add it to the `DisplayList`. Here, we create a method to perform all of these actions for us:

```
protected function setupTextField():void {
  traceFormat = new TextFormat();
  traceFormat.bold = true;
  traceFormat.font = "_sans";
  traceFormat.size = 44;
  traceFormat.align = "center";
  traceFormat.color = 0x333333;
  traceField = new TextField();
  traceField.defaultTextFormat = traceFormat;
  traceField.selectable = false;
  traceField.mouseEnabled = false;
  traceField.width = stage.stageWidth;
  traceField.height = stage.stageHeight;
  addChild(traceField);
}
```

4. Then, simply invoke `Multitouch.supportsGestureEvents` and `Multitouch.supportsTouchEvents` to check each of these capabilities as demonstrated in the following method:

```
protected function checkMultitouch():void {
    traceField.appendText(String("Gestures: " + Multitouch.
supportsGestureEvents) + "\n");
    traceField.appendText(String("Touch: " + Multitouch.
supportsTouchEvents));
}
```

5. Each of these properties will return a `Boolean` value of `true` or `false`, indicating device support as shown here:

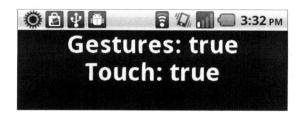

How it works...

Detecting whether the device supports either touch or gesture events will determine how much freedom you, as a developer, have in refining the user experience. If either of these items returns as false, then it is up to you to provide (if possible) an alternative way for the user to interact with the application. This is normally done through `Mouse` events:

▶ **Touch events**: Basic interactions such as a single finger tap.

▶ **Gesture events**: More complex interpretations of user interaction such as pinch, zoom, swipe, pan, and so forth.

There's more...

It is important to note that while a specific device may support either gesture events or touch events, when using Flash Platform tools, we must set the `Multitouch.inputMode` to one or the other specifically.

Verifying specific gesture support for common interactions

When dealing with Android devices, touch and gestures are the main mechanisms with which the user interacts with the device. If we want to use some of the predefined gestures in Flash Player and AIR, we can do so in the following manner.

How to do it...

To discover which specific gestures are supported on a device, perform the following actions:

1. First, import the following classes into your project:

```
import flash.display.StageScaleMode;
import flash.display.StageAlign;
```

```
import flash.display.Stage;
import flash.display.Sprite;
import flash.text.TextField;
import flash.text.TextFormat;
import flash.ui.Multitouch;
import flash.ui.MultitouchInputMode;
```

2. Declare a `TextField` and `TextFormat` object to allow visible output upon the device:

```
private var traceField:TextField;
private var traceFormat:TextFormat;
```

3. We will now set up our `TextField`, apply a `TextFormat`, and add it to the `DisplayList`. Here, we create a method to perform all of these actions for us:

```
protected function setupTextField():void {
    traceFormat = new TextFormat();
    traceFormat.bold = true;
    traceFormat.font = "_sans";
    traceFormat.size = 44;
    traceFormat.align = "center";
    traceFormat.color = 0x333333;
    traceField = new TextField();
    traceField.defaultTextFormat = traceFormat;
    traceField.selectable = false;
    traceField.mouseEnabled = false;
    traceField.width = stage.stageWidth;
    traceField.height = stage.stageHeight;
    addChild(traceField);
}
```

4. Set the specific input mode for the multitouch APIs to support gestures with the following command:

```
Multitouch.inputMode = MultitouchInputMode.GESTURE;
```

5. Invoking `Multitouch.supportedGestures` will return a `Vector` of `String` objects naming all the supported gestured exposed to Flash on the device:

```
var supportedGestures:Vector.<String> = Multitouch.
supportedGestures;
```

6. We can then look for a specific gesture or set of gestures to listen for, or fall back to other interaction events if necessary.

```
for(var i:int=0; i < supportedGestures.length; ++i) {
    trace(supportedGestures[i]);
}
```

7. We can perform all of these necessary functions within a single method:

```
protected function checkGestures():void {
  Multitouch.inputMode = MultitouchInputMode.GESTURE;
  if(Multitouch.supportedGestures){
    var supportedGestures:Vector.<String> =
        Multitouch.supportedGestures;
    for(var i:int=0; i <supportedGestures.length; ++i) {
      traceField.appendText(supportedGestures[i] + "\n");
    }
  }else{
    traceField.appendText("no gesture support!");
    }
}
```

8. The result will appear similar to the following:

How it works...

Flash player and AIR do a marvelous job of distilling information to essential details for an Android developer. Knowing which particular gestures are supported on a device will allow us to tailor event interactions on our applications and provide fallback interactions when necessary.

There's more...

In our example class, we also provide a check to be sure there are at least some gestures supported through `Multitouch.supportedGestures`. Chances are, if the device does provide gesture support, we will want to provide a warning to the user explaining that the application will not perform optimally because of hardware limitations.

Apart from the more common gestures such as zoom, swipe, rotate, and pan, which are included in the `flash.events.TransformGestureEvent` package, there are additional, yet less common gestures such as two-finger tap, found in the `flash.events.GestureEvent` and `flash.events.PressAndTapGestureEvent` classes. These will all be referenced by `Multitouch.supportedGestures` if available on the device.

Using gestures to zoom a display object

Pinching and pulling are gestures that are often used on touch screens that support multitouch input. Bringing two fingers closer together will shrink an object, while spreading two fingers apart makes the object larger on the device.

How to do it...

This example draws a square within a `Shape` object using the `Graphics` API, adds it to the `Stage`, and then sets up listeners for zoom gesture events in order to scale the `Shape` appropriately:

1. First, import the following classes into your project:

    ```
    import flash.display.StageScaleMode;
    import flash.display.StageAlign;
    import flash.display.Stage;
    import flash.display.Sprite;
    import flash.display.Shape;
    import flash.events.TransformGestureEvent;
    import flash.ui.Multitouch;
    import flash.ui.MultitouchInputMode;
    ```

2. Declare a `Shape` object, upon which we will perform the gestures:

    ```
    private var box:Shape;
    ```

3. Next, construct a method to handle the creation of our `Sprite` and add it to the `DisplayList`:

    ```
    protected function setupBox():void {
        box = new Shape();
        box.graphics.beginFill(0xFFFFFF, 1);
        box.x = stage.stageWidth/2;
        box.y = stage.stageHeight/2;
        box.graphics.drawRect(-150,-150,300,300);
        box.graphics.endFill();
        addChild(box);
    }
    ```

4. Set the specific input mode for the multitouch APIs to support touch input by setting `Multitouch.inputMode` to the `MultitouchInputMode.TOUCH_POINT` constant the `MultitouchInputMode.TOUCH_POINT` constant and register anevent listener for the `GESTURE_ZOOM` event. In this case, the `onZoom` method will fire whenever the application detects a zoom gesture:

```
protected function setupTouchEvents():void {
  Multitouch.inputMode = MultitouchInputMode.GESTURE;
  stage.addEventListener(TransformGestureEvent.
      GESTURE_ZOOM, onZoom);
}
```

5. To use the accepted behavior of pinch and zoom, we can adjust the scale of objects on stage based upon the scale factor returned by our event listener.

```
protected function onZoom(e:TransformGestureEvent):void {
  box.scaleX *= e.scaleX;
  box.scaleY *= e.scaleY;
}
```

6. The resulting gesture will affect our visual object in the following way:

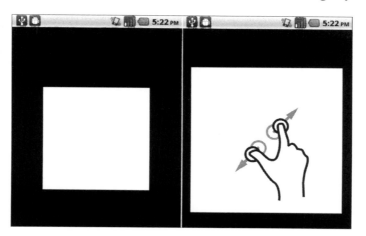

 Illustrations provided by Gestureworks (www.gestureworks.com).

How it works...

As we are setting our `Multitouch.inputMode` to gestures through `MultitouchInputMode.GESTURE`, we are able to listen for and react to a host of predefined gestures. In this example, we are listening for the `TransformGestureEvent.GESTURE_ZOOM` event in order to set the scale of our `Shape` object. By multiplying the current scale properties by the scale values reported through our event, we can adjust the scale of our object based upon this gesture.

There's more...

Note here that we are drawing our square in such a way that the `Shape` registration point is located in the center of the visible `Shape`. It is important that we do this, as the `DisplayObject` will scale up and down, based upon the registration point and transform point.

When using the drawing tools in Flash Professional, be sure to set the registration point of your `MovieClip` symbol to be centered in order for this to work correctly.

See also...

`TransformGestureEvent.GESTURE_ZOOM` is just one of a set of four primary transform gestures available to us when working with the Flash Platform runtimes and Android devices. Reference the following recipes for a complete overview of these gestures:

▸ *Using gestures to pan a display object*
▸ *Using gestures to swipe a display object*
▸ *Using gestures to rotate a display object*

Using gestures to pan a display object

Panning a `DisplayObject` is accomplished by touching the screen with two fingers simultaneously, and then moving both fingers across the screen in the direction we want to pan the object. This is normally used upon an object that occupies more real estate than the screen affords, or an object that has been zoomed in so far that only a portion of it is visible on the screen at any given time.

How to do it...

This example draws a square within a `Shape` object using the `Graphics` API, adds it to the `Stage`, and then sets up listeners for pan gesture events in order to scale the `Shape` appropriately.

1. First, import the following classes into your project:

```
import flash.display.StageScaleMode;
import flash.display.StageAlign;
import flash.display.Stage;
import flash.display.Sprite;
import flash.display.Shape;
import flash.events.TransformGestureEvent;
import flash.ui.Multitouch;
import flash.ui.MultitouchInputMode;
```

2. Declare a `Shape` object which we will perform the gestures upon:

```
private var box:Shape;
```

3. Next, construct a method to handle the creation of our `Shape` and add it to the `DisplayList`. We have made extra effort to be sure our `Shape` is much larger than the screen so that it can be panned effectively:

```
protected function setupBox():void {
  box = new Shape();
  box.graphics.beginFill(0xFFFFFF, 1);
  box.x = stage.stageWidth/2;
  box.y = stage.stageHeight/2;
  box.graphics.drawRect(-150,-150,300,300);
  box.graphics.endFill();
  box.graphics.lineStyle(10, 0x440000, 1);
  box.graphics.moveTo(0, -800);
  box.graphics.lineTo(0, 800);
  box.graphics.moveTo(-800, 0);
  box.graphics.lineTo(800, 0);
  addChild(box);
}
```

4. Set the specific input mode for the multitouch APIs to support touch input by setting `Multitouch.inputMode` to the `MultitouchInputMode.TOUCH_POINT` constant and register an event listener for the `GESTURE_PAN` event. In this case, the `onPan` method will fire whenever the application detects a zoom gesture:

```
protected function setupTouchEvents():void {
  Multitouch.inputMode = MultitouchInputMode.GESTURE;
  stage.addEventListener(TransformGestureEvent.
          GESTURE_PAN, onPan);
}
```

5. We can now respond to the data being returned by our pan event. In this case, we are simply shifting the x and y positions of our `Shape` based upon the pan offset data:

```
protected function onPan(e:TransformGestureEvent):void {
    box.x += e.offsetX;
    box.y += e.offsetY;
}
```

6. The resulting gesture will affect our visual object in the following way:

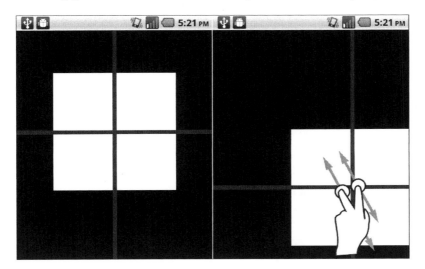

 Illustrations provided by Gestureworks (www.gestureworks.com).

How it works...

As we are setting our `Multitouch.inputMode` to gestures through `MultitouchInputMode.GESTURE`, we are able to listen for and react to a host of predefined gestures. In this example we are listening for the `TransformGestureEvent.GESTURE_PAN` event in order to shift the x and y position of our `Shape` object. By adjusting the coordinates of our `Shape` through the reported offset data, we can adjust the position of our object in a way that the user expects.

There's more...

Note that this is often a difficult gesture to perform on certain devices (As you must touch the screen with two fingers, simultaneously), and that other devices may not even support it. For a fallback, we can always use the `startDrag()` and `stopDrag()` methods to simulate a pan.

See also...

`TransformGestureEvent.GESTURE_PAN` is just one of a set of four primary transform gestures available to us when working with the Flash Platform runtimes and Android devices. Reference the following recipes for a complete overview of these gestures:

- *Using Gestures to Zoom a DisplayObject*
- *Using Gestures to Swipe a Display Object*
- *Using Gestures to Rotate a Display Object*

Using gestures to swipe a display object

Swipe is one of the most common gestures on Android devices, and with good reason. Whether flipping through a series of photographs, or simply moving between states in an application, the swipe gesture is something users have come to expect. A swipe gesture is accomplished by simply touching the screen and swiping up, down, left, or right across the screen quickly in the opposite direction.

How to do it...

This example draws a square within a `Shape` object using the `Graphics` API, adds it to the `Stage`, and then sets up a listener for swipe gesture events in order to move the `Shape` instance against the bounds of our screen in accordance with the direction of swipe:

1. First, import the following classes into your project:

```
import flash.display.StageScaleMode;
import flash.display.StageAlign;
import flash.display.Stage;
import flash.display.Sprite;
import flash.display.Shape;
import flash.events.TransformGestureEvent;
import flash.ui.Multitouch;
import flash.ui.MultitouchInputMode;
```

2. Declare a `Shape` object which we will perform the gestures upon:

```
private var box:Shape;
```

3. Next, construct a method to handle the creation of our `Shape` and add it to the `DisplayList`:

```
protected function setupBox():void {
  box = new Shape();
  box.graphics.beginFill(0xFFFFFF, 1);
  box.x = stage.stageWidth/2;
  box.y = stage.stageHeight/2;
  box.graphics.drawRect(-150,-150,300,300);
  box.graphics.endFill();
  addChild(box);
}
```

4. Set the specific input mode for the multitouch APIs to support touch input by setting `Multitouch.inputMode` to the `MultitouchInputMode.TOUCH_POINT` constant and register an event listener for `TransformGestureEvent.GESTURE_SWIPE` events:

```
protected function setupTouchEvents():void {
  Multitouch.inputMode = MultitouchInputMode.GESTURE;
  stage.addEventListener(TransformGestureEvent.
          GESTURE_SWIPE, onSwipe);
}
```

5. We can now respond to the data being returned by our swipe event. In this case, we are simply shifting the x and y position of our `Shape` based upon the swipe offset data:

```
protected function onSwipe(e:TransformGestureEvent):void {
  switch(e.offsetX){
    case 1:{
      box.x = stage.stageWidth - (box.width/2);
      break;
    }
    case -1:{
      box.x = box.width/2;
      break;
    }
  }
  switch(e.offsetY){
    case 1:{
      box.y = stage.stageHeight - (box.height/2);
      break;
    }
}
```

```
            case -1:{
                box.y = box.height/2;
                break;
            }
        }
    }
```

6. The resulting gesture will affect our visual object in the following way:

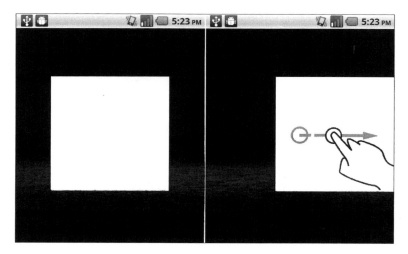

 Illustrations provided by Gestureworks (www.gestureworks.com).

How it works...

As we are setting our `Multitouch.inputMode` to gestures through `MultitouchInputMode.GESTURE`, we are able to listen for and react to a host of predefined gestures. In this example we are listening for the `TransformGestureEvent.GESTURE_SWIPE` event in order to shift the x and y position of our `Shape` object. By adjusting the coordinates of our `Shape` through the reported offset data, we can adjust the position of our object in a way that the user expects.

We can see through this example that the `offsetX` and `offsetY` values returned by our event listener will each either be 1 or -1. This makes it very simple for us to determine which direction the swipe has registered:

 ▸ **Swipe up**: offsetY = -1
 ▸ **Swipe down**: offsetY = 1

> ▸ **Swipe left**: offsetX = -1
> ▸ **Swipe right**: offsetX = 1

There's more...

When reacting to swipe events, it may be a good idea to provide a bit of transition animation, either by using built in tweening mechanisms, or an external tweening engine. There are many great tweening engines for ActionScript freely available as open source software. The use of these engines along with certain gestures can provide a more pleasant experience for the user of your applications.

We might consider the following popular tweening engines for use in our application:

TweenLite: `http://www.greensock.com/tweenlite/`

GTween: `http://www.gskinner.com/libraries/gtween/`

See also...

`TransformGestureEvent.GESTURE_SWIPE` is just one of a set of four primary transform gestures available to us when working with the Flash Platform runtimes and Android devices. Reference the following recipes for a complete overview of these gestures:

> ▸ *Using gestures to zoom a display object*
> ▸ *Using gestures to pan a display object*
> ▸ *Using gestures to rotate a display object*

Using gestures to rotate a display object

Rotation is performed by holding two fingers at different points on an object, and then moving one finger around the other in a clockwise or counter clockwise motion. This results in the rotation of the object on screen. Rotation can be used alongside the pan and zoom gestures to provide full control to the user over an image or other `DisplayObject`.

How to do it...

This example draws a square within a `Shape` object using the `Graphics` API, adds it to the `Stage`, and then sets up a listener for `Rotate` gesture events in order to appropriately rotate the `Shape` instance around its registration point:

1. First, import the following classes into your project:

    ```
    import flash.display.StageScaleMode;
    import flash.display.StageAlign;
    import flash.display.Stage;
    import flash.display.Sprite;
    import flash.display.Shape;
    import flash.events.TransformGestureEvent;
    import flash.ui.Multitouch;
    import flash.ui.MultitouchInputMode;
    ```

2. Declare a `Shape` object which we will perform the gestures upon:

    ```
    private var box:Shape;
    ```

3. Next, construct a method to handle the creation of our `Shape` and add it to the `DisplayList`.

    ```
    protected function setupBox():void {
      box = new Shape();
      box.graphics.beginFill(0xFFFFFF, 1);
      box.x = stage.stageWidth/2;
      box.y = stage.stageHeight/2;
      box.graphics.drawRect(-150,-150,300,300);
      box.graphics.endFill();
      addChild(box);
    }
    ```

4. Set the specific input mode for the multitouch APIs to support touch input by setting `Multitouch.inputMode` to the `MultitouchInputMode.TOUCH_POINT` constant and register an event listener for the `GESTURE_ROTATE` event. In this case, the `onRotate` method will fire whenever the application detects a rotation gesture:

    ```
    protected function setupTouchEvents():void {
      Multitouch.inputMode = MultitouchInputMode.GESTURE;
        stage.addEventListener(TransformGestureEvent.GESTURE_ROTATE,
        onRotate);
    }
    ```

5. We can now respond to the data being returned by our rotate event. In this case, we are simply assigning the `rotation` value returned from our event listener to the `rotation` parameter of our `Shape` in order to perform the appropriate rotation:

```
protected function onRotate(e:TransformGestureEvent):void {
  box.rotation += e.rotation;
}
```

6. The resulting gesture will affect our visual object in the following way:

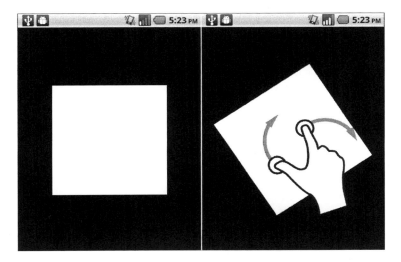

 Illustrations provided by Gestureworks (www.gestureworks.com).

How it works...

As we are setting our `Multitouch.inputMode` to gestures through `MultitouchInputMode.GESTURE`, we are able to listen for and react to a host of predefined gestures. In this example we are listening for the `TransformGestureEvent.GESTURE_ROTATE` event in order to assign the returned `rotation` value to our `Shape` object.

There is really no further calculation to make upon this data in most cases, but we could perform more advanced rotation interactions by allowing (for instance) the rotation of one `DisplayObject` to affect the rotation of an additional `DisplayObject`, or even multiple `DisplayObjects` on the `Stage`.

There's more...

Note here that we are drawing our square in such a way that the `Shape` registration point is located in the center of the visible `Shape`. It is important that we do this, as the `DisplayObject` will rotate based upon the registration point and transform point.

When using the drawing tools in Flash Professional, be sure to set the registration point of your `MovieClip` symbol to be centered in order for this to work correctly.

See also...

`TransformGestureEvent.GESTURE_ROTATE` is just one of a set of four primary transform gestures available to us when working with the Flash Platform runtimes and Android devices. Reference the following recipes for a complete overview of these gestures:

- *Using gestures to zoom a display object*
- *Using gestures to pan a display object*
- *Using gestures to swipe a display object*

Accessing raw touchpoint data

Sometimes the predefined gestures that are baked into Flash Player and AIR are not enough for certain application interactions. This recipe will demonstrate how to access raw touch data reported by the operating system through Flash Player or AIR APIs.

How to do it...

To read raw touch data in your project, perform the following steps:

1. First, import the following classes into your project:

    ```
    import flash.display.StageScaleMode;
    import flash.display.StageAlign;
    import flash.display.Stage;
    import flash.display.Sprite;
    import flash.events.TouchEvent;
    import flash.text.TextField;
    import flash.text.TextFormat;
    import flash.ui.Multitouch;
    import flash.ui.MultitouchInputMode;
    ```

2. Declare a `TextField` and `TextFormat` object to allow visible output upon the device:

```
private var traceField:TextField;
private var traceFormat:TextFormat;
```

3. We will now set up our `TextField`, apply a `TextFormat`, and add it to the `DisplayList`. Here, we create a method to perform all of these actions for us:

```
protected function setupTextField():void {
  traceFormat = new TextFormat();
  traceFormat.bold = true;
  traceFormat.font = "_sans";
  traceFormat.size = 44;
  traceFormat.align = "left";
  traceFormat.color = 0x333333;
  traceField = new TextField();
  traceField.defaultTextFormat = traceFormat;
  traceField.selectable = false;
  traceField.mouseEnabled = false;
  traceField.width = stage.stageWidth;
  traceField.height = stage.stageHeight;
  addChild(traceField);
}
```

4. Set the specific input mode for the multitouch APIs to support touch input by setting `Multitouch.inputMode` to the `MultitouchInputMode.TOUCH_POINT` constant. We will also register a set of listeners for `TouchEvent` data in the following method:

```
protected function setupTouchEvents():void {
  Multitouch.inputMode = MultitouchInputMode.TOUCH_POINT;
  stage.addEventListener(TouchEvent.TOUCH_MOVE, touchMove);
  stage.addEventListener(TouchEvent.TOUCH_END, touchEnd);
}
```

5. To clear out our `TextField` after each touch interaction ends, we will construct the following function:

```
protected function touchEnd(e:TouchEvent):void {
  traceField.text = "";
}
```

6. We can then read the various properties from the touch event to interpret in some way. Events such as pressure, coordinates, size, and more can be derived from the event object that is returned:

```
protected function touchMove(e:TouchEvent):void {
  traceField.text = "";
```

```
     traceField.appendText("Primary: " +
         e.isPrimaryTouchPoint + "\n");
     traceField.appendText("LocalX: " + e.localX + "\n");
     traceField.appendText("LocalY: " + e.localY + "\n");
     traceField.appendText("Pressure: " + e.pressure + "\n");
     traceField.appendText("SizeX: " + e.sizeX + "\n");
     traceField.appendText("SizeY: " + e.sizeY + "\n");
     traceField.appendText("StageX: " + e.stageX + "\n");
     traceField.appendText("StageY: " + e.stageY + "\n");
     traceField.appendText("TPID: " + e.touchPointID + "\n");
}
```

7. The result will appear similar to the following:

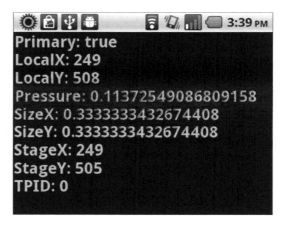

How it works...

Each touch point that is registered in the device has a number of specific properties associated with it. By registering a set of listeners to detect these interactions, we can read this data and the application can react appropriately. In our example, we are simply exposing these values via `TextField`, but this would be the exact data we would need to build a pressure-sensitive gaming mechanic or some other custom gesture.

Note that on a device that allows more than one touchpoint, we will be able to read the data from both touchpoints using the same listener. Multiple touchpoints are differentiated by location on the stage and by `touchPointID`. We would use these IDs to differentiate between touchpoints when devising complex gestures, or simply when we have the need to keep track of each touchpoint in a precise way.

There's more...

It is important to note that while `Multitouch.inputMode` is set to `MultitouchInputMode.TOUCH_POINT` that we will not be able to take advantage of the predefined gestures that Flash Player and AIR make available through the simplified gesture API. Setting the `Multitouch.inputMode` to `MultitouchInputMode.GESTURE` will allow us to take advantage of common, predefined gesture events within our application.

Creating a custom gesture based upon touchPoint data

Using raw touch data, we can define custom gestures to develop unique interactions used in our application. We do this by making calculations based upon data delivered through raw touch events.

How to do it...

In this example, we will create a diagonal swipe gesture that can have four separate values returned which let us know the direction of a diagonal swipe.

1. First, import the following classes into your project:

```
import flash.display.Shape;
import flash.display.Sprite;
import flash.display.Stage;
import flash.display.StageAlign;
import flash.display.StageScaleMode;
import flash.events.TouchEvent;
import flash.text.TextField;
import flash.text.TextFormat;
import flash.ui.Multitouch;
import flash.ui.MultitouchInputMode;
```

2. Declare a `TextField` and `TextFormat` object to allow visible text output upon the device:

```
private var traceField:TextField;
private var traceFormat:TextFormat;
```

3. We will set up two additional objects to help track our gestures, a `Shape` called `drawArea` to draw out the gestures through the graphics API, and `trackBeginObject`, which is a simple object we can use to preserve our beginning touch coordinates to compare with the coordinates of our touch end:

```
private var drawArea:Shape;
private var trackBeginObject:Object;
```

4. We will now set up our `TextField`, apply a `TextFormat`, and add it to the `DisplayList`. Here, we create a method to perform all of these actions for us:

```
protected function setupTextField():void {
  traceFormat = new TextFormat();
  traceFormat.bold = true;
  traceFormat.font = "_sans";
  traceFormat.size = 32;
  traceFormat.align = "center";
  traceFormat.color = 0x333333;
  traceField = new TextField();
  traceField.defaultTextFormat = traceFormat;
  traceField.selectable = false;
  traceField.mouseEnabled = false;
  traceField.width = stage.stageWidth;
  traceField.height = stage.stageHeight;
  addChild(traceField);
}
```

5. Next, we will set up our `Shape` within which we will draw out gestures using the `Graphics` API:

```
protected function setupDrawArea():void {
  drawArea = new Shape();
  addChild(drawArea);
}
```

6. Set the specific input mode for the multitouch APIs to support touch input by setting `Multitouch.inputMode` to the `MultitouchInputMode.TOUCH_POINT` constant. In this example, we will register a set of listeners to detect touch movement on the `Stage`. This will serve to provide visual feedback for our gesture tracking and also preserve our beginning touch coordinates to compare with the coordinates of our touch end.

7. We will also initialize out tracking `Object` through this same method:

```
protected function setupTouchEvents():void {
  Multitouch.inputMode = MultitouchInputMode.TOUCH_POINT;
  trackBeginObject = new Object();
  stage.addEventListener(TouchEvent.TOUCH_BEGIN, touchBegin);
  stage.addEventListener(TouchEvent.TOUCH_MOVE, touchMove);
```

```
        stage.addEventListener(TouchEvent.TOUCH_END, touchEnd);
    }
```

8. Construct a method called `touchBegin` to initialize the beginning of our gesture and preserve coordinate data for later comparison. We will make sure that the touchpoint being registered is the first touchpoint of what could be multiple by testing against the `TouchEvent.isPrimaryTouchPoint` boolean property.

```
protected function touchBegin(e:TouchEvent):void {
    if(e.isPrimaryTouchPoint){
        drawArea.graphics.clear();
        drawArea.graphics.lineStyle(20, 0xFFFFFF, 0.8);
        trackBeginObject.x = e.stageX;
        trackBeginObject.y = e.stageY;
        drawArea.graphics.moveTo(e.stageX, e.stageY);
    }
}
```

9. Construct another method called `touchMove` to accept the touch movement data and draw out our visual feedback:

```
protected function touchMove(e:TouchEvent):void {
    if(e.isPrimaryTouchPoint){
        drawArea.graphics.lineTo(e.stageX, e.stageY);
    }
}
```

10. Construct a final method called `touchEnd` to compare the end touch data coordinates with what we preserved at the beginning through our `trackBeginObject` and then determine what sort of gesture it is. In this case, we output the results as a `String` to a `TextField`, previously created:

```
protected function touchEnd(e:TouchEvent):void {
    if(e.isPrimaryTouchPoint){
        if(e.stageX > trackBeginObject.x && e.stageY >
            trackBeginObject.y){
            traceField.text = "Diagonal Gesture: TL -> BR";
    }elseif(e.stageX < trackBeginObject.x && e.stageY >
            trackBeginObject.y){
            traceField.text = "Diagonal Gesture: TR -> BL";

    }elseif(e.stageX < trackBeginObject.x && e.stageY <
            trackBeginObject.y){
            traceField.text = "Diagonal Gesture: BR -> TL";
    }elseif(e.stageX > trackBeginObject.x && e.stageY <
            trackBeginObject.y){
            traceField.text = "Diagonal Gesture: BL -> TR";
        }
    }
}
```

11. The result will appear similar to the following:

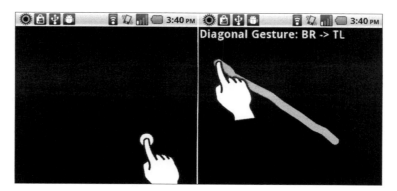

 Illustrations provided by Gestureworks (www.gestureworks.com).

How it works...

As we have access to all of the raw touchpoint data, we can track the life cycle of a touch interaction from beginning to end with the help of regular ActionScript elements such as `Object`, `Vector`, or `Array` instances. Based upon the data tracked, such as coordinate position, touch pressure, and so forth, we can make calculations and determine whether or not the interaction qualifies as the gesture we are looking to track.

In the case of our preceding example, we are being fairly loose with our determination of a qualifying gesture. To be more stringent, we could also calculate the distance of different touch points and even track the time from touch begin to touch end to be sure the gesture is exactly what we are looking for, and therefor intentional by the user.

There's more...

There are actually quite a few gesture libraries that we can use as alternatives to those built into the Flash Player and AIR runtimes. Performing a quick web search should allow us access to these libraries, many of which are free open source software. The most popular 3rd party gesture library is `Gesture Works`, which can be downloaded from `http://gestureworks.com/`.

Emulating the Android long-press interaction

One of the most useful interactions built into the Android operating system is the long press. This is achieved when a user taps a specific area and holds for a few seconds without releasing. While neither Flash Player nor AIR for Android have the long-press interaction as part of the multitouch gesture events library, it is fairly simple to emulate this interaction through either runtime.

How to do it...

We will emulate the Android long-press interaction through use of an ActionScript `Timer` object along with the use of `TouchPoint` events.

1. First, import the following classes into your project:

```
import flash.display.StageScaleMode;
import flash.display.StageAlign;
import flash.display.Stage;
import flash.display.Sprite;
import flash.events.TimerEvent;
import flash.events.TouchEvent;
import flash.geom.Rectangle;
import flash.ui.Multitouch;
import flash.ui.MultitouchInputMode;
import flash.utils.Timer;
```

2. Declare a `Sprite` object which we will perform the long-press upon, as well as a `Timer` object:

```
private var box:Sprite;
private var lpTimer:Timer;
```

3. Set up out `Timer` object to measure the amount of time it should take to register a long-press; in this case, 1000 milliseconds. Additionally, we will now register a listener to detect when the `Timer` cycle has completed:

```
protected function setupTimer():void {
  lpTimer = new Timer(1000,1);
  lpTimer.addEventListener(TimerEvent.TIMER_COMPLETE, timerEnd);
}
```

4. Next, construct a method to handle the creation of our `Sprite` and add it to the `DisplayList`:

```
protected function setupBox():void {
  box = new Sprite();
```

```
    box.graphics.beginFill(0xFFFFFF, 1);
    box.x = stage.stageWidth/2;
    box.y = stage.stageHeight/2;
    box.graphics.drawRect(-100,-100,200,200);
    box.graphics.endFill();
    addChild(box);
}
```

5. Set the specific input mode for the multitouch APIs to support touch input by setting `Multitouch.inputMode` to the `MultitouchInputMode.TOUCH_POINT` constant. To emulate a long-press, we must start a timer at each instance of a touch interaction through `TouchEvent.TOUCH_BEGIN`. The `Timer` will be stopped whenever a `TouchEvent.TOUCH_END` or some other touch cancelling event is fired, resetting our "long-press".

```
protected function setupTouchEvents():void {
    Multitouch.inputMode = MultitouchInputMode.TOUCH_POINT;
    box.addEventListener(TouchEvent.TOUCH_BEGIN, touchBegin);
    box.addEventListener(TouchEvent.TOUCH_END, touchEnd);
    box.addEventListener(TouchEvent.TOUCH_OUT, touchEnd);
    box.addEventListener(TouchEvent.TOUCH_ROLL_OUT, touchEnd);
}
```

6. Construct a method to modify our `Sprite` upon the start of our touch interaction. We will scale the `Sprite` slightly and change the alpha property to indicate that something has activated. At this point, we begin measuring the long-press through our `Timer`:

```
protected function touchBegin(e:TouchEvent):void {
    box.scaleX += 0.1;
    box.scaleY += 0.1;
    box.alpha = 0.8;
    lpTimer.start();
}
```

7. The `Timer` is set to complete after 1000 milliseconds, once fired. Upon this trigger, we can then perform whatever action is necessary within the application. In this case, we are making our `Sprite` dragable:

```
protected function timerEnd(e:TimerEvent):void {
    var dragBounds:Rectangle = new Rectangle(box.width/2,
    box.height/2, stage.stageWidth-box.width,
    stage.stageHeight-box.height);
    box.startDrag(true, dragBounds);
}
```

8. The method for a touch end should stop our `Timer` and cancel any drag events occurring with our `Sprite`. Here, we also rest the `scale` and `alpha` of our `Sprite` to return it to a rest state:

```
protected function touchEnd(e:TouchEvent):void {
    lpTimer.stop();
    box.stopDrag();
    box.scaleX = 1;
    box.scaleY = 1;
    box.alpha = 1;
}
```

9. The resulting gesture will affect our visual object in the following way:

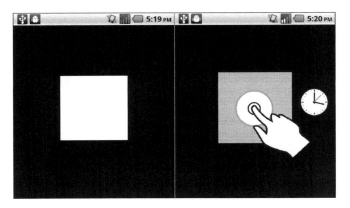

 Illustrations provided by Gestureworks (www.gestureworks.com).

How it works...

Our example requires a one second press and hold to trigger a function invocation, which causes a `Shape` object to become draggable across the `Stage`. This is accomplished by listening for a `TOUCH_BEGIN` event, then monitoring a `Timer` to decide whether this is an intentional long-press interaction. If one second goes by without a `TOUCH_END` event, then we make the `Shape` draggable. We have modified the scale and opacity of the `Shape` once the `Timer` is triggered to indicate that it now a draggable object. Releasing the `Shape` will complete the interaction.

There's more...

The most common uses of the long-press are to perform a repositioning of certain visual elements, as we have done here, or to invoke a menu operation as Android users are very comfortable with using this sort of interaction on their devices.

Invoking the virtual keyboard programmatically

In most cases, simply giving focus to a text input field will invoke the virtual keyboard. Losing focus will dismiss the virtual keyboard. Perhaps we require our application to do this without user interaction, or immediately when entering a certain application state for convenience.

How to do it...

We configure a `Shape` to toggle the Android virtual keyboard on and off through a `Tap` touch event assigned to it.

1. First, import the following classes into your project:

```
import flash.display.Sprite;
import flash.display.Stage;
import flash.display.StageAlign;
import flash.display.StageScaleMode;
import flash.events.SoftKeyboardEvent;
import flash.events.TouchEvent;
import flash.text.TextField;
import flash.text.TextFormat;
import flash.ui.Multitouch;
import flash.ui.MultitouchInputMode;
```

2. Declare a `Shape` alongside a `TextField` and `TextFormat` object. These will be used for interaction and visual feedback.

```
private var tapBox:Sprite;
private var tapBoxField:TextField;
private var tapBoxFormat:TextFormat;
```

3. Next, construct a method to handle the creation of our `Sprite` and add it to the `DisplayList`. Tapping this `Sprite` will allow us to invoke or hide the virtual keyboard. We will also construct a `TextField` and associated `TextFormat` object within the `Sprite` to allow us to provide stateful messages to the user.

```
protected function setupBox():void {
  tapBox = new Sprite();
```

```
tapBox.graphics.beginFill(0xFFFFFF, 1);
tapBox.x = stage.stageWidth/2;
tapBox.y = stage.stageHeight/2 - 200;
tapBox.graphics.drawRect(-200,-100,400,160);
tapBox.graphics.endFill();
tapBoxFormat = new TextFormat();
tapBoxFormat.bold = true;
tapBoxFormat.font = "_sans";
tapBoxFormat.size = 42;
tapBoxFormat.align = "center";
tapBoxFormat.color = 0x333333;
tapBoxField = new TextField();
tapBoxField.defaultTextFormat = tapBoxFormat;
tapBoxField.selectable = false;
tapBoxField.mouseEnabled = false;
tapBoxField.multiline = true;
tapBoxField.wordWrap = true;
tapBoxField.width = tapBox.width;
tapBoxField.height = tapBox.height;
tapBoxField.x = -200;
tapBoxField.y = -80;
tapBoxField.text = "Tap to Toggle Virtual Keyboard";
tapBox.addChild(tapBoxField);
addChild(tapBox);
}
```

4. Set the specific input mode for the multitouch APIs to support touch input by setting `Multitouch.inputMode` to the `MultitouchInputMode.TOUCH_POINT` constant and register an event listener on the `DisplayObject`, which will be used to trigger the activation and deactivation of the Android virtual keyboard. In this case, a `TouchEvent.TOUCH_TAP` event. A touch tap is the touch equivalent of a mouse click event. We can also register a number of listeners for a set of virtual keyboard events. In order for a `DisplayObject` to be able to invoke the virtual keyboard, we will need to set its `needsSoftKeyboard` property to `true`. The `SoftKeyboardEvent` listeners we register here are optional.

```
protected function setupTouchEvents():void {
  Multitouch.inputMode = MultitouchInputMode.TOUCH_POINT;
  tapBox.needsSoftKeyboard = true;
  tapBox.addEventListener(TouchEvent.TOUCH_TAP, touchTap);
  tapBox.addEventListener (SoftKeyboardEvent.
          SOFT_KEYBOARD_ACTIVATING, vkActivating);
  tapBox.addEventListener(SoftKeyboardEvent.
          SOFT_KEYBOARD_ACTIVATE, vkActivate);
  tapBox.addEventListener(SoftKeyboardEvent.
          SOFT_KEYBOARD_DEACTIVATE, vkDeactivate);
}
```

5. To make use of the `SoftKeyboardEvent` listeners defined in the preceding point, we must create a variety of methods to execute once each activity is detected. In this way, we can monitor, interact with, or even prevent certain events from firing by intercepting the virtual keyboard while in the midst of activating, or detecting when the virtual keyboard has completed activation or deactivation completely.

```
protected function vkActivating(e:SoftKeyboardEvent):void {
  trace("Virtual Keyboard ACTIVATING");
}
protected function vkActivate(e:SoftKeyboardEvent):void {
  trace("Virtual Keyboard ACTIVATED");
}
protected function vkDeactivate(e:SoftKeyboardEvent):void {
  trace("Virtual Keyboard DEACTIVATED");
}
```

6. To invoke the virtual keyboard, we simply invoke `requestSoftKeyboard()` on the `DisplayObject`, whose `needsSoftKeyboard` property has been set to `true`. Here, we are checking to see whether `needsSoftKeyboard` is set to true or not, and toggling this property based upon that.

```
protected function touchTap(e:TouchEvent):void {
  if(tapBox.needsSoftKeyboard == true){
    tapBox.requestSoftKeyboard();
    tapBoxField.text = "Virtual Keyboard is Up";
    tapBox.needsSoftKeyboard = false;
  }else{
    tapBox.needsSoftKeyboard = true;
    tapBoxField.text = "Virtual Keyboard is Down";
  }
}
```

7. To dismiss the virtual keyboard, the user will need to tap upon a `DisplayObject`, whose `needsSoftKeyboard` property has been set to `false`.

8. The result will appear similar to the following:

How it works...

In order to invoke the Android virtual keyboard through ActionScript, we must set an interactive `DisplayObjects.needsSoftKeyboard` property to `true`. This will allow us to register a tap touch listener and invoke `requestSoftKeyboard()` upon the tap touch event being fired, revealing the virtual keyboard on screen.

Touching any `DisplayObject` whose `needsSoftKeyboard` property is set to `false` (the default state), will dismiss the virtual keyboard. In our preceding example, we switch this property from `true` to `false` in order to make the `DisplayObject` function as a toggle control.

There's more...

While it is not necessary to use the `SoftKeyboardEvent` class to activate or dismiss the Android virtual keyboard through ActionScript, it is included in the example class as it allows us to respond to such events with an additional set of listener functions.

Responding to Android soft-key interactions

AIR for Android does not include support for invoking the native operating system options menu that often appears at the bottom of the screen. However, there are ways of simulating the native behaviour, which we will explore in this section.

The normal behaviour of the `back` button, on Android, is to step back through the application states until we arrive back home. A further press of the `back` button will exit the application. By default, AIR for Android applications behave in this way as well. If we want to override this default behaviour, we must set up a mechanism to intercept this interaction and then prevent it.

How to do it...

We can respond to soft-key events through standard ActionScript event listeners.

1. First, import the following classes into your project:

```
import flash.display.Sprite;
import flash.display.Stage;
import flash.display.StageAlign;
import flash.display.StageScaleMode;
import flash.events.KeyboardEvent;
import flash.text.TextField;
import flash.text.TextFormat;
import flash.ui.Keyboard;
```

2. Declare a `TextField` and `TextFormat` object to allow visible output upon the device:

```
private var traceField:TextField;
private var traceFormat:TextFormat;
```

3. We will then set up our `TextField`, apply a `TextFormat`, and add it to the `DisplayList`. Here, we create a method to perform all of these actions for us:

```
protected function setupTextField():void {
  traceFormat = new TextFormat();
  traceFormat.bold = true;
  traceFormat.font = "_sans";
  traceFormat.size = 32;
  traceFormat.align = "center";
  traceFormat.color = 0x333333;
  traceField = new TextField();
  traceField.defaultTextFormat = traceFormat;
  traceField.selectable = false;
  traceField.mouseEnabled = false;
```

```
        traceField.width = stage.stageWidth;
        traceField.height = stage.stageHeight;
        addChild(traceField);
    }
```

4. Now we need to set an event listener on the `Stage` to respond to keyboard presses:

```
protected function registerListeners():void {
    stage.addEventListener(KeyboardEvent.KEY_DOWN, keyDown);
}
```

5. We will then write a switch/case statement in our `keyDown` method that will perform different actions in response to specific soft-key events. In this case, we output the name of a specific menu item to our `TextField`:

```
protected function keyDown(e:KeyboardEvent):void {
    var key:uint = e.keyCode;
    traceField.text = key + " pressed!\n";
    switch(key){
        case Keyboard.BACK:{
        e.preventDefault();
        traceField.appendText("Keyboard.BACK");
        break;
    }
        case Keyboard.MENU:{
        traceField.appendText("Keyboard.MENU");
        break;
        }
        case Keyboard.SEARCH:{
        traceField.appendText("Keyboard.SEARCH");
        break;
        }
    }
}
```

6. The result will appear similar to the following:

How it works...

We register listeners for these Android device soft-keys just as we would for a physical or virtual keyboard in ActionScript. If developing Android applications using AIR for Android, we also have access to the BACK, MENU, and SEARCH constants through the Keyboard class.

Registering a keyboard keyDown listener and then responding to specific key values through a switch/case statement allows us to respond to the interaction appropriately. For instance, if the MENU soft-key interaction is detected, we can reveal an options menu.

There's more...

There is also a HOME soft-key on Android devices. This key press cannot be captured through ActionScript as it exists solely to return the user to the Android home screen from any opened application.

> We must use the keyDown event when we want to cancel the default Android behavior of the BACK key because the keyUp event will fire too late and not be caught at all.

Responding to trackball and D-Pad events

Some Android devices have additional physical inputs that we can take advantage of. For instance, the Motorola Droid has a slider keyboard, which includes a directional D-pad and the HTC Nexus One has a built-in trackball control.

How to do it...

We can respond to trackball and D-pad events through standard ActionScript event listeners.

1. First, import the following classes into your project:

```
import flash.display.Shape;
import flash.display.Sprite;
import flash.display.Stage;
import flash.display.StageAlign;
import flash.display.StageScaleMode;
import flash.events.KeyboardEvent;
import flash.text.TextField;
import flash.text.TextFormat;
import flash.ui.Keyboard;
```

2. Declare a `Shape` alongside a `TextField` and `TextFormat` object. These will be used for interaction and visual feedback.

```
private var traceField:TextField;
private var traceFormat:TextFormat;
private var box:Shape;
```

3. We will then set up our `TextField`, apply a `TextFormat`, and add it to the `DisplayList`. Here, we create a method to perform all of these actions for us:

```
protected function setupTextField():void {
  traceFormat = new TextFormat();
  traceFormat.bold = true;
  traceFormat.font = "_sans";
  traceFormat.size = 32;
  traceFormat.align = "center";
  traceFormat.color = 0x333333;
  traceField = new TextField();
  traceField.defaultTextFormat = traceFormat;
  traceField.selectable = false;
  traceField.mouseEnabled = false;
  traceField.width = stage.stageWidth;
  traceField.height = stage.stageHeight;
  addChild(traceField);
}
```

4. Next, construct a method to handle the creation of our `Shape` and add it to the `DisplayList`.

```
protected function setupBox():void {
  box = new Shape();
  box.graphics.beginFill(0xFFFFFF, 1);
  box.x = stage.stageWidth/2;
  box.y = stage.stageHeight/2;
  box.graphics.drawRect(-100,-100,200,200);
  box.graphics.endFill();
  addChild(box);
}
```

5. Set an event listener on the `Stage` to respond to keyboard presses:

```
protected function registerListeners():void {
  stage.addEventListener(KeyboardEvent.KEY_DOWN, keyDown);
}
```

6. Now, we simply need to write a switch/case statement that will perform different actions in response to D-pad/trackball events. In this case, we change the position of our Shape and output the keyCode to a TextField:

```
protected function keyDown(e:KeyboardEvent):void {
  var key:uint = e.keyCode;
  traceField.text = key + " pressed!";
  switch(key){
    case Keyboard.UP:{
      box.y -= 20;
      break;
    }
    case Keyboard.DOWN:{
      box.y += 20;
      break;
    }
    case Keyboard.LEFT:{
      box.x -= 20;
      break;
    }
    case Keyboard.RIGHT:{
      box.x += 20;
      break;
    }
    case Keyboard.ENTER:{
      box.x = stage.stageWidth/2;
      box.y = stage.stageHeight/2;
      break;
    }
  }
}
```

7. The result will appear similar to the following:

How it works...

We register listeners for these special controls just as we would the `Keyboard.UP`, `Keyboard.DOWN`, `Keyboard.LEFT`, `Keyboard.RIGHT`, and `Keyboard.ENTER` keys for any physical keyboard. In this example, we are shifting the target `Shape` in each direction and rest the location based upon the D-pad/trackball being pressed. We are also outputting the `keyCode` value to a text field.

There's more...

It is important to note that most Android devices do not have such specialized input mechanisms. If we do register events mapped to these keys, we should always supply and alternative as well.

3
Movement through Space: Accelerometer and Geolocation Sensors

This chapter will cover the following recipes:

- ▶ Detecting whether or not an Android device supports the accelerometer
- ▶ Detecting Android device movement in 3D space
- ▶ Adjusting the accelerometer sensor update interval
- ▶ Updating display object position through accelerometer sensor
- ▶ Switching between portrait and landscape based upon device tilt
- ▶ Detecting whether or not a device supports a geolocation sensor
- ▶ Detecting whether the geolocation sensor has been disabled by the user
- ▶ Retrieving device geolocation sensor data
- ▶ Adjusting the geolocation sensor update interval
- ▶ Retrieving map data through geolocation coordinates

Introduction

Android devices are not only equipped with touch panels, virtual keyboards, and other input mechanisms, but they also include sensors such as accelerometer for detecting change in 3D space, and geolocation on both a fine (satellite) and coarse (triangulation) level. This chapter will examine how to tap into these sensors in meaningful ways within Flash platform-based Android applications.

All of the recipes in this chapter are represented as pure ActionScript 3 classes and are not dependent upon external libraries or the Flex framework. Therefore, we will be able to use these examples in any IDE we wish.

Detecting whether or not an Android device supports the accelerometer

When developing projects which target the Android operating system, it is always a good idea to make sure that certain sensors, such as the accelerometer, are actually supported on the device. In the case of an Android phone, this will probably always be the case, but we should never assume the capabilities of any device.

How to do it...

We will need to use Accelerometer API classes to detect whether or not an accelerometer is supported:

1. First, import the following classes into your project:

    ```
    import flash.display.StageScaleMode;
    import flash.display.StageAlign;
    import flash.display.Stage;
    import flash.display.Sprite;
    import flash.text.TextField;
    import flash.text.TextFormat;
    import flash.sensors.Accelerometer;
    ```

2. Declare a `TextField` and `TextFormat` object pair to allow visible output upon the device:

    ```
    private var traceField:TextField;
    private var traceFormat:TextFormat;
    ```

3. We will now set up our `TextField`, apply a `TextFormat`, and add it to the `DisplayList`. Here, we create a method to perform all of these actions for us:

```
protected function setupTextField():void {
    traceFormat = new TextFormat();
    traceFormat.bold = true;
    traceFormat.font = "_sans";
    traceFormat.size = 44;
    traceFormat.align = "center";
    traceFormat.color = 0x333333;
    traceField = new TextField();
    traceField.defaultTextFormat = traceFormat;
    traceField.selectable = false;
    traceField.mouseEnabled = false;
    traceField.width = stage.stageWidth;
    traceField.height = stage.stageHeight;
    addChild(traceField);
}
```

4. Then, simply invoke `Accelerometer.isSupported` to confirm support for this capability:

```
protected function checkAccelerometer():void {
    traceField.appendText("Accelerometer: " +
        Accelerometer.isSupported + "\n");
}
```

5. This invocation will return a Boolean value of `true` or `false`, indicating device support for this sensor:

How it works...

Detecting whether the device includes an accelerometer sensor will determine whether or not a user can effectively utilize an application that is dependent upon such data. If our query returns as false, then it is up to us to notify the user or provide some sort of alternative to gathering accelerometer data from the device as a form of interaction.

Detecting Android device movement in 3D space

The `Accelerometer` class works in tandem with the device's motion sensor to measure and report movement and acceleration coordinates as the device is moved through 3D space. To measure this data and react to these measurements, we must perform certain actions to allow the gathering of accelerometer data within our application.

How to do it...

We will need to employ certain ActionScript classes to allow monitoring of accelerometer feedback:

1. First, import the following classes into your project:
```
import flash.display.Sprite;
import flash.display.Stage;
import flash.display.StageAlign;
import flash.display.StageScaleMode;
import flash.events.AccelerometerEvent;
import flash.sensors.Accelerometer;
import flash.text.TextField;
import flash.text.TextFormat;
```

2. Declare a `TextField` and `TextFormat` object pair to allow visible output upon the device, along with an `Accelerometer` object:
```
private var traceField:TextField;
private var traceFormat:TextFormat;
private var accelerometer:Accelerometer;
```

3. We will now set up our `TextField`, apply a `TextFormat`, and add it to the `DisplayList`. Here, we create a method to perform all of these actions for us:
```
protected function setupTextField():void {
  traceFormat = new TextFormat();
  traceFormat.bold = true;
  traceFormat.font = "_sans";
  traceFormat.size = 44;
  traceFormat.align = "center";
  traceFormat.color = 0x333333;
  traceField = new TextField();
  traceField.defaultTextFormat = traceFormat;
  traceField.selectable = false;
  traceField.mouseEnabled = false;
  traceField.width = stage.stageWidth;
```

```
    traceField.height = stage.stageHeight;
    addChild(traceField);
}
```

4. We must now instantiate an `Accelerometer` object to register an `AccelerometerEvent` listener to. In this case, we will have it invoke a function called `movementDetected`. We also first check to see whether or not the `Accelerometer` API is actually supported on the device by checking the `Accelerometer.isSupported` property:

```
protected function registerListeners():void {
    if(Accelerometer.isSupported) {
        accelerometer = new Accelerometer();
        accelerometer.addEventListener(AccelerometerEvent.UPDATE,
                movementDetected);
    }else{
        traceField.text = "Accelerometer not supported!";
    }
}
```

5. We are now able to monitor and respond to device movement through the `movementDetected` method:

```
protected function movementDetected(e:AccelerometerEvent):void {
    traceField.text = "";
    traceField.appendText("Time: " + e.timestamp + "\n");
    traceField.appendText("X: " + e.accelerationX + "\n");
    traceField.appendText("Y: " + e.accelerationY + "\n");
    traceField.appendText("Z: " + e.accelerationZ + "\n");
}
```

6. The output will look similar to this:

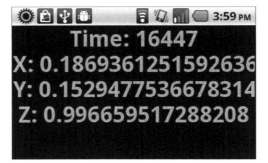

How it works...

By registering an event listener to `AccelerometerEvent.UPDATE` we are able to detect changes reported by the movement sensor on an Android device. There are four properties that are reported back through this event: `accelerationX`, `accelerationY`, `accelerationZ`, and `timestamp`.

- ▸ `accelerationX`: A `Number` which measures acceleration along the x-axis, which runs from left to right when the device is placed in an upright position. A positive acceleration is indicated when the device is moved to the right. Leftward movement is presented as a negative number.

- ▸ `accelerationY`: A `Number` which measures acceleration along the y-axis, which runs from bottom to top when the device is placed in an upright position. A positive acceleration is indicated when the device is moved upwards. Downward movement is presented as a negative number.

- ▸ `accelerationZ`: A `Number` which measures acceleration along the z-axis, which runs perpendicular to the face of the device. A positive acceleration is indicated when the device is moved so that the face points skyward. Movement positioning the face at an earthward angle will be represented as a negative number.

- ▸ `timestamp`: An `int` which measures the amount of milliseconds since the application has been initialized. This can be used to track update events over time.

There's more...

The accelerometer is often used when creating balance-based games on Android such as having a ball travel through a maze based upon device tilt, but we can use this data in any way we wish to monitor changes in space, tilt, or other movement-based actions.

Adjusting the accelerometer sensor update interval

While the default accelerometer sensor update interval may be just fine for most applications, what if we would like to speed up or slow down this interval for a specific purpose?

How to do it...

We will need to change the accelerometer sensor update interval using methods included with the `Accelerometer` class:

1. First, import the following classes into your project:

```
import flash.display.Sprite;
import flash.display.Stage;
import flash.display.StageAlign;
import flash.display.StageScaleMode;
import flash.events.AccelerometerEvent;
import flash.events.TouchEvent;
import flash.sensors.Accelerometer;
import flash.text.TextField;
import flash.text.TextFormat;
import flash.ui.Multitouch;
import flash.ui.MultitouchInputMode;
```

2. We'll now declare a number of objects to use in the example. First, a `TextField` and `TextFormat` object pair to allow visible output upon the device, along with an `Accelerometer` object.

3. Then we will need to also employ a `Number` to keep track of our interval amount.

4. Also needed are two `Sprite` objects for the user to interact with.

```
private var traceField:TextField;
private var traceFormat:TextFormat;
private var accelerometer:Accelerometer;
private var accelerometerInterval:Number;
private var boxUp:Sprite;
private var boxDown:Sprite;
```

5. We will now set up our `TextField`, apply a `TextFormat`, and add it to the `DisplayList`. Here, we create a method to perform all of these actions for us:

```
protected function setupTextField():void {
  traceFormat = new TextFormat();
  traceFormat.bold = true;
  traceFormat.font = "_sans";
  traceFormat.size = 44;
  traceFormat.align = "center";
  traceFormat.color = 0xFFFFFF;
  traceField = new TextField();
  traceField.defaultTextFormat = traceFormat;
  traceField.selectable = false;
  traceField.mouseEnabled = false;
```

```
        traceField.width = stage.stageWidth;
        traceField.height = stage.stageHeight;
        addChild(traceField);
    }
```

6. To detect user input through touch, we will create two `Sprite` instances and add each to the `Stage`. To differentiate between `Sprite` instances in any event listener we register with these objects, we will provide a unique `name` property upon each `Sprite`:

```
protected function setupBoxes():void {
    boxUp = new Sprite();
    boxUp.name = "boxUp";
    boxUp.graphics.beginFill(0xFFFFFF, 1);
    boxUp.x = 20;
    boxUp.y = stage.stageHeight/2;
    boxUp.graphics.drawRect(0,0,100,80);
    boxUp.graphics.endFill();
    addChild(boxUp);
    boxDown = new Sprite();
    boxDown.name = "boxDown";
    boxDown.graphics.beginFill(0xFFFFFF, 1);
    boxDown.x = stage.stageWidth - 120;
    boxDown.y = stage.stageHeight/2;
    boxDown.graphics.drawRect(0,0,100,80);
    boxDown.graphics.endFill();
    addChild(boxDown);
}
```

7. We also first check to see whether or not the Accelerometer API is actually supported on the device by checking the `Accelerometer.isSupported` property.

8. We will then need to set the specific input mode for the multitouch APIs to support touch input by setting `Multitouch.inputMode` to the `MultitouchInputMode.TOUCH_POINT` constant.

9. Each Sprite will register a `TouchEvent.TOUCH_TAP` listener so that it will be able to invoke a method to shift the update interval upon touch tap.

10. Now, we can instantiate an `Accelerometer` object and invoke the `setRequestedUpdateInterval` method, which requires an interval measured in milliseconds to be passed into the method call.

11. We'll also register an event listener to respond to any device movement:

```
protected function registerListeners():void {
    if(Accelerometer.isSupported) {
        Multitouch.inputMode = MultitouchInputMode.TOUCH_POINT;
```

```
    boxUp.addEventListener(TouchEvent.TOUCH_TAP, shiftInterval);
    boxDown.addEventListener(TouchEvent.TOUCH_TAP, shiftInterval);
    accelerometer = new Accelerometer();
    accelerometerInterval = 100;
    accelerometer.setRequestedUpdateInterval
            (accelerometerInterval);
    accelerometer.addEventListener(AccelerometerEvent.UPDATE,
            movementDetected);
    }else{
    traceField.text = "Accelerometer not supported!";
    }
}
```

12. Our `shiftInterval` method will now respond to any touch taps intercepted by the two `Sprite` boxes we created. We are checking to see what `name` property has been given to each `Sprite` and shift the `accelerometerInterval` accordingly:

```
protected function shiftInterval(e:TouchEvent):void {
  switch(e.target.name){
    case "boxUp":{
      accelerometerInterval += 100;
      break;
    }
    case "boxDown":{
      accelerometerInterval -= 100;
      break;
    }
  }
  if(accelerometerInterval < 0){
    accelerometerInterval = 0;
  }
  accelerometer.setRequestedUpdateInterval(accelerometerInterval);
}
```

13. The accelerometer sensor update interval will now invoke the following function, which will output detected movement and interval data through our `TextField`:

```
protected function movementDetected(e:AccelerometerEvent):void {
  traceField.text = "Interval: " + accelerometerInterval + "\n\n";
  traceField.appendText("Time: " + e.timestamp + "\n");
  traceField.appendText("X: " + e.accelerationX + "\n");
  traceField.appendText("Y: " + e.accelerationY + "\n");
  traceField.appendText("Z: " + e.accelerationZ + "\n");
}
```

14. The result will appear similar to the following:

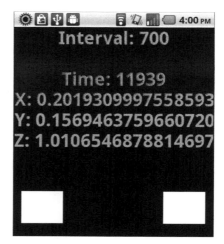

How it works...

By setting the accelerometer update interval through `setRequestedUpdateInterval()`, we are able to adjust this interval based upon circumstances in our particular application. In the preceding demonstration class, we have rendered two `Sprites` acting as an increase and decrease `TouchEvent.TOUCH_TAP` event receptors. Tapping upon these `DisplayObjects` will either increase or decrease the accelerometer update interval, which is monitored through our `TextField` on the screen.

There's more...

Note that the default accelerometer sensor update interval is dependent upon whichever device is running our application. This strategy can also be used to try and even out the interval across devices.

Updating display object position through accelerometer events

The accelerometer sensor can be used when creating all sorts of games or applications for an Android device. One of the more frequent uses of this data is to update the position of a `DisplayObject` on the `Stage` in response to accelerometer update event data.

How to do it...

We will need to employ certain ActionScript classes to allow monitoring of accelerometer feedback through a `DisplayObject` instance. In this example, we will employ a simple `Shape` object and change its position based upon this data:

1. First, import the following classes into your project:

    ```
    import flash.display.Shape;
    import flash.display.Sprite;
    import flash.display.Stage;
    import flash.display.StageAlign;
    import flash.display.StageScaleMode;
    import flash.events.AccelerometerEvent;
    import flash.sensors.Accelerometer;
    import flash.text.TextField;
    import flash.text.TextFormat;
    ```

2. We'll now declare a number of objects to use in the example. First, a `TextField` and `TextFormat` object pair, along with a `Shape` to allow visible output upon the device.

3. We must also declare an `Accelerometer` object in order to monitor and respond to device movement:

    ```
    private var traceField:TextField;
    private var traceFormat:TextFormat;
    private var box:Shape;
    private var accelerometer:Accelerometer;
    ```

4. We will now set up our `TextField`, apply a `TextFormat`, and add it to the `DisplayList`. Here, we create a method to perform all of these actions for us:

    ```
    protected function setupTextField():void {
      traceFormat = new TextFormat();
      traceFormat.bold = true;
      traceFormat.font = "_sans";
      traceFormat.size = 44;
      traceFormat.align = "center";
      traceFormat.color = 0xFFFFFF;
      traceField = new TextField();
      traceField.defaultTextFormat = traceFormat;
      traceField.selectable = false;
      traceField.mouseEnabled = false;
      traceField.width = stage.stageWidth;
      traceField.height = stage.stageHeight;
      addChild(traceField);
    }
    ```

5. Create a new `Shape` object called `box`, draw a rectangle with the `Graphics` API, and add it to the `Stage`:

```
protected function setupBox():void {
  box = new Shape();
  box.graphics.beginFill(0xFFFFFF, 1);
  box.x = stage.stageWidth/2;
  box.y = stage.stageHeight/2;
  box.graphics.drawRect(-100,-100,200,200);
  box.graphics.endFill();
  addChild(box);
}
```

6. We must now instantiate an `Accelerometer` object to register an `AccelerometerEvent` listener to. In this case, we will have it invoke a function called `movementDetected`. We also first check to see whether or not the Accelerometer API is actually supported on the device by checking the `Accelerometer.isSupported` property:

```
protected function registerListeners():void {
  if(Accelerometer.isSupported) {
    accelerometer = new Accelerometer();
    accelerometer.addEventListener(AccelerometerEvent.UPDATE,
          movementDetected);
  }else{
    traceField.text = "Accelerometer not supported!";
  }
}
```

7. We are now able to monitor and respond to device movement through the `movementDetected` method by adjusting the x and y coordinates of our `Shape` object, based upon the `accelerationX` and `accelerationY` data reported through the `AccelerometerEvent.UPDATE` data being reported.

8. In the following function, we are going to perform a number of checks to be sure our `Shape` does not move off of the `Stage` as the device is tilted. We will also output the x and y properties of our `Sprite` to a `TextField`

```
protected function movementDetected(e:AccelerometerEvent):void {
  traceField.text = "";
  var speed:Number = 20;
  if(box.x > box.width/2){
    box.x -= Math.floor(e.accelerationX*speed);
  }else{
    box.x = box.width/2;
  }
  if(box.x < stage.stageWidth-(box.width/2)){
    box.x -= Math.floor(e.accelerationX*speed);
```

```
  }else{
    box.x = stage.stageWidth-(box.width/2);
  }
  if(box.y > box.height/2){
    box.y += Math.floor(e.accelerationY*speed);
  }else{
    box.y = box.height/2;
  }
  if(box.y < stage.stageHeight-(box.height/2)){
    box.y += Math.floor(e.accelerationY*speed);
  }else{
    box.y = stage.stageHeight-(box.height/2);
  }
  traceField.appendText("box.x: " + box.x + "\n");
  traceField.appendText("box.y: " + box.y + "\n");
}
```

9. The resulting output will appear similar to the following:

How it works...

By registering an event listener to `AccelerometerEvent.UPDATE` we are able to detect changes reported by the movement sensor on an Android device. Using ActionScript, we can then respond to these changes in movement and tilt, as the code example demonstrates, by moving a `DisplayObject` around the screen based upon the reported sensor data.

In the example, not only are we moving the Shape object around the screen, but we are also being mindful to never allow the shape to leave the screen through a number of conditional statements taking into account object width, height, and detected screen dimensions.

Switching between portrait and landscape based upon device tilt

Most Android devices will allow both portrait and landscape views for the user to interact with. The portrait mode is enabled when the device is held with the y-axis aligned from top to bottom, while landscape mode is enabled by holding the device so that the y-axis is measured from left to right. By using data reported from the accelerometer sensor, we can know when these movements have occurred and respond to them within our application.

How to do it...

We will need to employ the Accelerometer API to detect device rotation and tilt:

1. First, import the following classes into your project:

```
import flash.display.Sprite;
import flash.display.Stage;
import flash.display.StageAlign;
import flash.display.StageScaleMode;
import flash.events.AccelerometerEvent;
import flash.sensors.Accelerometer;
import flash.text.TextField;
import flash.text.TextFormat;
```

2. We'll now declare a number of objects to use in the example. First, a TextField and TextFormat object pair to allow visible output upon the device.

3. We must also declare an Accelerometer object in order to monitor and respond to device movement:

```
private var traceField:TextField;
private var traceFormat:TextFormat;
private var accelerometer:Accelerometer;
```

4. We will now set up our TextField, apply a TextFormat, and add it to the DisplayList. Here, we create a method to perform all of these actions for us:

```
protected function setupTextField():void {
  traceFormat = new TextFormat();
  traceFormat.bold = true;
  traceFormat.font = "_sans";
  traceFormat.size = 44;
```

```
      traceFormat.align = "center";
      traceFormat.color = 0xFFFFFF;
      traceField = new TextField();
      traceField.defaultTextFormat = traceFormat;
      traceField.selectable = false;
      traceField.mouseEnabled = false;
      traceField.width = stage.stageWidth;
      traceField.height = stage.stageHeight;
      addChild(traceField);
   }
```

5. Then, we must create an `Accelerometer` instance and assign an event listener of type `AccelerometerEvent.UPDATE` to it. This will trigger the `movementDetected` method whenever a change in accelerometer data is detected. We also first check to see whether or not the Accelerometer API is actually supported on the device by checking the `Accelerometer.isSupported` property:

```
protected function registerListeners():void {
   if(Accelerometer.isSupported) {
      accelerometer = new Accelerometer();
      accelerometer.addEventListener(AccelerometerEvent.UPDATE,
            movementDetected);
   }else{
      traceField.text = "Accelerometer not supported!";
   }
}
```

6. Within our `movementDetected` method, we simply need to monitor the acceleration data reported by the sensor and adjust our application accordingly. We'll also output data to our `TextField` to monitor device movement:

```
protected function movementDetected(e:AccelerometerEvent):void {
   traceField.text = "";
   traceField.appendText("Time: " + e.timestamp + "\n");
   traceField.appendText("X: " + e.accelerationX + "\n");
   traceField.appendText("Y: " + e.accelerationY + "\n");
   traceField.appendText("Z: " + e.accelerationZ + "\n");
   if(e.accelerationY > 0.5){
      traceField.appendText("\n\n\nPORTRAIT");
   }else{
      traceField.appendText("\n\n\nLANDSCAPE");
   }
}
```

7. The result will appear similar to the following:

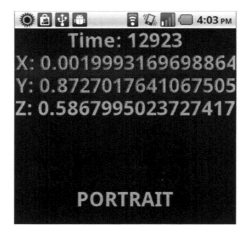

How it works...

As the accelerometer movement is detected within our application, the `movementDetected` method will report data regarding the x, y, and z axis of the device. If we monitor the acceleration value that is reported, we can respond to device tilt in a way that takes into account the vertical orientation and thus know whether or not to adjust elements on the `Stage` for portrait or landscape viewing.

There's more...

In this example, we are using pure ActionScript to detect accelerometer senor data and respond to it. When using the mobile Flex framework in developing our application, we can allow the framework to handle device orientation for us when setting up our **Flex Mobile Project** by choosing the **Automatically reorient** option in the **Mobile Settings** dialog.

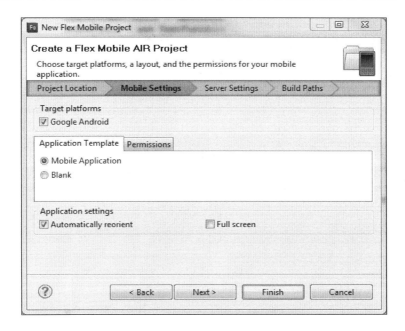

See also...

Chapter 6, Structural Adaptation: Handling Device Layout and Scaling, also has more information on adapting to device orientation changes using alternative detection methods.

Detecting whether or not a device supports a geolocation sensor

When developing projects which target the Android operating system, it is always a good idea to make sure that certain sensors, such as the geolocation sensor, are actually supported on the device. In the case of an Android device, this will probably always be the case, but we should never assume the capabilities of any device.

How to do it...

We will need to use internal classes to detect whether or not the geolocation API is supported:

1. First, import the following classes into your project:

```
import flash.display.StageScaleMode;
import flash.display.StageAlign;
import flash.display.Stage;
```

```
import flash.display.Sprite;
import flash.text.TextField;
import flash.text.TextFormat;
import flash.sensors.Geolocation;
```

2. Declare a `TextField` and `TextFormat` object pair to allow visible output upon the device:

```
private var traceField:TextField;
private var traceFormat:TextFormat;
```

3. We will now set up our `TextField`, apply a `TextFormat`, and add the `TextField` to the `DisplayList`. Here, we create a method to perform all of these actions for us:

```
protected function setupTextField():void {
  traceFormat = new TextFormat();
  traceFormat.bold = true;
  traceFormat.font = "_sans";
  traceFormat.size = 44;
  traceFormat.align = "center";
  traceFormat.color = 0x333333;
  traceField = new TextField();
  traceField.defaultTextFormat = traceFormat;
  traceField.selectable = false;
  traceField.mouseEnabled = false;
  traceField.width = stage.stageWidth;
  traceField.height = stage.stageHeight;
  addChild(traceField);
}
```

4. Then, simply invoke `Geolocation.isSupported` to confirm support for this capability:

```
protected function checkGeolocation():void {
  traceField.appendText("Geolocation: " +
      Geolocation.isSupported);
}
```

5. This invocation will return a Boolean value of `true` or `false`, indicating device support for this sensor. This result will be output to the `TextField` we created:

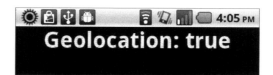

How it works...

Detecting whether the device includes a geolocation sensor will determine whether or not a user can effectively utilize an application that is dependent upon such data. If our query returns as false, then it is up to us to notify the user or provide some sort of alternative to gathering such data from the user. This is normally handled by the user inputting specific location data manually.

See also...

The availability of the geolocation sensors must be requested by the application developer through an Android manifest file. In order for our application to use these sensors, permissions must be stated within the manifest file. See *Chapter 9, Manifest Assurance: Security and Android Permissions*, for more information.

Detecting whether the geolocation sensor has been disabled by the user

There are many reasons why the Android geolocation sensor may not be available for use in our application. The user could have simply switched this sensor off to conserve battery life, or perhaps we, as developers, did not provide adequate permissions through the Android manifest file to allow geolocation access. In any case, it is a good idea to check and respond with a kind prompt if the sensor has been disabled.

How to do it...

We will need to check the `muted` property included with the `Geolocation` class:

1. First, import the following classes into your project:

```
import flash.display.Sprite;
import flash.display.Stage;
import flash.display.StageAlign;
import flash.display.StageScaleMode;
import flash.events.StatusEvent;
import flash.sensors.Geolocation;
import flash.text.TextField;
import flash.text.TextFormat;
```

2. Declare a `TextField` and `TextFormat` object pair to allow visible output upon the device along with a `Geolocation` object:

```
private var traceField:TextField;
private var traceFormat:TextFormat;
private var geo:Geolocation;
```

3. We will now set up our `TextField`, apply a `TextFormat`, and add the `TextField` to the `DisplayList`. Here, we create a method to perform all of these actions for us:

```
protected function setupTextField():void {
    traceFormat = new TextFormat();
    traceFormat.bold = true;
    traceFormat.font = "_sans";
    traceFormat.size = 44;
    traceFormat.align = "center";
    traceFormat.color = 0x333333;
    traceField = new TextField();
    traceField.defaultTextFormat = traceFormat;
    traceField.selectable = false;
    traceField.mouseEnabled = false;
    traceField.width = stage.stageWidth;
    traceField.height = stage.stageHeight;
    addChild(traceField);
}
```

4. Now, we must instantiate a `Geolocation` instance and register an event listener to determine whether geolocation becomes disabled while our application is running.

 We could also simply check the `muted` property at any time now that we have defined a `Geolocation` instance.

```
protected function registerListeners():void {
    geo = new Geolocation();
    geo.addEventListener(StatusEvent.STATUS,
            checkGeolocationMuted);
    traceField.appendText("Geolocation Disabled? \n\n" + geo.muted);
}
```

5. Once we invoke the method, check the muted property. If this returns `true`, we can access the device geolocation sensor; if it returns `false`, then we know the sensor has been disabled:

```
protected function checkGeolocationMuted(e:StatusEvent):void {
    traceField.appendText("Geolocation Disabled? \n\n" + geo.muted);
}
```

6. The result will be output to the device screen as shown in the following screenshot:

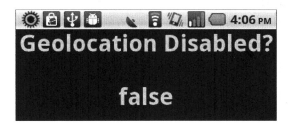

How it works...

Once we construct a `Geolocation` instance, we then are able to access the `muted` property of that class. By checking the `muted` property of a `Geolocation` object, we can either disable geolocation features in our application, prompt the user to manually enter their location, or simply notify the user that they must enable the geolocation sensor on the device in order to proceed.

There's more...

As demonstrated in our example, the `Geolocation` object can have a `status` event registered to it, which will alert us when the `muted` property changes. We can use this to detect changes in the property while running the application and respond accordingly.

See also...

The availability of the geolocation sensors must be requested by the application developer through an Android manifest file. In order for our application to use these sensors, permissions must be stated within the manifest file. See *Chapter 9* for more information.

Retrieving device geolocation sensor data

The `Geolocation` class can be used to reveal a full set of properties for tracking device position on the globe. This is useful for mapping, weather, travel, and other location-aware applications. To measure this data and react to these measurements, we must perform certain actions.

How to do it...

We will need to employ certain ActionScript classes to allow monitoring of geolocation feedback:

1. First, import the following classes into your project:

```
import flash.display.Sprite;
import flash.display.Stage;
import flash.display.StageAlign;
import flash.display.StageScaleMode;
import flash.events.GeolocationEvent;
import flash.sensors.Geolocation;
import flash.text.TextField;
import flash.text.TextFormat;
```

2. Declare a `TextField` and `TextFormat` object pair to allow visible output upon the device along with a `Geolocation` object:

```
private var traceField:TextField;
private var traceFormat:TextFormat;
private var geolocation:Geolocation;
```

3. We will now set up our `TextField`, apply a `TextFormat`, and add the `TextField` to the `DisplayList`. Here, we create a method to perform all of these actions for us:

```
protected function setupTextField():void {
  traceFormat = new TextFormat();
  traceFormat.bold = true;
  traceFormat.font = "_sans";
  traceFormat.size = 44;
  traceFormat.align = "center";
  traceFormat.color = 0x333333;
  traceField = new TextField();
  traceField.defaultTextFormat = traceFormat;
  traceField.selectable = false;
  traceField.mouseEnabled = false;
  traceField.width = stage.stageWidth;
  traceField.height = stage.stageHeight;
  addChild(traceField);
}
```

4. We must now instantiate a `Geolocation` object to register a `GeolocationEvent` listener to. In this case, we will have it invoke a function called `geolocationUpdate`. We also first check to see whether or not the Geolocation API is actually supported on the device by checking the `Geolocation.isSupported` property:

```
protected function registerListeners():void {
  if(Geolocation.isSupported) {
    geolocation = new Geolocation();
```

```
      geolocation.addEventListener(GeolocationEvent.UPDATE,
                geolocationUpdate);
   }else{
      traceField.text = "Geolocation not supported!";
   }
}
```

5. We are now able to monitor and respond to device movement through the
    `geolocationUpdate` method. In this case, we are outputting the collected data to a
    `TextField`:

```
protected function geolocationUpdate(e:GeolocationEvent):void {
   traceField.text = "";
   traceField.appendText("altitude: " + e.altitude + "\n");
   traceField.appendText("heading: " + e.heading + "\n");
   traceField.appendText("horizontal accuracy: " +
         e.horizontalAccuracy + "\n");
   traceField.appendText("latitude: " + e.latitude + "\n");
   traceField.appendText("longitude: " + e.longitude + "\n");
   traceField.appendText("speed: " + e.speed + "\n");
   traceField.appendText("timestamp: " + e.timestamp + "\n");
   traceField.appendText("vertical accuracy: " +
         e.verticalAccuracy);
}
```

6. The output will look something like this:

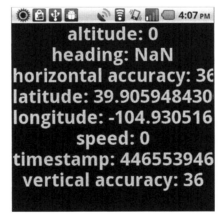

How it works...

By registering an event listener to `GeolocationEvent.UPDATE` we are able to detect changes reported by the geolocation sensor on an Android device. Note that not every Android device will be able to report upon all of these properties; it will vary based upon device being used. There are eight possible properties that are reported back through this event: `altitude`, `heading`, `horizontalAccuracy`, `latitude`, `longitude`, `speed`, `timestamp`, and `verticalAccuracy`.

- `altitude`: A `Number` measuring current altitude, in meters.
- `heading`: A `Number` representative of the direction of movement, in degrees.
- `horizontalAccuracy`: A `Number` measuring the horizontal accuracy of the sensor measurement, in meters.
- `latitude`: A `Number` representative of the current device latitude, in degrees.
- `longitude`: A `Number` representative of the current device longitude, in degrees.
- `speed`: A `Number` measuring speed in meters per second.
- `timestamp`: An `int` representative of the number of milliseconds since application initialization.
- `verticalAccuracy`: A `Number` measuring the vertical accuracy of the sensor measurement, in meters.

Adjusting the geolocation sensor update interval

While the default geolocation sensor update interval may be just fine for most applications, what if we would like to speed up or slow down this interval for a specific purpose?

How to do it...

We will need to change the geolocation sensor update interval using methods included with the `Geolocation` class:

1. First, import the following classes into your project:

```
import flash.display.Sprite;
import flash.display.Stage;
import flash.display.StageAlign;
import flash.display.StageScaleMode;
import flash.events.GeolocationEvent;
import flash.events.TouchEvent;
import flash.sensors.Geolocation;
```

```
import flash.text.TextField;
import flash.text.TextFormat;
import flash.ui.Multitouch;
import flash.ui.MultitouchInputMode;
```

2. We'll now declare a number of objects to use in the example. First, a `TextField` and `TextFormat` object to allow visible output upon the device, along with an `Geolocation` object.

3. Then we will need to also employ a `Number` to keep track of our interval amount. Also needed are two `Sprite` objects for the user to interact with.

```
private var traceField:TextField;
private var traceFormat:TextFormat;
private var geolocation:Geolocation;
private var geolocationInterval:Number;
private var boxUp:Sprite;
private var boxDown:Sprite;
```

4. We will now set up our `TextField`, apply a `TextFormat`, and add the `TextField` to the `DisplayList`. Here, we create a method to perform all of these actions for us:

```
protected function setupTextField():void {
  traceFormat = new TextFormat();
  traceFormat.bold = true;
  traceFormat.font = "_sans";
  traceFormat.size = 44;
  traceFormat.align = "center";
  traceFormat.color = 0x333333;
  traceField = new TextField();
  traceField.defaultTextFormat = traceFormat;
  traceField.selectable = false;
  traceField.mouseEnabled = false;
  traceField.width = stage.stageWidth;
  traceField.height = stage.stageHeight;
  addChild(traceField);
}
```

5. To detect user input through touch, we will create two `Sprite` instances and add each to the `Stage`. To differentiate between `Sprite` instances in any event listener we register with these objects, we will provide a unique name property upon each `Sprite`:

```
protected function setupBoxes():void {
  boxUp = new Sprite();
  boxUp.name = "boxUp";
  boxUp.graphics.beginFill(0xFFFFFF, 0.6);
  boxUp.x = 20;
```

```
        boxUp.y = stage.stageHeight/2;
        boxUp.graphics.drawRect(0,0,100,80);
        boxUp.graphics.endFill();
        addChild(boxUp);
        boxDown = new Sprite();
        boxDown.name = "boxDown";
        boxDown.graphics.beginFill(0xFFFFFF, 0.6);
        boxDown.x = stage.stageWidth - 120;
        boxDown.y = stage.stageHeight/2;
        boxDown.graphics.drawRect(0,0,100,80);
        boxDown.graphics.endFill();
        addChild(boxDown);
    }
```

6. We first check to see whether or not the Geolocation API is actually supported on the device by checking the `Geolocation.isSupported` property.

7. We will then need to set the specific input mode for the multitouch APIs to support touch input by setting `Multitouch.inputMode` to the `MultitouchInputMode.TOUCH_POINT` constant. Each `Sprite` will register a `TouchEvent.TOUCH_TAP` listener so that it will be able to invoke a method to shift the update interval upon touch tap.

8. Now, we can also instantiate a `Geolocation` object and invoke the `setRequestedUpdateInterval` method, which requires an interval measured in milliseconds to be passed into the method call.

9. We'll register an event listener to respond to any device movement:

```
protected function registerListeners():void {
  if(Geolocation.isSupported) {
    Multitouch.inputMode = MultitouchInputMode.TOUCH_POINT;
    boxUp.addEventListener(TouchEvent.TOUCH_TAP, shiftInterval);
    boxDown.addEventListener(TouchEvent.TOUCH_TAP, shiftInterval);
    geolocation = new Geolocation();
    geolocationInterval = 100;
  geolocation.setRequestedUpdateInterval(geolocationInterval);
    geolocation.addEventListener(GeolocationEvent.UPDATE,
              geolocationUpdate);
  }else{
    traceField.text = "Geolocation not supported!";
  }
}
```

10. Our `shiftInterval` method will now respond to any touch taps intercepted by the two `Sprite` boxes we created. We are checking to see what name property has been given to each `Sprite` and shift the `accelerometerInterval` accordingly:

```
protected function shiftInterval(e:TouchEvent):void {
  switch(e.target.name){
    case "boxUp":{
      geolocationInterval += 100;
      break;
    }
    case "boxDown":{
      geolocationInterval -= 100;
      break;
    }
  }
  if(geolocationInterval < 0){
    geolocationInterval = 0;
  }
  geolocation.setRequestedUpdateInterval(geolocationInterval);
}
```

11. The geolocation sensor update interval will now invoke the following function which will output detected movement and interval data through our `TextField`:

```
protected function geolocationUpdate(e:GeolocationEvent):void {
  traceField.text = "Interval: " + geolocationInterval + "\n\n";
  traceField.appendText("altitude: " + e.altitude + "\n");
  traceField.appendText("heading: " + e.heading + "\n");
  traceField.appendText("horizontal accuracy: " +
          e.horizontalAccuracy + "\n");
  traceField.appendText("latitude: " + e.latitude + "\n");
  traceField.appendText("longitude: " + e.longitude + "\n");
  traceField.appendText("speed: " + e.speed + "\n");
  traceField.appendText("timestamp: " + e.timestamp + "\n");
  traceField.appendText("vertical accuracy: " +
          e.verticalAccuracy);
}
```

12. The result will appear similar to the following screenshot:

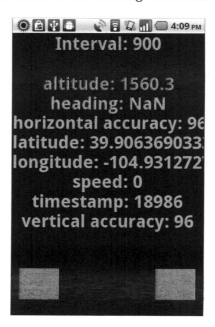

How it works...

By setting the geolocation update interval through `setRequestedUpdateInterval()`, we are able to adjust this interval based upon circumstances in our particular application. In the `demonstration` class in the preceding section, we have rendered two `Sprites` acting as an increase and decrease `TouchEvent.TOUCH_TAP` event receptors. Tapping upon these `DisplayObjects` will either increase or decrease the geolocation update interval, which is monitored through our `TextField` on the screen.

There's more...

Note that the default geolocation sensor update interval is dependent upon whichever device is running our application. This strategy can also be used to try and even out the interval across devices. Some things, however, are totally out of our control. For instance, if a user is located deep inside of a building and has a poor GPS signal, the update interval can actually be well over a minute. Various factors such as this should be kept in mind.

Retrieving map data through geolocation coordinates

To retrieve a map through the use of geolocation coordinates is one of the fundamental uses of the ActionScript Geolocation API. In this recipe, we will examine how to render a map on the Stage and generate a marker based on latitude and longitude coordinates reported by the device geolocation sensors using the Google Maps API for Flash.

Getting ready...

There are a few steps we will need to take before getting into the recipe itself. These steps will prepare our project with the proper code libraries and allow us access to the Google Maps services:

1. First, we must download the Google Maps API for Flash from `http://code.google.com/apis/maps/documentation/flash/`

2. The package will include two separate `.swc` files. One for Flex, and the other for ActionScript projects. In this example, we will extract the pure `AS3` `.swc` to our local hard drive.

3. From the same URL (in the first point) click on the link that reads **Sign up for a Google Maps API Key** to generate an API key and register a URL. You will need both of these items to complete the example.

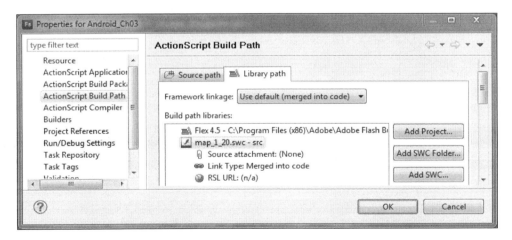

4. Now, include the Google Maps SDK into your development environment by either adding the .swc through the **ActionScript Build Path** properties dialog in the case of Flash Builder (you can also simply drag the .swc into the libs directory) or FDT or through the **Advanced ActionScript Properties** dialog in Flash Professional:

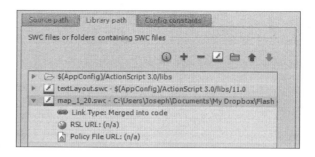

5. We are now ready to proceed with the recipe.

How to do it...

We will need to create our map DisplayObject, **generate event listeners for** Geolocation API updates, and adjust map properties based upon our current location:

1. First, import the following classes into your project:

```
import flash.display.Sprite;
import flash.display.Stage;
import flash.display.StageAlign;
import flash.display.StageScaleMode;
import flash.events.GeolocationEvent;
import flash.geom.Point;
import flash.sensors.Geolocation;
import flash.text.TextField;
import flash.text.TextFormat;
```

2. Next, we will want to import a number of classes included in the Google Maps SDK. These classes will allow us to render a Map on the Stage, listen for map-specific events, and render a Marker on our current location:

```
import com.google.maps.LatLng;
import com.google.maps.Map;
import com.google.maps.MapEvent;
import com.google.maps.MapType;
import com.google.maps.overlays.Marker;
```

3. We will now create a number of object references to be used in this example. First, a `TextField` and `TextFormat` object pair to allow visible output upon the device, along with a `Geolocation` object.

4. Then we will need to also employ `Map` and `LatLng` objects to render a map of our location:

```
private var traceField:TextField;
private var traceFormat:TextFormat;
private var geolocation:Geolocation;
private var map:Map;
private var coordinates:LatLng;
```

5. We are now ready to create our `Map` by passing in the API key and URL we set up when registering with Google, and adding the `Map` to the display list:

```
protected function setupMap():void {
  map = new Map();
  map.key = "{GOOGLE_MAPS_API_KEY}";
  map.url = "{APP_URL}";
  map.sensor = "true";
  map.setSize(new Point(stage.stageWidth, stage.stageHeight));
  addChild(map);
}
```

6. We will now set up our `TextField`, apply a `TextFormat`, and add the `TextField` to the `DisplayList`. Here, we create a method to perform all of these actions for us:

```
protected function setupTextField():void {
  traceFormat = new TextFormat();
  traceFormat.bold = true;
  traceFormat.font = "_sans";
  traceFormat.size = 44;
  traceFormat.align = "center";
  traceFormat.color = 0x333333;
  traceField = new TextField();
  traceField.defaultTextFormat = traceFormat;
  traceField.selectable = false;
  traceField.mouseEnabled = false;
  traceField.width = stage.stageWidth;
  traceField.height = stage.stageHeight;
  addChild(traceField);
}
```

7. It is important that we register listeners for both geolocation updates, and `Map` completion events, so that we are able to read coordinate data, and know when our `Map` is ready for interaction. We also first check to see whether or not the Geolocation API is actually supported on the device by checking the `Geolocation.isSupported` property:

```
protected function registerListeners():void {
  if(Geolocation.isSupported) {
    geolocation = new Geolocation();
    geolocation.addEventListener(GeolocationEvent.UPDATE,
               geolocationUpdate);
    map.addEventListener(MapEvent.MAP_READY, mapReady);
  }else{
    traceField.text = "Geolocation not supported!";
  }
}
```

8. As the geolocation updates are being handled locally, this will most likely be our first event listener to fire. We will grab the `longitude` and `latitude` from data provided by the device geolocation sensor through this event and create a `LatLong` object from this which will be fed into the `Map` upon initialization:

```
protected function geolocationUpdate(e:GeolocationEvent):void {
  traceField.text = "";
  traceField.appendText("latitude:\n" + e.latitude + "\n\n");
  traceField.appendText("longitude:\n" + e.longitude);
    coordinates = new LatLng(e.latitude, e.longitude);
}
```

9. Once our `mapReady` listener method fires, we will already have the coordinate information needed to display our current coordinates through the `Map` and also render a simple `Marker` at this precise location:

```
protected function mapReady(e:MapEvent):void {
  map.setCenter(coordinates, 16, MapType.NORMAL_MAP_TYPE);
  var marker:Marker = new Marker(map.getCenter());
  map.addOverlay(marker);
}
```

10. The result will look similar to this:

How it works...

By tapping into a mapping service such as Google Maps, we can listen for local device geolocation updates and feed the necessary data into the mapping service to perform numerous tasks.

In the case of this example, we simply center the `Map` to our device coordinates and place a `Marker` overlay upon the `Map`. Whenever you are using a service such as this, it is always a good idea to thoroughly read the documentation to know both the possibilities and limitation n of the service.

The `url` property should be set to an online location where the purpose and scope of the application is described, as per Google's request.

> We are setting the `sensor` property of our `Map` instance to `true`. This is required if the `Map` is reacting to data based upon device geolocation sensors by Google. If we were simply allowing the user to input coordinates and adjust the `Map` location in that way, we would set the `sensor` property to `false`.

There's more...

In this case, we are using the Google Maps API for Flash. It is quite robust, but you may want to use another mapping system such as Yahoo! Maps, MapQuest, or some other service. That is fine since they will all require similar information; only the specific API setup will differ.

4
Visual and Audio Input: Camera and Microphone Access

This chapter will cover the following recipes:

- ▶ Detecting camera and microphone support
- ▶ Using the traditional camera API to save a captured image
- ▶ Using the Mobile CameraUI API to save a captured photograph
- ▶ Using the Mobile CameraUI API to save a captured video
- ▶ Using the device microphone to monitor audio sample data
- ▶ Recording microphone audio sample data

Introduction

Camera and microphone are standard accessories on most mobile devices and Android devices are no exception to this. The present chapter will cover everything from accessing the camera and taking photos, recording video data, and encoding raw audio captured from the device microphone and encoding it to WAV or MP3 for use on other platforms and systems.

All of the recipes in this chapter are represented as pure ActionScript 3 classes and are not dependent upon external libraries or the Flex framework. Therefore, we will be able to use these examples in any IDE we wish.

Detecting camera and microphone support

Nearly all Android devices come equipped with camera hardware for capturing still images and video. Many devices now have both front and rear-facing cameras. It is important to know whether the default device camera is usable through our application. We should never assume the availability of certain hardware items, no matter how prevalent across devices.

Similarly, we will want to be sure to have access to the device microphone as well, when capturing video or audio data.

How to do it...

We will determine which audio and video APIs are available to us on our Android device:

1. First, import the following classes into your project:

```
import flash.display.Sprite;
import flash.display.Stage;
import flash.display.StageAlign;
import flash.display.StageScaleMode;
import flash.media.Camera;
import flash.media.CameraUI;
import flash.media.Microphone;
import flash.text.TextField;
import flash.text.TextFormat;
```

2. Declare a `TextField` and `TextFormat` object pair to allow visible output upon the device:

```
private var traceField:TextField;
private var traceFormat:TextFormat;
```

3. We will now set up our `TextField`, apply a `TextFormat`, and add the `TextField` to the `DisplayList`. Here, we create a method to perform all of these actions for us:

```
protected function setupTextField():void {
  traceFormat = new TextFormat();
  traceFormat.bold = true;
  traceFormat.font = "_sans";
  traceFormat.size = 44;
  traceFormat.align = "center";
  traceFormat.color = 0x333333;
  traceField = new TextField();
  traceField.defaultTextFormat = traceFormat;
  traceField.selectable = false;
  traceField.mouseEnabled = false;
```

```
        traceField.width = stage.stageWidth;
        traceField.height = stage.stageHeight;
        addChild(traceField);
    }
```

4. Now, we must check the isSupported property of each of these objects. We create a method here to perform this across all three and write results to a TextField:

```
protected function checkCamera():void {
    traceField.appendText("Camera: " + Camera.isSupported + "\n");
    traceField.appendText("CameraUI: " +
            CameraUI.isSupported + "\n");
    traceField.appendText("Microphone: " +
            Microphone.isSupported + "\n");
}
```

5. We now know the capabilities of video and audio input for a particular device and can react accordingly:

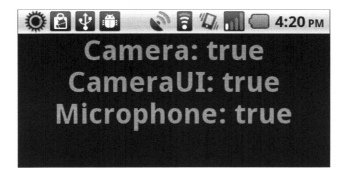

How it works...

Each of these three classes has a property isSupported, which we may invoke at any time to verify support on a particular Android device. The traditional Camera and mobile-specific CameraUI both refer to the same hardware camera, but are entirely different classes for dealing with the interaction between Flash and the camera itself, as CameraUI relies upon the default device camera applications to do all the capturing, and Camera works exclusively within the Flash environment.

> The traditional Microphone object is also supported in this manner.

There's more...

It is important to note that even though many Android devices come equipped with more than one camera, only the primary camera (and microphone) will be exposed to our application. Support for multiple cameras and other sensors will likely be added to the platform as Android evolves.

Using the traditional camera API to save a captured image

When writing applications for the web through Flash player, or for a desktop with AIR, we have had access to the `Camera` class through ActionScript. This allows us to access different cameras attached to whatever machine we are using. On Android, we can still use the `Camera` class to access the default camera on the device and access the video stream it provides for all sorts of things. In this example, we will simply grab a still image from the `Camera` feed and save it to the Android `CameraRoll`.

How to do it...

We will construct a `Video` object to bind the `Camera` stream to, and use `BitmapData` methods to capture and then save our rendered image using the mobile `CameraRoll` API:

1. At a minimum, we need to import the following classes into our project:

```
import flash.display.BitmapData;
import flash.display.Sprite;
import flash.display.Stage;
import flash.display.StageAlign;
import flash.display.StageScaleMode;
import flash.events.TouchEvent;
import flash.media.Camera;
import flash.media.CameraRoll;
import flash.media.Video;
import flash.ui.Multitouch;
import flash.ui.MultitouchInputMode;
```

2. Now we must declare the object instances necessary for camera access and file reference:

```
private var video:Video;
private var camera:Camera;
private var capture:BitmapData;
private var cameraRoll:CameraRoll;
private var videoHolder:Sprite;
```

3. Initialize a `Video` object, passing in the desired width and height, and add it to the `DisplayList`:

```
protected function setupVideo():void {
  videoHolder = new Sprite();
  videoHolder.x = stage.stageWidth/2;
  videoHolder.y = stage.stageHeight/2;
  video = new Video(360, 480);
  videoHolder.addChild(video);
  video.x = -180;
  video.y = -240;
  videoHolder.rotation = 90;
  addChild(videoHolder);
}
```

4. Initialize a `Camera` object and employ `setMode` to specify width, height, and frames per second before attaching the `Camera` to our `Video` on the `DisplayList`:

```
protected function setupCamera():void {
  camera = Camera.getCamera();
  camera.setMode(480, 360, 24);
  video.attachCamera(camera);
}
```

5. We will now register a `TouchEvent` listener of type `TOUCH_TAP` to the `Stage`. This will enable the user to take a snapshot of the camera display by tapping the device screen:

```
protected function registerListeners():void {
  Multitouch.inputMode =
  MultitouchInputMode.TOUCH_POINT;
  stage.addEventListener(TouchEvent.TOUCH_TAP, saveImage);
}
```

6. To capture an image from the camera feed, we will initialize our `BitmapData` object, matching the width and height of our `Video` object, and employ the `draw` method to translate the `Video` pixels to `BitmapData`.

7. To save our acquired image to the device, we must initialize a `CameraRoll` object and invoke `addBitmapData()`, passing in the `BitmapData` object we have created using `Video` object pixels. We will also determine whether or not this device supports the `addBitmapData()` method by verifying `CameraRoll`. `supportsAddBitmapData` is equal to `true`:

```
protected function saveImage(e:TouchEvent):void {
  capture = new BitmapData(360, 480);
  capture.draw(video);
  cameraRoll = new CameraRoll();
```

```
if(CameraRoll.supportsAddBitmapData){
  cameraRoll.addBitmapData(capture);
}
}
```

8. If we now check our Android Gallery, we will find the saved image:

How it works...

Most of this is performed exactly as it would be with normal Flash Platform development on the desktop. Attach a `Camera` to a `Video`, add the `Video` to the `DisplayList`, and then do whatever you need for your particular application. In this case, we simply capture what is displayed as `BitmapData`.

The `CameraRoll` class, however, is specific to mobile application development as it will always refer to the directory upon which the device camera stores the photographs it produces. If you want to save these images within a different directory, we could use a `File` or `FileReference` object to do so, but this involves more steps for the user.

Note that while using the `Camera` class, the hardware orientation of the camera is landscape. We can deal with this by either restricting the application to landscape mode, or through rotations and additional manipulation as we've performed in our example class. We've applied a 90 degree rotation to the image in this case using `videoHolder.rotation` to account for this shift when reading in the `BitmapData`. Depending on how any specific application handles this, it may not be necessary to do so.

There's more...

Other use cases for the traditional Camera object are things such as sending a video stream to Flash Media Server for live broadcast, augmented reality applications, or real-time peer to peer chat.

See also...

In order to access the camera and storage, we will need to add some Android permissions for `CAMERA` and `WRITE_EXTERNAL_STORAGE`. Refer to *Chapter 11, Final Considerations: Application Compilation and Distribution* for information on how to go about this.

Using the Mobile CameraUI API to save a captured photograph

Using the new `CameraUI` API (available in the mobile AIR SDK), we can perform and alternative capture process to the normal `Camera` API. The `Mobile CameraUI` class will make use of the default Android camera application, alongside our custom app, to capture a photograph.

How to do it...

We will set up a `CameraUI` object to invoke the native Android camera to capture a photograph:

1. First, import the following classes into your project:

```
import flash.display.Sprite;
import flash.display.StageAlign;
import flash.display.StageScaleMode;
import flash.events.Event;
import flash.events.MediaEvent;
import flash.events.TouchEvent;
import flash.media.CameraUI;
import flash.media.MediaType;
import flash.media.MediaPromise;
import flash.ui.Multitouch;
import flash.ui.MultitouchInputMode;
import flash.text.TextField;
import flash.text.TextFormat;
```

2. Declare a `TextField` and `TextFormat` object pair to allow visible output upon the device. A `CameraUI` object must also be declared for this example:

```
private var camera:CameraUI;
private var traceField:TextField;
private var traceFormat:TextFormat;
```

3. We will now set up our `TextField`, apply a `TextFormat`, and add the `TextField` to the `DisplayList`. Here, we create a method to perform all of these actions for us:

```
protected function setupTextField():void {
  traceFormat = new TextFormat();
  traceFormat.bold = true;
  traceFormat.font = "_sans";
  traceFormat.size = 22;
  traceFormat.align = "center";
  traceFormat.color = 0xFFFFFF;
  traceField = newTextField();
  traceField.defaultTextFormat = traceFormat;
  traceField.selectable = false;
  traceField.mouseEnabled = false;
  traceField.width = stage.stageWidth;
  traceField.height = stage.stageHeight;
  addChild(traceField);
}
```

4. Instantiate a new `CameraUI` instance, which will be used to launch the device camera application and return file information back to us. If the `CameraUI` object is not supported on a particular device, a message is output to our `TextField` indicating this:

```
protected function setupCamera():void {
  if(CameraUI.isSupported) {
    camera = new CameraUI();
    registerListeners();
  }else{
    traceField.appendText("CameraUI is not supported...");
  }
}
```

5. Add an event listener to the `CameraUI` object so that we know when the capture is complete. We will also register a touch event on the `Stage` to initiate the capture:

```
protected function registerListeners():void {
  Multitouch.inputMode = MultitouchInputMode.TOUCH_POINT;
  camera.addEventListener(MediaEvent.COMPLETE, photoReady);
  stage.addEventListener(TouchEvent.TOUCH_TAP, launchCamera);
    }
```

6. To employ the default camera application on our Android device, we will need to invoke the `launch` method, passing in the `MediaType.IMAGE` constant to specify that we wish to capture a photograph:

```
protected function launchCamera(e:TouchEvent):void {
  camera.launch(MediaType.IMAGE);
}
```

7. Now, the default Android camera will initialize, allowing the user to capture a photograph. Once the user hits **OK**, focus will return to our application.

8. Finally, once we complete the capture process, an event of type MediaEvent. COMPLETE will fire, invoking our photoReady method. From this, we can ascertain certain details about our captured photograph.

```
protected function photoReady(e:MediaEvent):void {
  var promise:MediaPromise = e.data;
  traceField.appendText("mediaType: " + promise.mediaType + "\n");
  traceField.appendText("relativePath: " +
          promise.relativePath + "\n");
  traceField.appendText("creationDate: " +
          promise.file.creationDate + "\n");
  traceField.appendText("extension: " +
          promise.file.extension + "\n");
  traceField.appendText("name: " + promise.file.name + "\n");
  traceField.appendText("size: " + promise.file.size + "\n");
  traceField.appendText("type: " + promise.file.type + "\n");
  traceField.appendText("nativePath: " +
          promise.file.nativePath + "\n");
  traceField.appendText("url: " + promise.file.url + "\n");
    }
```

9. The output will look something like this:

How it works...

Invoking the `CameraUI.launch` method will request the Android device to open the default camera application and allow the user to take a photograph. Upon completing the capture process and confirming the captured photograph, focus is then returned to our application along with a set of data about the new file contained within the `MediaEvent.COMPLETE` event object.

At this point, our application can do all sorts of things with the data returned, or even open the file within the application, assuming that the file type can be loaded and displayed by the runtime.

There's more...

The default camera application will not load if the device does not have a storage card mounted. It is also important to note that if the device becomes low on memory during the capture process, Android may terminate our application before the process is complete.

See also...

We will discuss the display of images through an AIR for Android application in *Chapter 5: Rich Media Presentation: Working with Images, Video, and Audio.*

Using the Mobile CameraUI API to save a captured video

Using the new `CameraUI` API (available in the mobile AIR SDK) we can perform and alternative capture process to the normal `Camera` API. The mobile `CameraUI` class will make use of the default Android camera application, alongside our custom app to capture a video.

How to do it...

We will set up a `CameraUI` object to invoke the native Android camera to capture a video:

1. First, import the following classes into your project:

```
import flash.display.Sprite;
import flash.display.StageAlign;
import flash.display.StageScaleMode;
import flash.events.Event;
import flash.events.MediaEvent;
import flash.events.TouchEvent;
import flash.media.CameraUI;
import flash.media.MediaPromise;
import flash.media.MediaType;
import flash.text.TextField;
import flash.text.TextFormat;
import flash.ui.Multitouch;
import flash.ui.MultitouchInputMode;
```

2. Declare a `TextField` and `TextFormat` object pair to allow visible output upon the device. A `CameraUI` object must also be declared for this example:

```
private var camera:CameraUI;
private var traceField:TextField;
private var traceFormat:TextFormat;
```

3. We will now set up our `TextField`, apply a `TextFormat`, and add the `TextField` to the `DisplayList`. Here, we create a method to perform all of these actions for us:

```
protected function setupTextField():void {
  traceFormat = new TextFormat();
  traceFormat.bold = true;
  traceFormat.font = "_sans";
  traceFormat.size = 22;
  traceFormat.align = "center";
  traceFormat.color = 0xFFFFFF;
```

```
    traceField = new TextField();
    traceField.defaultTextFormat = traceFormat;
    traceField.selectable = false;
    traceField.mouseEnabled = false;
    traceField.width = stage.stageWidth;
    traceField.height = stage.stageHeight;
    addChild(traceField);
}
```

4. Instantiate a new `CameraUI` instance, which will be used to launch the device camera application and return file information back to us. If the `CameraUI` object is not supported on a particular device, a message is output to our `TextField` indicating this.

```
protected function setupCamera():void {
    if(CameraUI.isSupported) {
        camera = new CameraUI();
        registerListeners();
    }else{
        traceField.appendText("CameraUI is not supported...");
    }
}
```

5. Add an event listener to the `CameraUI` object so that we know when the capture is complete. We will also register a touch event on the `Stage` to initiate the capture:

```
protected function registerListeners():void {
    Multitouch.inputMode = MultitouchInputMode.TOUCH_POINT;
    camera.addEventListener(MediaEvent.COMPLETE, videoReady);
    stage.addEventListener(TouchEvent.TOUCH_TAP, launchCamera);
}
```

6. To employ the default camera application on our Android device, we will need to invoke the `launch` method, passing in the `MediaType.VIDEO` constant to specify that we wish to capture a video file:

```
protected function launchCamera(e:TouchEvent):void {
    camera.launch(MediaType.VIDEO);
}
```

7. Now, the default Android camera will initialize, allowing the user to take some video. Once the user hits **OK**, focus will return to our application:

8. Finally, once we complete the capture process, an event of type `MediaEvent.COMPLETE` will fire, invoking our `videoReady` method. From this, we can ascertain certain details about our captured video file:

```
protected function videoReady(e:MediaEvent):void {
    var promise:MediaPromise = e.data;
    traceField.appendText("mediaType: " + promise.mediaType + "\n");
    traceField.appendText("relativePath: " +
            promise.relativePath + "\n");
    traceField.appendText("creationDate: " +
            promise.file.creationDate + "\n");
    traceField.appendText("extension: " +
            promise.file.extension + "\n");
    traceField.appendText("name: " + promise.file.name + "\n");
    traceField.appendText("size: " + promise.file.size + "\n");
    traceField.appendText("type: " + promise.file.type + "\n");
    traceField.appendText("nativePath: " +
            promise.file.nativePath + "\n");
    traceField.appendText("url: " + promise.file.url + "\n");
}
```

9. The output will look something like this:

How it works...

Invoking the `CameraUI.launch` method will request that the Android device open the default camera application and allow the user to capture some video. Upon completing the capture process and confirming the captured video file, focus is then returned to our application along with a set of data about the new file contained within the `MediaEvent.COMPLETE` event object.

At this point, our application can do all sorts of things with the data returned, or even open the file within the application, assuming that the file type can be loaded and displayed by the runtime. This is very important when it comes to video as certain devices will use a variety of codecs to encode the captured video, not all of them Flash Platform compatible.

There's more...

The default camera application will not load if the device does not have a storage card mounted. It is also important to note that if the device becomes low on memory during the capture process, Android may terminate our application before the process is complete.

Also, there are many other events aside from `MediaEvent.COMPLETE` that we can use in such a process. For instance, register an event listener of type `Event.CANCEL` in order to react to the user canceling a video save.

See also...

We will discuss the playback of video files through an AIR for Android application in *Chapter 5*.

Using the device microphone to monitor audio sample data

By monitoring the sample data being returned from the Android device microphone through the ActionScript `Microphone` API, we can gather much information about the sound being captured, and perform responses within our application. Such input can be used in utility applications, learning modules, and even games.

How to do it...

We will set up an event listener to respond to sample data reported through the `Microphone` API:

1. First, import the following classes into your project:

   ```
   import flash.display.Sprite;
   import flash.display.Stage;
   import flash.display.StageAlign;
   import flash.display.StageScaleMode;
   import flash.events.SampleDataEvent;
   import flash.media.Microphone;
   import flash.text.TextField;
   import flash.text.TextFormat;
   ```

2. Declare a `TextField` and `TextFormat` object pair to allow visible output upon the device. A `Microphone` object must also be declared for this example:

   ```
   private var mic:Microphone;
   private var traceField:TextField;
   private var traceFormat:TextFormat;
   ```

3. We will now set up our `TextField`, apply a `TextFormat`, and add the `TextField` to the `DisplayList`. Here, we create a method to perform all of these actions for us:

   ```
   protected function setupTextField():void {
     traceFormat = new TextFormat();
     traceFormat.bold = true;
     traceFormat.font = "_sans";
     traceFormat.size = 44;
     traceFormat.align = "center";
   ```

```
traceFormat.color = 0x333333;
traceField = new TextField();
traceField.defaultTextFormat = traceFormat;
traceField.selectable = false;
traceField.mouseEnabled = false;
traceField.width = stage.stageWidth;
traceField.height = stage.stageHeight;
addChild(traceField);
}
```

4. Now, we must instantiate our `Microphone` object and set it up according to our needs and preferences with adjustments to `codec`, `rate`, `silenceLevel`, and so forth. Here we use `setSilenceLevel()` to determine what the minimum input level our application should consider to be "sound" and the `rate` property is set to **44**, indicating that we will capture audio data at a rate of 44kHz. Setting the `setLoopBack ()` property to false will keep the captured audio from being routed through the device speaker:

```
protected function setupMic():void {
    mic = Microphone.getMicrophone();
    mic.setSilenceLevel(0);
    mic.rate = 44;
    mic.setLoopBack(false);
}
```

5. Once we have instantiated our `Microphone` object, we can then register a variety of event listeners. In this example, we'll be monitoring audio sample data from the device microphone, so we will need to register our listener for the `SampleDataEvent.SAMPLE_DATA` constant:

```
protected function registerListeners():void {
    mic.addEventListener(SampleDataEvent.SAMPLE_DATA, onMicData);
}
```

6. As the `Microphone` API generates sample data from the Android device input, we can now respond to this in a number of ways, as we have access to information about the `Microphone`object itself, and more importantly, we have access to the sample bytes with which we can perform a number of advanced operations:

```
public function onMicData(e:SampleDataEvent):void {
    traceField.text = "";
    traceField.appendText("activityLevel: " +
            e.target.activityLevel + "\n");
    traceField.appendText("codec: " + e.target.codec + "\n");
    traceField.appendText("gain: " + e.target.gain + "\n");
```

```
traceField.appendText("bytesAvailable: " +
        e.data.bytesAvailable + "\n");
traceField.appendText("length: " + e.data.length + "\n");
traceField.appendText("position: " + e.data.position + "\n");
}
```

7. The output will look something like this. The first three values are taken from the `Microphone` itself, the second three from `Microphone` sample data:

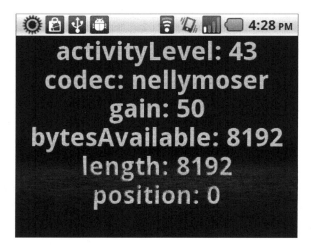

How it works...

When we instantiate a `Microphone` object and register a `SampleDataEvent.SAMPLE_ DATA` event listener, we can easily monitor various properties of our Android device microphone and the associated sample data being gathered. We can then respond to that data in many ways. One example would be to move objects across the `Stage` based upon the `Microphone.activityLevel` property. Another example would be to write the sample data to a `ByteArray` for later analysis.

What do all these properties mean?

- ▶ `activityLevel`: This is a measurement indicating the amount of sound being received
- ▶ `codec`: This indicates the codec being used: Nellymoser or Speex
- ▶ `gain`: This is an amount of boosting provided by the microphone to the sound signal
- ▶ `bytesAvailable`: This reveals the number of bytes from the present position until the end of our sample data `byteArray`

- ▶ `length`: Lets us know the total length of our sample data `byteArray`
- ▶ `position`: This is the current position, in bytes, within our sample data `byteArray`

See also...

In order to access the microphone, we will need to add some Android permissions for `RECORD_AUDIO`. Refer to *Chapter 11* for information on how to go about this.

Recording Microphone Audio Sample Data

One of the most fundamental things a developer would want to be able to do with audio sample data gathered from an Android microphone, would be to capture the data and use it in some way within an application. This recipe will demonstrate how to preserve and play back captured microphone audio sample data.

How to do it...

We will employ an event listener to respond to sample data reported through the `Microphone` API by writing captured audio data to a `ByteArray` and then playing it back internally through the `Sound` object:

1. First, import the following classes into your project:

```
import flash.display.Sprite;
import flash.display.Stage;
import flash.display.StageAlign;
import flash.display.StageScaleMode;
import flash.events.SampleDataEvent;
import flash.events.TouchEvent;
import flash.media.Microphone;
import flash.media.Sound;
import flash.media.SoundChannel;
import flash.utils.ByteArray;
import flash.ui.Multitouch;
import flash.ui.MultitouchInputMode;
import flash.text.TextField;
import flash.text.TextFormat;
```

2. Declare a `TextField` and `TextFormat` object pair to allow visible output upon the device. A `Microphone` object must also be declared for this example. To store and play back the sample data, we will need to declare a `ByteArray`, along with a `Sound` and `SoundChannel` pair:

```
private var mic:Microphone;
private var micRec:ByteArray;
```

```
private var output:Sound;
private var outputChannel:SoundChannel;
private var traceField:TextField;
private var traceFormat:TextFormat;
```

3. We will now set up our `TextField`, apply a `TextFormat`, and add the `TextField` to the `DisplayList`. Here, we create a method to perform all of these actions for us:

```
protected function setupTextField():void {
    traceFormat = new TextFormat();
    traceFormat.bold = true;
    traceFormat.font = "_sans";
    traceFormat.size = 44;
    traceFormat.align = "center";
    traceFormat.color = 0x333333;
    traceField = new TextField();
    traceField.defaultTextFormat = traceFormat;
    traceField.selectable = false;
    traceField.mouseEnabled = false;
    traceField.width = stage.stageWidth;
    traceField.height = stage.stageHeight;
    addChild(traceField);
}
```

4. Then, instantiate a `Microphone` object and set it up according to our needs and preferences with adjustments to `codec`, `rate`, `silenceLevel`, and so forth. Here we use `setSilenceLevel()` to determine what the minimum input level our application should consider to be "sound" and the `rate` property is set to **44**, indicating that we will capture audio data at a rate of 44kHz. Setting the `setLoopBack ()` property to false will keep the captured audio from being routed through the device speaker. We'll also instantiate a `ByteArray` to hold all of our audio samples as they are intercepted:

```
protected function setupMic():void {
    mic = Microphone.getMicrophone();
    mic.setSilenceLevel(0);
    mic.rate = 44;
    mic.setLoopBack(false);
    micRec = new ByteArray();
}
```

5. Once we have instantiated our `Microphone` and `ByteArray` objects, we can then register an event listener to enable touch interactions. A simple tap will suffice:

```
protected function registerListeners():void {
    Multitouch.inputMode = MultitouchInputMode.TOUCH_POINT;
```

```
    stage.addEventListener(TouchEvent.TOUCH_TAP, startRecording);
    traceField.text = "Tap to Record";
}
```

6. Once recording has been invoked by the user, we'll be monitoring audio sample data from the device microphone, so will need to register our listener for the `SampleDataEvent.SAMPLE_DATA` constant:

```
protected function startRecording(e:TouchEvent):void {
    stage.removeEventListener(TouchEvent.TOUCH_TAP, startRecording);
    stage.addEventListener(TouchEvent.TOUCH_TAP, stopRecording);
    mic.addEventListener(SampleDataEvent.SAMPLE_DATA, onMicData);
    traceField.text = "Recording Audio \nTap to Stop";
}
```

7. As the `Microphone` API generates sample data from the Android device input, we have access to the audio sample data bytes, which we can write to a `ByteArray` for later use:

```
protected function onMicData(e:SampleDataEvent):void {
    micRec.writeBytes(e.data);
}
```

8. To stop recording, we will need to remove the `SampleDataEvent.SAMPLE_DATA` event listener from our `Microphone` object:

```
protected function stopRecording(e:TouchEvent):void {
    mic.removeEventListener(SampleDataEvent.SAMPLE_DATA, onMicData);
    stage.removeEventListener(TouchEvent.TOUCH_TAP, stopRecording);
    stage.addEventListener(TouchEvent.TOUCH_TAP, playBackAudio);
    traceField.text = "Tap to Playback";
}
```

9. To prepare for playback, we will instantiate a new `Sound` object and register a `SampleDataEvent.SAMPLE_DATA` event upon it just as we had done for the `Microphone` object previously. We will also instantiate a `SoundChannel` object and invoke the `play()` method of our `Sound` object to play back the captured `Microphone` audio:

```
protected function playBackAudio(e:TouchEvent):void {
    stage.removeEventListener(TouchEvent.TOUCH_TAP, playBackAudio);
    micRec.position = 0;
    output = new Sound();
    output.addEventListener(SampleDataEvent.SAMPLE_DATA,
                onSampleDataRequest);
    outputChannel = output.play();
    traceField.text = "Playing Audio";
}
```

10. Once we invoke the `play()` method upon our `Sound` object, it will begin gathering generated sample data from a method called `onSampleDataRequest`. We need to create this method now, and allow it to loop over the bytes we previously wrote to our `ByteArray` object. This is, effectively, the inverse of our capture process.

11. In order to provide proper playback within our application we must provide between 2048 and 8192 samples of data. It is recommended to use as many samples as possible, but this will also depend upon the sample frequency.

> Note that we invoke `writeFloat()` twice within the same loop because we need our data expressed in stereo pairs, one for each channel.

12. When using `writeBytes()` in this example, we are actually channeling sound data back out through our `SampleDataEvent` and through a `Sound` object, thus enabling the application to produce sound:

```
protected function
  onSampleDataRequest(e:SampleDataEvent):void {
  var out:ByteArray = new ByteArray();
  for(var i:int = 0; i < 8192  && micRec.bytesAvailable; i++ ) {
  var micsamp:Number = micRec.readFloat();
    // left channel
    out.writeFloat(micsamp);
    // right channel
    out.writeFloat(micsamp);
  }
  e.data.writeBytes(out);
}
```

13. Output to our `TextField` will change depending upon the current application state:

How it works...

When we instantiate a `Microphone` object and register a `SampleDataEvent.SAMPLE_DATA` event listener, we can easily monitor the associated sample data being gathered and write this data to a `ByteArray` for later playback. As new samples come in, more data is added to the `ByteArray`, building up the sound data over time.

By registering a `SampleDataEvent.SAMPLE_DATA` event listener to a `Sound` object, we instruct it to actively seek audio data generated from a specific method as soon as we invoke `play()`. In our example, we move through the constructed `ByteArray` and send audio data back out through this method, effectively playing back the recorded audio through the `Sound` object and associated `SoundChannel`.

See also...

The use of bytes within ActionScript is a complex subject. To read more about this topic, we recommend Thibault Imbert's book "*What can you do with bytes?*", which is freely available from `http://www.bytearray.org/?p=711`.

To read recipes concerning the playback of audio files, have a look at *Chapter 5*. For information on saving captured audio data to the Android device, refer to *Chapter 8*: *Abundant Access*: *File System and Local Database*.

5
Rich Media Presentation: Working with Images, Video, and Audio

This chapter will cover the following recipes:

- ▶ Loading photographs from the device cameraRoll
- ▶ Applying Pixel Bender Shader effects to loaded images
- ▶ Playing video files from the local file system or over HTTP
- ▶ Playing remote video files over RTMP
- ▶ Playing audio files from the local file system or over HTTP
- ▶ Generating an audio spectrum visualizer
- ▶ Generating audio tones for your application

Introduction

This chapter will include a variety of recipes for the display of image data and playback of both video and audio streams. Included among these recipes are examples demonstrating the ability to load images from the device camera repository, applying Pixel Bender Shaders to loaded images, the playback of audio and video over different protocols, as well as the generation of visual data from sound and the generation of raw sound data.

The Flash platform is well known as the premiere video distribution platform worldwide. In the following pages, we will see that this experience and reach is in no way confined to desktop and browser-based computing. With new features such as StageVideo available in AIR 2.6 and Flash Player 10.2, Flash is becoming an even stronger platform for delivering video while preserving device battery life and providing a better user experience.

Loading photographs from the device cameraRoll

The Android operating system has a central repository for storing photographs captured by the variety of camera applications a user may have installed. There are APIs within AIR for Android, which allows a Flash developer to specifically target and pull from this repository for display within an application.

How to do it...

We must use the mobile `CameraRoll` API to browse directly to the device camera roll and select a photograph for display:

1. First, import the following classes into your project:

```
import flash.display.Loader;
import flash.display.Sprite;
import flash.display.StageAlign;
import flash.display.StageScaleMode;
import flash.events.Event;
import flash.events.MediaEvent;
import flash.events.TouchEvent;
import flash.filesystem.File;
import flash.media.CameraRoll;
import flash.media.MediaPromise;
import flash.ui.Multitouch;
import flash.ui.MultitouchInputMode;
```

2. Declare a `CameraRoll` object and a `Loader`, which will be used to display the photograph, once selected:

```
private var loader:Loader;
private var cameraRoll:CameraRoll;
```

3. We will create our `Loader` object, add it to the `Stage`, and register an event listener to properly scale the photo once it has been loaded:

```
protected function setupLoader():void {
  loader = new Loader();
```

```
    loader.contentLoaderInfo.addEventListener(Event.COMPLETE,
        sizePhoto);
    stage.addChild(loader);
}
```

4. For the `CameraRoll` itself, all we need to do is instantiate it and then add an event listener to fire once the user has selected a photograph to display. We should always check to see whether the device supports `CameraRoll.browseForImage()` by checking the `supportsBrowseForImage` property:

```
protected function setupCameraRoll():void {
    if(CameraRoll.supportsBrowseForImage){
        cameraRoll = new CameraRoll();
        cameraRoll.addEventListener(MediaEvent.SELECT, imageSelected);
        registerListeners();
    }else{
        trace("CameraRoll does not support browse for image!");
    }
}
```

5. We will now register a `TouchEvent` listener of type `TOUCH_TAP` to the `Stage`. This will enable the user to invoke a browse dialog in order to select a photograph from the `CameraRoll` by tapping the device screen.

 We are setting `Multitouch.inputMode` to the `MultitouchInputMode.TOUCH_POINT` constant in order for our application to accept touch events.

```
protected function registerListeners():void {
    Multitouch.inputMode = MultitouchInputMode.TOUCH_POINT;
    stage.addEventListener(TouchEvent.TOUCH_TAP,
        loadFromCameraRoll);
}
```

6. Once the following method is invoked from a user interaction, we can invoke the `browseForImage()` method upon the `CameraRoll` object we had set up earlier. This will open the default gallery application on an Android device and allow the user to select a photograph from their collection. If there is more than one gallery application on the device, the user will first choose which one to use for this event through a native Android dialog. Our application will lose focus and this will be handled by the operating system, returning to our application once a selection is made.

```
protected function loadFromCameraRoll(e:TouchEvent):void {
```

```
    cameraRoll.browseForImage();
}
```

7. Here, we can see the default gallery application on Android. A user can spend as much time as they wish browsing the various collections and photographs before a selection is made.

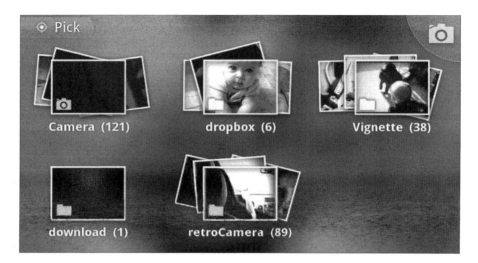

8. When the user has performed a valid selection in the native Android gallery application, focus returns to our application and an event containing a MediaPromise object is returned. The Loader class has a specific method called loadFilePromise() specifically for this sort of thing. We will now pass the MediaPromise through this method.

```
protected function imageSelected(e:MediaEvent):void {
    var promise:MediaPromise = e.data;
    loader.loadFilePromise(promise);
}
```

9. Once we've passed the MediaPromise object through the Loader using loadFilePromise(), it will load up onto the Stage. We will perform one more action here to adjust the Loader size to fit within the constraints of our Stage:

```
protected function sizePhoto(e:Event):void {
    loader.width = stage.stageWidth;
    loader.scaleY = loader.scaleX;
}
```

10. The resulting image, when loaded upon the Stage, will appear as follows:

How it works...

The ActionScript `CameraRoll` API specifically targets the on device storage location for photographs on Android. Whenever a user performs some interaction that invokes a `CameraRoll.browseForImage()` method in our application, the default Android gallery application will launch, allowing the user to select an image file from within their collection.

Once the user has selected a photograph from the gallery application, they will be returned to our AIR for Android application along with a `MediaPromise` object with which we can ascertain certain information about the file, or even load the photograph directly into our application.

There's more...

In this example, we examine how to load an image from the `CameraRoll` into a `Loader` on the `Stage`. There are, of course, many things we could do to the photograph once it has been loaded up. For an example of this, have a look at the next recipe: *Applying Pixel Bender Shader effects to loaded images.*

Applying Pixel Bender Shader effects to loaded images

Once we load a visual object into our application, as this is all Flash-based, we can do all sorts of robust visual manipulation. In this example, we will load a preselected photograph from the local file system, and then apply a variety of Pixel Bender Shaders to it, drastically changing its appearance.

Getting ready...

This recipe makes use of Pixel Bender Shaders. You can download `.pbj` files from the Adobe Exchange or create your own.

If you decide to write your own Pixel Bender kernels, you can download the Pixel Bender Toolkit for free from `http://www.adobe.com/devnet/pixelbender.html` and use it to compile all sorts of shaders for use in Flash and AIR projects.

The toolkit allows you to write kernels using the Pixel Bender kernel language (formerly known as Hydra) and provides mechanisms for image preview and separate property manipulation that can be exposed to ActionScript.

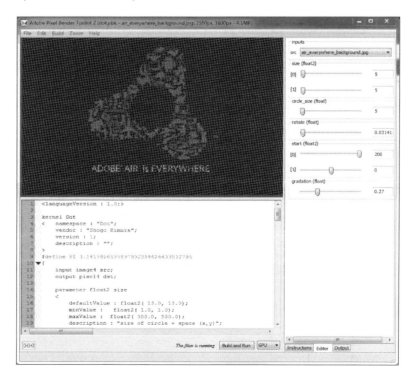

For a good resource on writing Pixel Bender Shaders, check out the documentation located at `http://www.adobe.com/devnet/pixelbender.html`.

In this recipe, we are also referencing a photograph that exists within the Android image gallery, which we previously captured with the default camera application. You may do the same, or simply bundle an image file along with the application for later reference.

How to do it...

We will now load a predetermined image from the local device storage and apply multiple Pixel Bender Shaders to it:

1. First, import the following classes into your project:

```
import flash.display.Loader;
import flash.display.Shader;
import flash.display.Sprite;
import flash.display.StageAlign;
import flash.display.StageScaleMode;
import flash.events.Event;
import flash.events.TouchEvent;
import flash.filters.ShaderFilter;
import flash.net.URLLoader;
import flash.net.URLLoaderDataFormat;
import flash.net.URLRequest;
import flash.ui.Multitouch;
import flash.ui.MultitouchInputMode;
```

2. For this recipe, we must declare a number of different objects up front. We will declare a `String` constant to hold the path to our image and a `Loader`, which will be used to display the photograph. A `URLRequest` and `URLLoader` object pair will be used to load in our `.pbj` files. The `Array` will be set up to hold the names of each `.pbj` we will be loading. An `int` is employed to keep track of the shader we have currently loaded from our `Array` set. Finally, a `Shader` and `ShaderFilter` pair are declared to apply the loaded `.pbj` onto our `Loader`.

```
private const photoURL:String = "
        {local file path or http address}";
private var loader:Loader;
private var urlRequest:URLRequest;
private var urlLoader:URLLoader;
private var pbjArray:Array;
private var currentFilter:int;
private var shader:Shader;
private var shaderFilter:ShaderFilter;
```

3.   The next step is to initialize our `Array` and populate it with the Pixel Bender Shader file references we will be loading into our application. These files can be obtained through the Adobe Exchange, other locations on the web, or authored using the Pixel Bender Toolkit:

```
protected function setupArray():void {
  pbjArray = new Array();
  pbjArray[0] = "dot.pbj";
  pbjArray[1] = "LineSlide.pbj";
  pbjArray[2] = "outline.pbj";
}
```

4.   Then, we create our `Loader` object, add it to the `Stage`, and register an event listener to properly scale the photo once it has been loaded:

```
protected function setupLoader():void {
  loader = new Loader();
  loader.contentLoaderInfo.addEventListener(Event.COMPLETE,
             sizePhoto);
  stage.addChild(loader);
}
```

5.   We will now register a `TouchEvent` listener of type `TOUCH_TAP` to the `Loader`. This will enable the user to tap the loaded image to cycle through a variety of Pixel Bender Shaders. We also set the `currentFilter` int to 0, which will indicate the first position of our `Array`:

```
protected function registerListeners():void {
  Multitouch.inputMode = MultitouchInputMode.TOUCH_POINT;
  loader.addEventListener(TouchEvent.TOUCH_TAP, loadShader);
  currentFilter = 0;
}
```

6.   To load the photograph into the `Loader` instance for display within our application, we will invoke the `load()` method and pass in a new `URLRequest` along with the `photoURL` `String` constant that was declared earlier:

```
protected function loadPhotograph():void {
  loader.load(new URLRequest(photoURL));
}
```

7.   Once the file has loaded, we will perform one more action to adjust the `Loader` size to fit within the constraints of our `Stage`:

```
protected function sizePhoto(e:Event):void {
  loader.width = stage.stageWidth;
  loader.scaleY = loader.scaleX;
}
```

8. The resulting image, when loaded upon the Stage, without any shaders applied, will appear as follows:

9. Each time the users performs a touch tap upon the Loader instance, this method will execute. Basically, we are setting up a URLRequest using values from the Array of shader locations that was set up earlier, pulling the value from whatever current index that has been recorded to the currentFilter object.

10. Before we invoke the URLLoader.load() method, we must explicitly set the dataFormat property to the URLLoaderDataFormat.BINARY constant. This ensures that when our file is loaded up, it is treated as binary and not text.

11. An Event.COMPLETE listener is registered to invoke the applyFilter method once our shader has been loaded up.

12. Finally, we can either increment our currentFilter value, or set it back to 0, depending upon where we are along the length of the Array:

```
protected function loadShader(e:TouchEvent):void {
    urlRequest = new URLRequest(pbjArray[currentFilter]);
    urlLoader = new URLLoader();
    urlLoader.dataFormat = URLLoaderDataFormat.BINARY;
    urlLoader.addEventListener(Event.COMPLETE, applyFilter);
```

```
urlLoader.load(urlRequest);
if(currentFilter < pbjArray.length-1){
  currentFilter++;
}else{
  currentFilter = 0;
}
}
```

13. To actually apply the loaded `.pbj` onto our `Loader`, we will first assign the binary data to a new `Shader` object. This is subsequently passed through the constructor of a `ShaderFilter`, which is then applied to the filters property of our `Loader` as an `Array`:

```
protected function applyFilter(e:Event):void {
  shader = new Shader(e.target.data);
  shaderFilter = new ShaderFilter(shader);
  loader.filters = [shaderFilter];
}
```

14. When the user has tapped the image, we cycle through the available Pixel Bender Shaders and apply then, in turn, to the loaded photograph. The resulting image cycle can be seen as follows:

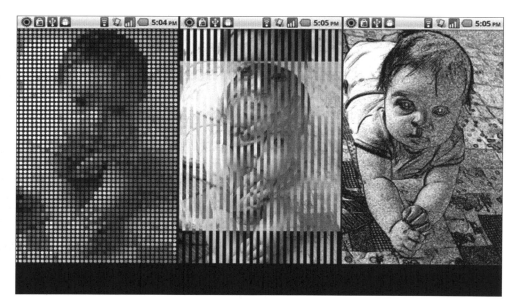

How it works...

Using Pixel Bender Shaders is a simple and direct way of enabling some really powerful visual manipulation within an application. In this recipe, we load an image into a `Loader` object, construct an `Array` of `.pbj` file references to pass through a `URLLoader`. When the user interacts with our loaded image, we will load a `.pbj` file and construct a `Shader` based upon the received data. Finally we can construct a `ShaderFilter` based off of this object and pass this onto our image through the `Loader.filters` property.

There's more...

In this example, we examine how to load an image into a `Loader` on the `Stage` and look at applying Pixel Bender Shaders to it upon user interaction. You can, of course, apply such shaders to any `DisplayObject` you like, including video!

A good place to locate a variety of Pixel Bender files to use in such an example, is the Adobe Exchange. Visit the Exchange website at `http://www.adobe.com/exchange`.

Playing video files from the local filesystem or over HTTP

As we have the full Flash Player (and Adobe AIR) on Android devices, playback of video files is as simple as it normally is on the desktop. The main consideration is whether the video is optimized for playback on mobile, or not.

Getting ready...

This recipe involves the playback of a video file that has been packaged along with our application. We could just as easily reference an HTTP address or even local storage on the Android device, so long as it is a file format and codec, which can be played back through Flash Platform runtimes. You will want to prepare this file ahead of time.

How to do it...

We will create a `Video` object, add it to the `Stage`, and stream a file in through a basic `NetConnection` and `NetStream` pair:

1. First, import the following classes into your project:

    ```
    import flash.display.Sprite;
    import flash.display.StageAlign;
    import flash.display.StageScaleMode;
    import flash.events.NetStatusEvent;
    ```

```
import flash.media.Video;
import flash.net.NetConnection;
import flash.net.NetStream;
import flash.text.TextField;
import flash.text.TextFormat;
```

2. For this recipe, we must declare a number of different objects up front. We are, in this case, packaging a video file along with the application itself; we will declare a `String` constant referring to this file.

3. The next set of objects pertains to the actual video stream. Declare a `Video` object to display the `NetStream` data coming in over our local `NetConnection`. We will also declare an `Object` to bind specific, necessary functions to for video playback.

4. Finally, we will declare a `TextField` and `TextFormat` pair to relay text messages onto the device display:

```
private const videoPath:String = "assets/test.m4v";
private var video:Video;
private var streamClient:Object;
private var connection:NetConnection;
private var stream:NetStream;
private var traceField:TextField;
private var traceFormat:TextFormat;
```

5. We will now set up our `TextField`, apply a `TextFormat`, and add it to the `DisplayList`. Here, we create a method to perform all of these actions for us:

```
protected function setupTextField():void {
  traceFormat = new TextFormat();
  traceFormat.bold = true;
  traceFormat.font = "_sans";
  traceFormat.size = 24;
  traceFormat.align = "center";
  traceFormat.color = 0xCCCCCC;
  traceField = new TextField();
  traceField.defaultTextFormat = traceFormat;
  traceField.selectable = false;
  traceField.mouseEnabled = false;
  traceField.width = stage.stageWidth;
  traceField.height = stage.stageHeight;
  addChild(traceField);
}
```

6. Now to set up our video connection; we will create a new Object called `streamClient`, which we will use to bind a number of helper functions to our stream objects. A `Video` object must be created and added to the `DisplayList` in order for the user to actually view the video stream. Finally, we create a `NetConnection`, assign `streamClient` to its `client` property, register an event listener to monitor connection status, and then invoke the `connect()` method, passing in `null` as the connection argument, since we are not using any sort of media server in this example.

7. We may not always want to set the `Video.smoothing` property to true; in this case, since we are unsure exactly how large the video is, we will enable it in order to smooth any potential artifacting that may occur through scaling:

```
protected function setupVideoConnection():void {
   streamClient = new Object();
   streamClient.onTextData = onTextData;
   streamClient.onMetaData = onMetaData;
   streamClient.onCuePoint = onCuePoint;
   video = new Video();
   video.smoothing = true;
   addChild(video);
   connection = new NetConnection();
   connection.client = streamClient;
   connection.addEventListener(NetStatusEvent.NET_STATUS,
              onNetStatus);
   connection.connect(null);
}
```

8. The following method will be called from our `onNetStatus` function once we are sure the `NetConnection` has connected successfully. Within this method, create a new `NetStream` object to stream the video over our `NetConnection`. We will also assign `streamClient` to the `client` property and register an event listener to monitor stream status. To display the stream through our `Video` object, use the `attachStream()` method and pass in our `NetStream` object. Now, simply invoke the `play()` method, passing in our `videoPath` constant, and pointing to the video file location:

```
protected function connectStream():void {
   stream = new NetStream(connection);
   stream.addEventListener(NetStatusEvent.NET_STATUS, onNetStatus);
   stream.client = streamClient;
   video.attachNetStream(stream);
   stream.play(videoPath);
}
```

9. The `onNetStatus` method, as defined in the following code snippet, can be used with both our `NetStream` and `NetConnection` objects in order to make decisions based upon the different status messages returned. In this example, we are either firing the `connectStream` method once a `NetConnection` is successfully connected, or performing some scaling and layout once we are sure the `NetStream` is playing successfully.

10. For a comprehensive list of all supported `NetStatusEvent` info codes, have a look at: `http://help.adobe.com/en_US/FlashPlatform/reference/ actionscript/3/flash/events/NetStatusEvent.html#info`.

```
protected function onNetStatus(e:NetStatusEvent):void {
  traceField.appendText(e.info.code + "\n");
  switch (e.info.code) {
    case "NetConnection.Connect.Success":
      connectStream();
      break;
    case "NetStream.Buffer.Full":
      video.width = stage.stageWidth;
      video.scaleY = video.scaleX;
      traceField.y = video.height;
      break;
  }
}
```

11. The next three steps include methods which have been bound to the client property of either the `NetConnection` or `NetStream`. These must exist as part of the client object, or else errors may be thrown as they are expected methods. The `onTextData` method fires whenever text is encountered within the file being streamed:

```
public function onTextData(info:Object):void {
  traceField.appendText("Text!\n");
}
```

12. The `onMetaData` method fires when the stream metadata is loaded into the application. This provides us with many useful pieces of information, such as stream width, height, and duration:

```
public function onMetaData(info:Object):void {
  traceField.appendText("Duration: " + info.duration + "\n");
  traceField.appendText("Width: " + info.width + "\n");
  traceField.appendText("Height: " + info.height + "\n");
  traceField.appendText("Codec: " + info.videocodecid + "\n");
  traceField.appendText("FPS: " + info.videoframerate + "\n");
}
```

13. The `onCuePoint` method fires whenever embedded cue points are encountered within the file being streamed:

```
public function onCuePoint(info:Object):void {
    traceField.appendText("Cuepoint!\n");
}
```

14. The resulting application will look similar to the following screen render:

How it works...

The entire workflow is almost exactly what would be used when developing for the desktop. When playing back video over Flash, we must first establish a `NetConnection` for our `NetStream` to travel across. Once the `NetConnection` is connected, we create our `NetStream` and bind the two of them together. Adding a `Video` object to the `Stage` will enable the stream to be viewable on our device, so long as we attach out `NetStream` to it. At this point, we can then play any files we wish over that `NetStream` by simply invoking the `play()` method.

When dealing with `NetConnection` and `NetStream`, there is always the need to create a number of helper functions. These functions include the registration of event listeners to detect particular status events, and the definition of a custom `client` property with associated methods that will be expected by the established workflow.

There's more...

In this example, we are playing a file packaged with our application. It would be just as simple to play a video file from the device gallery (assuming the codec used to compress the video is supported by Flash and AIR) or progressively stream a video over HTTP from a location available over a wireless network connection.

The video file we are playing back through Flash player or AIR must be of a type which is supported by the Flash Platform runtimes.

Valid video file types include:

- FLV
- MP4
- M4V
- F4V
- 3GPP

Flash Platform runtimes support every level and profile of the H.264 standard and retain full FLV support as well. However, recommended resolutions specific to Android are as follows:

- **4:3 video**: 640 × 480, 512 × 384, 480 × 360
- **16:9 video**: 640 × 360, 512 x 288, 480 × 272

When packaging such an application, which utilizes files that are distributed as part of the application package, we will also need to be sure and include them through the use of a GUI (if your IDE supports this) or as extra files in the command line compilation process.

Playing remote video streams over RTMP

Aside from the playback of video available through the local file system or from a remote HTTP web address, we also have the ability to stream video files onto Android devices using Flash Media Server and the RTMP protocol. If a streaming server such as this is available, you can make great use of this when deploying video across mobile Android devices.

Getting ready...

This recipe involves the playback of a video file that has been deployed to a Flash Media Server. You can actually set up a developer version of FMS for free if you do not have access to a production server. To find out more information about streaming video over **Real Time Messaging Protocol** (**RTMP**), you can have a look at the resources available at: `http://www.adobe.com/products/flashmediaserver/`

How to do it...

We will create a `Video` object, add it to the `Stage`, and stream a file in through a `NetConnection` and `NetStream` pair over RTMP:

1. First, import the following classes into your project:

    ```
    import flash.display.Sprite;
    import flash.display.StageAlign;
    import flash.display.StageScaleMode;
    import flash.events.NetStatusEvent;
    import flash.media.Video;
    import flash.net.NetConnection;
    import flash.net.NetStream;
    import flash.text.TextField;
    import flash.text.TextFormat;
    ```

2. For this recipe, we must declare a number of different objects up front. We are, in this case, using a Flash Media Server to perform a stream over RTMP; we will declare a `String` constant referring to the FMS application path.

3. The next set of objects pertains to the actual video stream. Declare a `Video` object to display the `NetStream` data coming in over our local `NetConnection`. We will also declare an `Object` to bind specific, necessary function to for video playback.

4. Finally, we will declare a `TextField` and `TextFormat` pair to relay text messages onto the device display:

    ```
    private const fmsPath:String = "rtmp://fms/vod";
    private var video:Video;
    private var streamClient:Object;
    private var connection:NetConnection;
    private var stream:NetStream;
    private var traceField:TextField;
    private var traceFormat:TextFormat;
    ```

5. We will now set up our `TextField`, apply a `TextFormat`, and add it to the `DisplayList`. Here, we create a method to perform all of these actions for us:

```
protected function setupTextField():void {
  traceFormat = new TextFormat();
  traceFormat.bold = true;
  traceFormat.font = "_sans";
  traceFormat.size = 24;
  traceFormat.align = "center";
  traceFormat.color = 0xCCCCCC;
  traceField = new TextField();
  traceField.defaultTextFormat = traceFormat;
  traceField.selectable = false;
  traceField.mouseEnabled = false;
  traceField.width = stage.stageWidth;
  traceField.height = stage.stageHeight;
  addChild(traceField);
}
```

6. Now to set up our video connection; we will create a new Object called `streamClient`, which we will use to bind a number of helper functions to our stream objects. A `Video` object must be created and added to the `DisplayList` in order for the user to actually view the video stream.

7. Finally, we create a `NetConnection`, assign `streamClient` to its `client` property, register an event listener to monitor connection status, and then invoke the `connect()` method, passing in the predefined `fmsPath` constant as the connection argument. This is because we must make a connection to this application instance on the Flash Media Server before proceeding.

```
protected function setupVideoConnection():void {
  streamClient = new Object();
  streamClient.onBWDone = onTextData;
  streamClient.onTextData = onTextData;
  streamClient.onMetaData = onMetaData;
  streamClient.onCuePoint = onCuePoint;
  video = new Video();
  video.smoothing = true;
  addChild(video);
  connection = new NetConnection();
  connection.client = streamClient;
  connection.addEventListener(NetStatusEvent.NET_STATUS,
                onNetStatus);
  connection.connect(fmsPath);
}
```

8. The following method will be called from our `onNetStatus` function once we are sure the `NetConnection` has connected successfully. Within this method, create a new `NetStream` object to stream the video over our `NetConnection`. We will also assign `streamClient` to the `client` property and register an event listener to monitor stream status.

9. To display the stream through our `Video` object, use the `attachStream()` method and pass in our `NetStream` object.

10. Now, simply invoke the `play()` method, passing in a `String` identifying the particular stream or file to play over RTMP. You will notice that since we are using an H.264 based file format, we must prefix the stream name with `mp4:`. If streaming live or via FLV, the prefix is not necessary.

```
protected function connectStream():void {
  stream = new NetStream(connection);
  stream.addEventListener(NetStatusEvent.NET_STATUS, onNetStatus);
  stream.client = streamClient;
  video.attachNetStream(stream);
  stream.play("mp4:test.m4v");
}
```

11. The `onNetStatus` method, as defined in the following code snippet, can be used with both our `NetStream` and `NetConnection` objects in order to make decisions based upon the different status messages returned. In this example, we are either firing the `connectStream` method once a `NetConnection` is successfully connected, or performing some scaling and layout once we are sure the `NetStream` is playing successfully:

```
protected function onNetStatus(e:NetStatusEvent):void {
  traceField.appendText(e.info.code + "\n");
  switch (e.info.code) {
    case "NetConnection.Connect.Success":
      connectStream();
      break;
    case "NetStream.Buffer.Full":
      video.width = stage.stageWidth;
      video.scaleY = video.scaleX;
      traceField.y = video.height;
      break;
  }
}
```

12. The next three steps include methods which have been bound to the client property of either the `NetConnection` or `NetStream`. These must exist as part of the client object, else errors may be thrown as they are expected methods. The `onBWDone` method is particular to files streamed over RTMP. It fires whenever the streaming server has completed an estimation of client bandwidth available.

```
public function onBWDone():void {
    traceField.appendText("BW Done!\n");
}
```

13. The `onTextData` method fires whenever text is encountered within the file being streamed.

```
public function onTextData(info:Object):void {
    traceField.appendText("Text!\n");
}
```

14. The `onMetaData` method fires when the stream metadata is loaded into the application. This provides us with many useful pieces of information, such as stream width, height, and duration:

```
public function onMetaData(info:Object):void {
    traceField.appendText("Duration: " + info.duration + "\n");
    traceField.appendText("Width: " + info.width + "\n");
    traceField.appendText("Height: " + info.height + "\n");
    traceField.appendText("Codec: " + info.videocodecid + "\n");
    traceField.appendText("FPS: " + info.videoframerate + "\n");
}
```

15. The `onCuePoint` method fires whenever embedded cue points are encountered within the file being streamed:

```
public function onCuePoint(info:Object):void {
    traceField.appendText("Cuepoint!\n");
}
```

16. The resulting application will look similar to the following screen render:

How it works...

When playing back RTMP streams, we must first establish a NetConnection for our NetStream to travel across. The NetConnection will attempt to connect to the specified application defined on a Flash Media Server address. Once the NetConnection is connected, we create our NetStream and bind the two of them together. Adding a Video object to the Stage will enable the stream to be viewable on our device, as long as we attach out NetStream to it. At this point, we can then play any files we wish over that NetStream by simply invoking the play() method.

When dealing with NetConnection and NetStream, there is always the need to create a number of helper functions. These functions include the registration of event listeners to detect particular status events, and the definition of a custom client property with associated methods that will be expected by the established workflow.

There's more...

In this example, we are streaming a video file through an RTMP location over the Internet through Flash Media Server. You can use this same technique to stream audio files over RTMP or write a video chat application using the device camera. While we demonstrate here how to generate a `Video` object from scratch, keep in mind that there are various component solutions available such as the `FLVPlayBack` control that ships with Flash Professional, and the `VideoDisplay` and `VideoPlayer` components, which are part of the Flex framework. There are endless possibilities with this technology!

Playing audio files from the local filesystem or over HTTP

The playback of audio files through Flash Platform runtimes on Android devices is fairly straightforward. We can point to files bundled with our application, as this recipe demonstrates, files on the device storage, or files over a remote network connection. No matter where the file is located, playback is accomplished in the same way.

How to do it...

We must load the audio file into a `Sound` object and will then have the ability to manipulate playback, volume, pan, among other properties. In this recipe, we will allow the user to control volume through the rotation of a basic dial:

1. First, import the following classes into your project:

    ```
    import flash.display.Sprite;
    import flash.display.StageAlign;
    import flash.display.StageScaleMode;
    import flash.events.TransformGestureEvent;
    import flash.media.Sound;
    import flash.media.SoundChannel;
    import flash.media.SoundTransform;
    import flash.net.URLRequest;
    import flash.text.TextField;
    import flash.text.TextFormat;
    import flash.ui.Multitouch;
    import flash.ui.MultitouchInputMode;
    ```

2. For this recipe, we must declare a number of different objects up front. We will begin with a sound object group consisting of Sound, SoundChannel, and SoundTransform. These objects will allow us to take full control over the audio for this recipe. We will also create a Sprite, which will serve as a user interaction point. Finally, we will declare a TextField and TextFormat pair to relay text messages onto the device display:

```
private var sound:Sound;
private var channel:SoundChannel;
private var sTransform:SoundTransform;
private var dial:Sprite;
private var traceField:TextField;
private var traceFormat:TextFormat;
```

3. We will now set up our TextField, apply a TextFormat, and add it to the DisplayList. Here, we create a method to perform all of these actions for us:

```
protected function setupTextField():void {
    traceFormat = new TextFormat();
    traceFormat.bold = true;
    traceFormat.font = "_sans";
    traceFormat.size = 24;
    traceFormat.align = "center";
    traceFormat.color = 0xCCCCCC;
    traceField = new TextField();
    traceField.defaultTextFormat = traceFormat;
    traceField.selectable = false;
    traceField.mouseEnabled = false;
    traceField.width = stage.stageWidth;
    traceField.height = stage.stageHeight;
    addChild(traceField);
}
```

4. To create our volume dial, we will initialize a new Sprite and use the graphics API to draw a representation of a dial within it. We then add this Sprite to the Stage:

```
protected function setupDial():void {
    dial = new Sprite();
    dial.graphics.beginFill(0xFFFFFF, 1);
    dial.x = stage.stageWidth/2;
    dial.y = stage.stageHeight/2;
    dial.graphics.drawCircle(0,0,150);
    dial.graphics.endFill();
    dial.graphics.lineStyle(5,0x440000);
    dial.graphics.moveTo(0, -150);
    dial.graphics.lineTo(0, 0);
    addChild(dial);
}
```

5. Now we will go about setting up our audio related objects. Initialize our `Sound` and load a `MP3` file into it through `URLRequest`.

6. Next, we will set the initial volume of the sound to 50% by creating a `SoundTransform` and passing in a value of `0.5` as the `volume` in ActionScript is registered in a range of `0 - 1`.

7. To play the `Sound`, we will create a `SoundChannel` object, assign our `SoundTransform` to its `soundTransform` property, and finally set the `SoundChannel` through the `Sound.Play()` method:

```
protected function setupSound():void {
    sound = new Sound();
    sound.load(new URLRequest("assets/test.mp3"));
    sTransform = new SoundTransform(0.5, 0);
    channel = new SoundChannel();
    channel.soundTransform = sTransform;
    channel = sound.play();
    traceField.text = "Volume: " + sTransform.volume;
}
```

8. Set the specific input mode for the multitouch APIs to support touch input by setting `Multitouch.inputMode` to the `MultitouchInputMode.GESTURE` constant. We will also register a listener for `TransformGestureEvent.GESTURE_ROTATE` events upon our `Sprite` to intercept user interaction:

```
protected function registerListeners():void {
    Multitouch.inputMode = MultitouchInputMode.GESTURE;
            dial.addEventListener(TransformGestureEvent.
            GESTURE_ROTATE, onRotate);
}
```

9. When the `Sprite` is rotated by a user, we want to adjust playback volume accordingly. To accomplish this, we will adjust the `Sprite rotation` based upon the data received from our gesture event. We can then convert the `Sprite rotation` into a valid `volume Number` and modify the `SoundTransform` to reflect this, which will raise or lower the volume of our audio:

```
protected function onRotate(e:TransformGestureEvent):void {
    dial.rotation += e.rotation;
    sTransform.volume = (dial.rotation+180)/360;
    channel.soundTransform = sTransform;
    traceField.text = "Volume: " + sTransform.volume;
}
```

10. The resulting application will look similar to the following screen render:

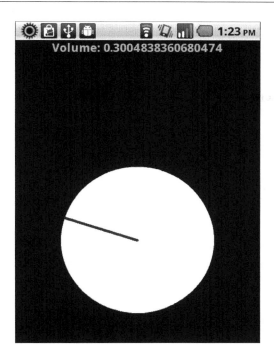

How it works...

We load an audio file into a Sound object in ActionScript through a URLRequest to make it available to our application. Simple playback can be achieved by invoking the play() method upon the Sound, but we retain a greater amount of control by assigning the sound playback onto a SoundChannel object, as we can then control things aspects such as pan and volume through the construction and assignment of a SoundTransform object. In this recipe, we modify the volume of the SoundTransform and then assign it to the SoundChannel. soundTransform property upon which our Sound is playing, thus modifying the sound.

There's more...

In this example, we are playing a file packaged with our application. It would be just as simple to play an audio file from the device file system (assuming the codec used to compress the audio is supported by Flash and AIR) or progressively stream a file over HTTP from a location available over a network connection.

The audio file we are playing back through Flash Player or AIR must be of a type that is supported by the Flash Platform runtimes.

Valid audio formats include:

- FLV
- MP3
- AAC+
- HE-AAC
- AAC v1
- AAC v2

When packaging such an application, which utilizes files which are distributed as part of the application package, we will also need to be sure and include them through the use of a GUI (if your IDE supports this) or as extra files in the command line compilation process.

Generating an audio spectrum visualizer

The ability to generate some sort of visual feedback when playing audio is very useful to the user, as they will be able to see that playback occurs even if the device volume has been muted or turned down. Generating visuals from audio is also useful in certain games, or in monitoring audio input levels.

How to do it...

We will load a MP3 file into a Sound object. By employing the SoundMixer. computeSpectrum() method, we can access the actual bytes being played back and construct visualizations with this data using the Sprite graphics API:

1. First, import the following classes into your project:

```
import flash.display.Sprite;
import flash.display.StageAlign;
import flash.display.StageScaleMode;
import flash.events.TimerEvent;
import flash.media.Sound;
import flash.media.SoundChannel;
import flash.media.SoundMixer;
import flash.net.URLRequest;
import flash.ui.Multitouch;
import flash.ui.MultitouchInputMode;
import flash.utils.ByteArray;
import flash.utils.Timer;
```

2. For this recipe, we must declare a number of different objects up front. We will begin with a sound object pair consisting of `Sound` and `SoundChannel`. These objects will allow us to take full control over the audio for this recipe. We will also create a `Sprite`, which will serve as a canvas to draw out audio spectrum data. Finally, we will declare a `Timer` in order to refresh the sound spectrum visualization every few milliseconds:

    ```
    private var sound:Sound;
    private var channel:SoundChannel;
    private var spectrum:Sprite;
    private var timer:Timer;
    ```

3. To construct the canvas within which we will draw out visualization elements, we must initialize a `Sprite`, define a particular line style on the `graphics` API, and add it to the `Stage`:

    ```
    protected function setupSpectrum():void {
      spectrum = new Sprite();
      addChild(spectrum);
    }
    ```

4. A `Timer` will be used to determine how often we will refresh the visualization within our container `Sprite`. In this case, we will set it to fire a `TIMER` event every 100 milliseconds, or 10 times every second.

    ```
    protected function registerTimer():void {
      timer = new Timer(100);
      timer.addEventListener(TimerEvent.TIMER, onTimer);
    }
    ```

5. Now we will go about setting up our audio related objects. Initialize our `Sound` and load a MP3 file into it through `URLRequest`. To play the `Sound`, we will create a `SoundChannel` object, assign our `SoundTransform` to its `soundTransForm` property, and finally set the `SoundChannel` through the `Sound.Play()` method. As we now have our `Sound` loaded and ready to go, we can start running our `Timer`.

    ```
    protected function setupSound():void {
      sound = new Sound();
      sound.load(new URLRequest("assets/test.mp3"));
      channel = new SoundChannel();
      channel = sound.play();
      timer.start();
    }
    ```

6. Finally, construct a method similar to the following, which will extract byte data from the global Flash `SoundMixer`, and use the `graphics` API to draw out visualizations based upon this data. We first initialize a number of variables to be used in this method and run `computeSpectrum()` off of the `SoundMixer` class. This will populate our `ByteArray` with all of the sound sample data needed to create our visuals.

7. In looping through the data, we can use the `graphics` API to draw lines, circles, or anything we desire into our `Sprite` container. In this case, we draw a series of lines to create a spectrum visualization. As this is set to update every 100 milliseconds, it becomes an ever-shifting visual indicator of the sound being played back.

```
protected function onTimer(e:TimerEvent):void {
  var a:Number = 0;
  var n:Number = 0;
  var i:int = 0;
  var ba:ByteArray = new ByteArray();
  SoundMixer.computeSpectrum(ba);
  spectrum.graphics.clear();
  spectrum.graphics.lineStyle(4, 0xFFFFFF, 0.8, false);
  spectrum.graphics.moveTo(0, (n/2)+150);
  for(i=0; i<=256; i++) {
    a = ba.readFloat();
    n = a*300;
    spectrum.graphics.lineTo(i*(stage.stageWidth/256), (n/2)+150);
  }
  spectrum.graphics.endFill();
}
```

8. The resulting application will look similar to the following screen render:

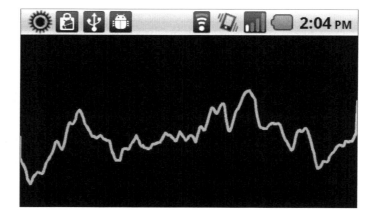

How it works...

The SoundMixer class provides access to the computeSpectrum() method, which is able to take a snapshot of the any sound being played through Flash Player or AIR and write it into a ByteArray object. There are 512 total Number values written to the ByteArray; the first 256 represent the left channel, and the remaining 256 represent the right. Depending upon what sort of visualization you need, the full 512 values may not be needed, as in the case here.

To generate the values which determine where to draw our lines using the graphics API, we use ByteArray.readFloat(), which reads a 32-bit floating-point value from the byte stream, and converts it to a Number. As this value indicates the specific sound data for that particular sample, we can use that to draw out a series of lines through the graphics API and form our visible spectrum.

There's more...

You can find a large amount of additional methods and formulae online by doing a simple search. The possibilities for doing this sort of generative visualization are truly endless, but we must take into account the lower than normal hardware specifications on these devices when deciding how far to push any visualization engine.

Generating audio tones for your application

Packing a lot of sound files into an application is one method of including audio. Another method is the runtime generation of sound data. We'll produce some simple sine tones in this recipe, which vary based upon detected touch pressure.

How to do it...

We will examine how to generate audio sample byte data based upon user touch pressure and feed this into a Sound object to generate a variety of tones:

1. First, import the following classes into your project:

```
import flash.display.Sprite;
import flash.display.StageAlign;
import flash.display.StageScaleMode;
import flash.events.SampleDataEvent;
import flash.events.TouchEvent;
import flash.media.Sound;
import flash.media.SoundChannel;
import flash.ui.Multitouch;
import flash.ui.MultitouchInputMode;
```

```
import flash.utils.ByteArray;
import flash.text.TextField;
import flash.text.TextFormat;
```

2. For this recipe, we must declare a number of different objects up front. We will begin with a sound object pair consisting of `Sound` and `SoundChannel`. These objects will allow us full control over the audio for this recipe. We will also create a `Number`, which will retain pressure information obtained through user touch. Finally, we will declare a `TextField` and `TextFormat` pair to relay text messages onto the device display:

```
private var sound:Sound;
private var channel:SoundChannel;
private var touchPressure:Number;
private var traceField:TextField;
private var traceFormat:TextFormat;
```

3. We will now set up our `TextField`, apply a `TextFormat`, and add it to the `DisplayList`. Here, we create a method to perform all of these actions for us:

```
protected function setupTextField():void {
  traceFormat = new TextFormat();
  traceFormat.bold = true;
  traceFormat.font = "_sans";
  traceFormat.size = 24;
  traceFormat.align = "center";
  traceFormat.color = 0xCCCCCC;
  traceField = new TextField();
  traceField.defaultTextFormat = traceFormat;
  traceField.selectable = false;
  traceField.mouseEnabled = false;
  traceField.width = stage.stageWidth;
  traceField.height = stage.stageHeight;
  addChild(traceField);
}
```

4. Now we will go about setting up our audio related objects. Initialize a `Sound` and `SoundChannel` object pair. These will be employed later on to play back our generated audio data:

```
protected function setupSound():void {
  sound = new Sound();
  channel = new SoundChannel();
}
```

5. Set the specific input mode for the multitouch APIs to support touch input by setting `Multitouch.inputMode` to the `MultitouchInputMode.TOUCH_POINT` constant. We will also register a listener for `SampleDataEvent.SAMPLE_DATA` events, which requests will begin once we set out `Sound` object to `play()` through the previously established `SoundChannel`:

```
protected function registerListeners():void {
    Multitouch.inputMode = MultitouchInputMode.TOUCH_POINT;
    stage.addEventListener(TouchEvent.TOUCH_BEGIN, onTouch);
    sound.addEventListener(SampleDataEvent.SAMPLE_DATA,
            onSampleDataRequest);
    channel = sound.play();
}
```

6. Whenever a touch event is detected, we will monitor it through the following method. Basically, we modify the `touchPressure Number`, which will be used to calculate our sine wave generation:

```
protected function onTouch(e:TouchEvent):void {
    touchPressure = e.pressure;
    traceField.text = "Pressure: " + touchPressure;
}
```

7. Our final method will execute whenever the currently playing `Sound` object requests new sample data to play back. We will employ the `ByteArray.writeFloat()` method to send generated audio data back to our `Sound` object for playback upon each sample request:

```
protected function
    onSampleDataRequest(e:SampleDataEvent):void {
    var out:ByteArray = new ByteArray();
    for( var i:int = 0 ; i < 8192; i++ ) {
    out.writeFloat(Math.sin((Number(i+e.position)/
        Math.PI/2))*touchPressure);
    out.writeFloat(Math.sin((Number(i+e.position)/
        Math.PI/2))*touchPressure);
    }
    e.data.writeBytes(out);
}
```

8. The resulting application will produce a variable tone depending upon the amount of pressure applied through touch and should look similar to the following screen render:

How it works...

The ActionScript `Sound` object, when registered with a `SampleDataEvent` event listener, will act as a socket when playback is initiated. We must provide sample data to pass along to this `Sound` object through a function, which generates this data, and passes samples to the waiting `Sound` object. The number of samples can vary between 2048 and 8192, in this case, we provide as much sample data as possible. The general formula provided by Adobe for generating a sine wave is: `Math.sin((Number(loopIndex+SampleDataEvent.position)/Math.PI/2))` multiplied by 0.25. Since we are modifying the formula based upon recorded touch point pressure, we multiply by this recorded value, instead. This modifies the generated audio that is produced by the application.

There's more...

For a more controlled library of generated sound tones, there exist ActionScript libraries, which can be used free of charge, or for a fee, depending on the library. I'd recommend checking out Sonoport at `http://www.sonoport.com/`.

6
Structural Adaptation: Handling Device Layout and Scaling

This chapter will cover the following recipes:

- ▶ Detecting useable screen bounds and resolution
- ▶ Detecting screen orientation changes
- ▶ Scaling visual elements across devices at runtime
- ▶ Scaling visual elements based on stage resize in Flash Professional CS5.5
- ▶ Employing the project panel in Flash Professional CS5.5
- ▶ Freezing a Flex application to landscape or portrait mode
- ▶ Defining a blank Flex mobile application
- ▶ Defining a Flex mobile view-based application
- ▶ Defining a Flex mobile tabbed application with multiple sections
- ▶ Using a splash screen within a Flex mobile application
- ▶ Configuring the ActionBar within a Flex mobile project for use with ViewNavigator
- ▶ Hiding the ActionBar Control in a single view for a Flex mobile project
- ▶ Hiding the ActionBar Control in all views for a Flex mobile project

Introduction

With such a variety of hardware devices running Android, developing applications that look and function properly across different resolutions can be a challenge. Thankfully, this is something the Flash platform is well-suited for. Whether using the default layout mechanisms as part of the Flex SDK or writing your own layout and scaling logic, there are many things to consider.

In this chapter we will look at layout mechanisms when dealing with the Flex framework for mobile application development, and also explore a variety of considerations for pure ActionScript projects.

Detecting useable screen bounds and resolution

When producing applications for a desktop or laptop computer, we don't have to give too much thought on the actual screen real estate we have to work with, or the **Pixels Per Inch(PPI)** resolution for that matter. It can be generally assumed that we will have at least a 1024x768 screen to work against, and we can be sure that it is a 72 PPI display. With mobile, that it all out the window.

With mobile device displays, our applications can basically be full screen or almost full screen; that is, but for the notification bar. These device screens can vary in size from just a few pixels, to hundreds. Then we must take into account different aspect ratios and the fact that the screen will certainly display 250 PPI or above. We must have a new set of checks in place to perform application layout modifications depending upon the device.

How to do it...

At runtime, we can monitor many device capabilities and react by modifying our various visual elements across the screen:

1. First, import the following classes into your project:

```
import flash.display.Sprite;
import flash.display.StageAlign;
import flash.display.StageScaleMode;
import flash.system.Capabilities;
import flash.text.TextField;
import flash.text.TextFormat;
```

2. We will now declare a `TextField` and `TextFormat` pair to relay text messages onto the device display:

```
private var traceField:TextField;
private var traceFormat:TextFormat;
```

3. Now, we will continue to set up our `TextField`, apply a `TextFormat`, and add it to the `DisplayList`. Here, we create a method to perform all of these actions for us:

```
protected function setupTextField():void {
    traceFormat = new TextFormat();
    traceFormat.bold = true;
    traceFormat.font = "_sans";
    traceFormat.size = 24;
    traceFormat.align = "center";
    traceFormat.color = 0xCCCCCC;
    traceField = new TextField();
    traceField.defaultTextFormat = traceFormat;
    traceField.selectable = false;
    traceField.mouseEnabled = false;
    traceField.width = stage.stageWidth;
    traceField.height = stage.stageHeight;
    addChild(traceField);
}
```

4. The final step is to create a method to gather all of the data we need to make any further modifications to our layout or UI components. In this example, we are reading both the `Stage.stageHeight` and `Stage.stageWidth` to get the usable area. We can contract this with `Capabilities.screenResolutionX` and `Capabilities.screenResolutionY` to get the actual display resolution.

5. Other important pieces of information are the `Capabilities.touchscreenType` to determine whether the touch screen expects a finger or stylus, `Capabilities.pixelAspectRatio` to retrieve pixel aspect ratio (though this is generally always 1:1), and most importantly that we use `Capabilities.screenDPI` to discover the PPI measurement of our display:

```
protected function readBounds():void {
    traceField.appendText("Stage Width: " +
            stage.stageWidth + "\n");
    traceField.appendText("Stage Height: " +
            stage.stageHeight + "\n");
    traceField.appendText("Pixel AR: " +
            Capabilities.pixelAspectRatio + "\n");
    traceField.appendText("Screen DPI: " +
            Capabilities.screenDPI + "\n");
    traceField.appendText("Touch Screen Type: " +
            Capabilities.touchscreenType + "\n");
```

```
traceField.appendText("Screen Res X: " +
        Capabilities.screenResolutionX + "\n");
traceField.appendText("Screen Res Y: " +
        Capabilities.screenResolutionY);
}
```

6. The resulting application will display as shown in the following screenshot:

How it works...

Through the `flash.display.Stage` and `flash.system.Capabilities` classes, we can learn a lot about the particular device display our application is running on and have the application react to that in some way. In this example, we are outputting the gathered information to a `TextField`, but this data could be also used to adjust the location, size, or arrangement of visual elements based on `Stage` resolution.

Detecting screen orientation changes

As most Android devices have at least two screen orientations, that is, portrait and landscape, it is useful when developing for these devices to know what the current orientation is in order to properly display application user interface elements.

How to do it...

We will register an event listener on our `Stage` to listen for `StageOrientationEvent` changes:

1. First, import the following classes into your project:
    ```
    import flash.display.Sprite;
    import flash.display.StageAlign;
    import flash.display.StageOrientation;
    import flash.display.StageScaleMode;
    ```

```
import flash.events.StageOrientationEvent;
import flash.text.TextField;
import flash.text.TextFormat;
```

2. We will now declare a `TextField` and `TextFormat` pair to relay text messages onto the device display:

```
private var traceField:TextField;
private var traceFormat:TextFormat;
```

3. Now, we will continue to set up our `TextField`, apply a `TextFormat`, and add it to the `DisplayList`. Here, we create a method to perform all of these actions for us:

```
protected function setupTextField():void {
    traceFormat = new TextFormat();
    traceFormat.bold = true;
    traceFormat.font = "_sans";
    traceFormat.size = 24;
    traceFormat.align = "center";
    traceFormat.color = 0xCCCCCC;
    traceField = new TextField();
    traceField.defaultTextFormat = traceFormat;
    traceField.selectable = false;
    traceField.mouseEnabled = false;
    traceField.width = stage.stageWidth;
    traceField.height = stage.stageHeight;
    addChild(traceField);
}
```

4. The next step will be to register an event listener to detect changes in screen orientation. We do this by listening for `StageOrientationEvent.ORIENTATION_CHANGE` events on the `Stage`:

```
protected function registerListeners():void {
    stage.addEventListener(StageOrientationEvent.ORIENTATION_CHANGE,
            onOrientationChange);
}
```

5. When a `StageOrientationEvent.ORIENTATION_CHANGE` event is detected, it will invoke a method named `onOrientationChange`. We will create this method and use it to write a text constant representing the new orientation to the `TextField`. We will also invoke a method to adjust our layout at this point:

```
protected function
    onOrientationChange(e:StageOrientationEvent):void {
    traceField.appendText(e.afterOrientation+"\n");
    reformLayout();
}
```

6. Finally, we will use the `reformLayout` method to adjust any visual components on screen to match our new `Stage` dimensions. Here, we simply adjust the sizes of our `TextField` object:

```
protected function reformLayout():void {
  traceField.width = stage.stageWidth;
  traceField.height = stage.stageHeight;
}
```

7. The resulting application will display as shown in the following screenshot:

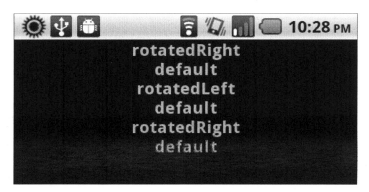

How it works...

Basically this is a simple event listener that is tied to devices, which have a variety of possible orientations. We register an event listener of type `StageOrientationEvent.ORIENTATION_CHANGE` on the `Stage` and receive two important pieces of data back: `StageOrientationEvent.beforeOrientation` and `StageOrientationEvent.afterOrientation`. The values contained within these event results will report device orientation constants.

There are four constants that can possibly be reported:

1. `StageOrientation.DEFAULT`
2. `StageOrientation.ROTATED_LEFT`
3. `StageOrientation.ROTATED_RIGHT`
4. `StageOrientation.UPSIDE_DOWN`

Again, these are simply possibilities. There are some devices which do not support all four of these constants so we must be cautious and not assume otherwise.

There's more...

There are actually a number of ways in which we could detect screen orientation changes. One would be to monitor the `Stage.orientation` through a `Timer` and react accordingly. Another would involve testing `Accelerometer` values for orientation changes. Using `StageOrientationEvent` is the most direct way, however, and supplies us with information about both the orientation before and after the event fires, which can be very useful.

See also...

For an example of how you might go about a similar task through the `Accelerometer` API, have a look at *Chapter 3, Movement through Space: Accelerometer and Geolocation Sensors.*

Scaling visual elements across devices at runtime

The wide variety of Pixels Per Inch (PPI) measurements and overall screen resolution differences across Android devices can make it difficult to make sizing and layout decisions when creating visual elements, especially interactive elements, as these must be large enough for users to touch with their fingertips easily. It is generally accepted that a physical measurement of a half inch square is ideal for proper touch. In this recipe, we will demonstrate how to ensure the same physical specifications across devices.

How to do it...

We will create some visual elements on the screen that are sized to physical measurements based upon the detected device display PPI:

1. First, import the following classes into your project:

```
import flash.display.Shape;
import flash.display.Sprite;
import flash.display.StageAlign;
import flash.display.StageScaleMode;
import flash.display.StageOrientation;
import flash.events.StageOrientationEvent;
import flash.system.Capabilities;
```

2. The next step will be to declare a number of objects to use in our application. We will create three `Shape` objects, which will be used to demonstrate this particular layout and sizing technique. We also set up two `Number` objects to hold specific measurements for use when determining size and position across the application:

```
private var boxTopLeft:Shape;
private var boxTopRight:Shape;
private var boxBottom:Shape;
private var halfInch:Number;
private var fullInch:Number;
```

3. Now, we must draw out our visual elements onto the `Stage`. As mentioned earlier, we are targeting a physical resolution of one half inch as the smallest measurement. Therefore, we begin by performing a calculation to determine the representation, measured in pixels, of both half inch and one full inch.

4. We will be creating a box in the upper left, and another in the upper right; each will be a half inch square and positioned based upon the available `Stagewidth` and `height`. A larger box will be positioned at the very bottom of our screen and will extend across the width of the `Stage`:

```
protected function setupBoxes():void {
    halfInch = Capabilities.screenDPI * 0.5;
    fullInch = Capabilities.screenDPI * 1;
    boxTopLeft = new Shape();
    boxTopLeft.graphics.beginFill(0xFFFFFF, 1);
    boxTopLeft.x = 0;
    boxTopLeft.y = 0;
    boxTopLeft.graphics.drawRect(0, 0, halfInch, halfInch);
    boxTopLeft.graphics.endFill();
    addChild(boxTopLeft);
    boxTopRight = new Shape();
    boxTopRight.graphics.beginFill(0xFFFFFF, 1);
    boxTopRight.x = stage.stageWidth - halfInch;
    boxTopRight.y = 0;
    boxTopRight.graphics.drawRect(0, 0, halfInch, halfInch);
    boxTopRight.graphics.endFill();
    addChild(boxTopRight);
    boxBottom = new Shape();
    boxBottom.graphics.beginFill(0xFFFFFF, 1);
    boxBottom.x = 0;
    boxBottom.y = stage.stageHeight - fullInch;
    boxBottom.graphics.drawRect(0, 0, stage.stageWidth, fullInch);
    boxBottom.graphics.endFill();
    addChild(boxBottom);
}
```

5. Register an event listener of type `StageOrientationEvent.ORIENTATION_` `CHANGE` upon the `Stage`. This will detect device orientation changes and alert us so that we may resize and reposition our visual elements appropriately:

```
protected function registerListeners():void {
    stage.addEventListener(StageOrientationEvent.ORIENTATION_CHANGE,
            onOrientationChange);
}
```

6. The following method will fire upon each orientation change detected by our application. In this case, we do not care so much what our present orientation actually is, but will reposition (and resize, when necessary) any visual element on the `Stage` to properly reflow the screen. We once again use our numeric measurements to perform these actions:

```
protected function
    onOrientationChange(e:StageOrientationEvent):void {
    boxTopLeft.x = 0;
    boxTopLeft.y = 0;
    boxTopRight.x = stage.stageWidth - halfInch;
    boxTopRight.y = 0;
    boxBottom.x = 0;
    boxBottom.y = stage.stageHeight - fullInch;
    boxBottom.width = stage.stageWidth;
}
```

7. The resulting application will display similar to what we see in the following screenshot:

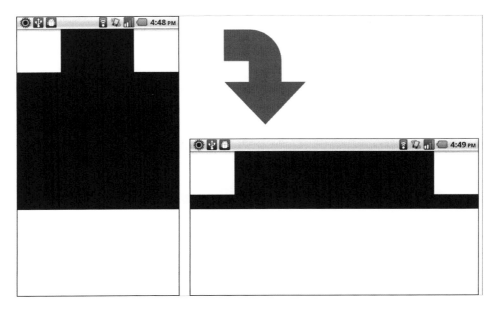

How it works...

A good trick to sizing visual components is to multiply the reported `Capabilities.screenDPI` times whatever physical measurement you want to achieve. For instance, if we want to be sure that certain touch elements are exactly half inch in width across devices, you can use the following formula:

```
private var halfInch:Number = Capabilities.screenDPI * 0.5;
```

In this example, we set up some variables, which represent measurements of physical half-inch and full-inch calculations, and then apply these upon the creation of our elements for layout and sizing. If a change in device orientation is detected, we adjust our layout based upon the new `Stage` dimensions and also resize visual elements as appropriate. As the two top `Shapes` are half inch squares, we simply adjust their `x` and `y` coordinates, but the bottom shape has the additional requirement of adjusting its `width` upon every orientation change to fill the width of the screen.

Scaling visual elements based on stage resize in Flash Professional CS5.5

One of the features introduced in Flash Professional CS5.5 that makes targeting various device resolutions easier is the ability for Flash to resize and reposition visual elements upon `Stage` resize. This allows us to modify our FLA files targeting specific resolutions and devices quite easily.

How to do it...

We will demonstrate how to employ **Scale content with stage** in order to target different screen resolutions:

1. Here we see a demo application laid out at **480x800**, targeting a Nexus S device. In the **Properties** panel, click upon the wrench icon next to the **Size** controls:

2. We want to adjust the display resolution to match that of a Droid2 so we change the **Document Settings** to reflect a **480x854** display resolution to match this device. Additionally, we can select **Scale content with stage**, which will scale our visual elements proportionately:

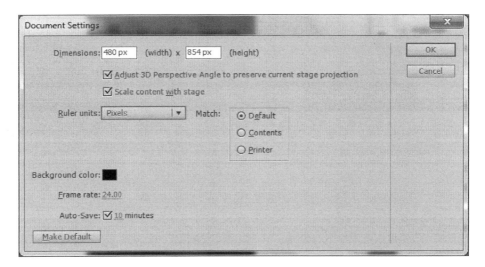

3. Upon hitting the **OK** button, we can see that the `Stage` has resized and our visual elements are now centered upon the `Stage`. Since we only adjusted the **height** of this application, the layout of the visual elements is repositioned according to settings which can be adjusted in **Edit | Preferences | General | Scale Content,** where we can choose to **Align top left** or not. Leaving this box unselected will center our elements upon rescaling the stage and selecting to scale contents, as we can see below.

4. To demonstrate this further, we will resize our `Stage` to match the resolution of a fictional Android tablet device. In the **Properties** panel, once again click upon the wrench icon next to the **Size** controls:

5. Our fictional tablet has a resolution of **800x1000**, so we will once again adjust the width and height settings and select **Scale content with stage** followed by a click of the button marked **OK**:

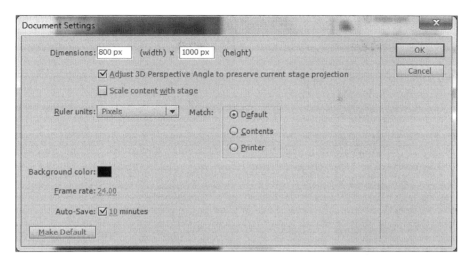

6. The new scaling feature is much more apparent now, and we can even see how much our application assets have been scaled by referring to the guides, which were originally marking our initial resolution. At this point, we can make any further adjustments to our application layout to be sure it appears exactly as we want upon the target device:

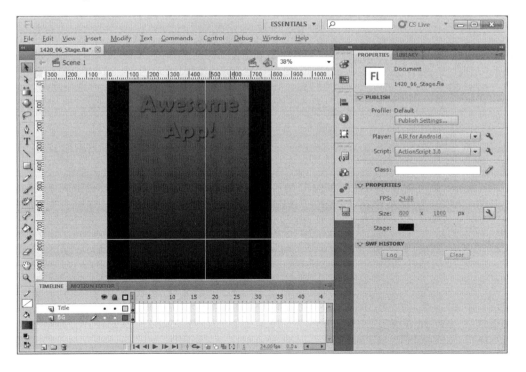

If we wanted to target a number of devices in a visual way, we could construct an FLA for each one using this technique, along with a shared codebase. Although many devices would be able to use an application generated from the exact same .fla, it all depends upon target device resolution and how much tweaking we want to do for each one.

How it works...

With Flash Professional CS5.5 and above, we now have the added feature of scaling content on our Stage when we adjust the Stage dimensions. This is excellent for mobile Android development purposes since there exists such a variety of display resolutions across devices. The ability to scale our content allows for rapid layout adjustments of FLA documents which, when compiled to .APK, target certain devices.

There's more...

It is important to note that the scaling of our visual elements will always be done in a way that preserves their original aspect ratio. If the new aspect ratio differs from the original, there will be further adjustments, which will be needed to be made in order to make the layout suitable to whichever device we are targeting.

Employing the Project panel in Flash Professional CS5.5

It has traditionally been troublesome when attempting to design application layout in Flash Professional since it required the manual organization of various FLA files, along with some mechanism of synchronizing changes between them in code and asset management. Flash Professional CS5.5 attempts to alleviate much of this burden with a new Project structure, including the ability to share author time Flash Library assets across project documents.

How to do it...

We will configure a Flash Project, which will allow us to target multiple screen resolutions using the same shared asset pool across device-targeted FLAs:

1. Create a new Flash Professional project by opening the **Project panel** by selecting **Create New | Flash Project** on the welcome screen, or through **File | New... | Flash Project** from the application menu:

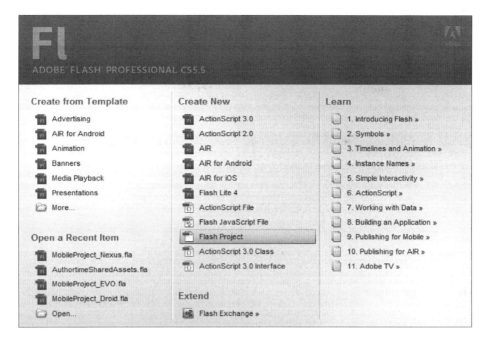

2. The **Create New Project** panel will appear, allowing us to configure a new **Flash Project**. We will provide a **Project name**, define a **Root folder** for the project files to reside, and choose a **Player**. In the case of AIR for Android, we will want to be sure to choose **AIR 2.6** or the latest version of AIR you wish to target:

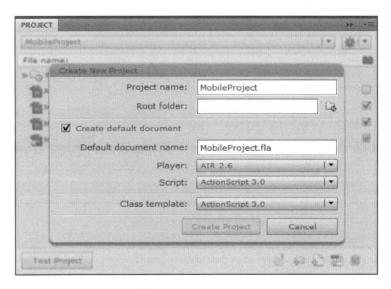

3.   The Flash Project structure allows us to define a number of different FLA documents within one project, which target a variety of resolutions and layouts. Here, for example, we have created specific documents targeting the Droid, EVO, and Nexus One mobile Android devices. In addition to these documents we also have an `AuthortimeSharedAssets.fla` file, which is generated for us automatically by Flash Professional. This will contain any assets which are shared across our other documents.

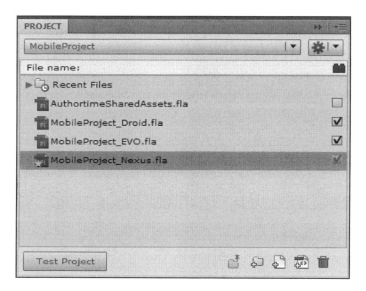

4.   Now, as we design and develop our application assets, we can mark each one as an author-time shared asset, which can be linked across all of our documents, making asset management within this particular project much more organized than it would be, otherwise. To mark a **Library** asset as shared, simply click on the checkbox next to it:

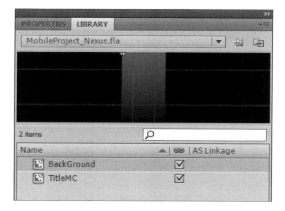

5. While marking a particular asset to be shared across documents in a project does make it sharable, we must also be sure to include the **Library** asset within the document in question to be able to access it within a particular device document at author time.

6. For instance, if we have two `.fla` files that we want to share a MovieClip symbol called "RedBall", we will first define "RedBall" in one `.fla`, and mark it as shared within that Library. This will place the symbol into our `AuthortimeSharedAssets.fla` file, but it will not be available to any other `.fla` until we actually bring it into the **Library** of the second `.fla`. At this point, any modifications made in either `.fla` will be shared across both because of the shared asset linkage in our project.

How it works...

The `AuthortimeSharedAssets.fla` file contains all of the Flash **Library** assets that are shared across our multiple FLA files. This allows us to modify a shared asset in one file, and have those changes cascade across all project documents in which it is used. The ability to define a variety of screen resolution layouts through multiple, targeted FLA files allows a designer great flexibility when structuring the application user interface. Having all of those interface elements linked through this new project structure keeps the work organized and clean.

There's more...

Not only does the new Flash Project panel and associated project structure allow for author time asset sharing and multi-device targeting through multiple FLA files, but the file structure is now totally compatible with Flash Builder. This allows developers to start a Flash Project in Flash Professional, and continue editing it in Flash Builder by importing the project folder within that environment.

Freezing a Flex application to landscape or portrait mode

It is sometimes desirable to constrain your application layout to a specific aspect ratio, landscape, or portrait. When building Android projects using the Flex framework, it is a simple matter to accomplish this.

How to do it...

We can freeze a particular aspect ratio for our application by modifying the AIR application descriptor file:

1. By default, when we define a new Flex mobile project, an application descriptor XML file is created. This file includes a node dedicated to the application `initialWindow` configuration. It will appear similar to the following code:

```
<initialWindow>
    <autoOrients>true</autoOrients>
    <fullScreen>false</fullScreen>
    <visible>true</visible>
    <softKeyboardBehavior>none</softKeyboardBehavior>
</initialWindow>
```

2. We want to modify the contents of this node in two ways. First, set the `autoOrients` tag to `false`. This will prevent the application from re-orienting itself upon device rotation:

```
<initialWindow>
    <autoOrients>false</autoOrients>
    <fullScreen>false</fullScreen>
    <visible>true</visible>
    <softKeyboardBehavior>none</softKeyboardBehavior>
</initialWindow>
```

3. Now, we will add an `aspectRatio` tag and provide it with one of two values, `landscape` or `portrait`:

```
<initialWindow>
    <autoOrients>false</autoOrients>
    <aspectRatio>landscape</aspectRatio>
    <fullScreen>false</fullScreen>
    <visible>true</visible>
    <softKeyboardBehavior>none</softKeyboardBehavior>
</initialWindow>
```

4. When we test this application on our device, even when holding it upright, in portrait mode, our application remains locked to landscape:

How it works...

The application descriptor file is very powerful as it can define many elements of our application without even editing any MXML or ActionScript. In this example, we are modifying tags within the project `initialWindow` node; setting `autoOrients` to false and adding an `aspectRation` tag, setting the aspect ratio of our application to `landscape` or `portrait`. Performing these edits will ensure that our application runs in a fixed aspect ratio no matter how the device is rotated by the user.

There's more...

Users of Flash professional CS5.5 will find that they can easily adjust these properties through the **AIR for Android Settings** dialog. This can be accessed from either the **Properties** panel or from **File | AIR for Android Settings**:

See also...

We will explore the application descriptor file in greater depth within *Chapter 9, Manifest Assurance: Security and Android Permissions*.

Defining a blank Flex mobile application

When you create a **Flex Mobile Project** in Flash Builder, there are a number of default view and layout controls that come along with it, including the `ActionBar` control and `ViewNavigator` container. These are very useful controls for many types of projects, but not all will benefit from these extra structures. Sometimes it is better to start with a blank project and build from there.

How to do it...

There are two ways to go about defining a blank Flex Mobile Application.

When creating a **New Flex Mobile Project** in Flash Builder:

1. Define your **Project Location** and click **Next**.
2. Now simply choose **Blank** in the **Application Template** area and proceed with your project setup:

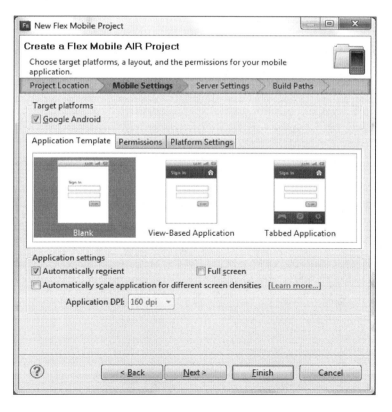

The second way is to modify an existing **Flex Mobile Project** to remove certain mobile-related structures:

1. Your mobile project will initially include the following MXML:

    ```
    <?xml version="1.0" encoding="utf-8"?>
    <s:ViewNavigatorApplication xmlns:fx=
                    "http://ns.adobe.com/mxml/2009"
        xmlns:s="library://ns.adobe.com/flex/spark"
      firstView="views.MainHomeView">
    </s:ViewNavigatorApplication>
    ```

2. We will now modify this in a number of ways. First, change your `ViewNavigatorApplication` tags to read as `Application` tags:

    ```
    <?xml version="1.0" encoding="utf-8"?>
      <s:Application
            xmlns:fx="http://ns.adobe.com/mxml/2009"
          xmlns:s="library://ns.adobe.com/flex/spark"
            firstView="views.MainHomeView">
      </s:Application>
    ```

3. Remove all `View` references in your code:

    ```
    <?xml version="1.0" encoding="utf-8"?>
    <s:Application xmlns:fx="http://ns.adobe.com/mxml/2009"
                    xmlns:s="library://ns.adobe.com/flex/spark">
    </s:Application>
    ```

Either of these methods will enable a blank Flex Mobile application:

How it works...

What defines whether the `ActionBar` and other mobile-related structures are present within a Flex Mobile Project is whether or not the application is of type `spark.components.ViewNavigatorApplication` or `spark.components.TabbedViewNavigatorApplication`. When using the more traditional `spark.components.Application` for your Flex Mobile project, the `ActionBar`, `TabBar`, and `ViewStack` are no longer present or usable within the project.

For more information about the structures mentioned above, have a look at the next few recipes, which describe ways of working in projects with `ViewNavigator` enabled.

There's more...

It is not a good idea to modify a Flex mobile project after working on it for some time, as you will most likely be tied deeply into the `ViewStack` at that point.

Defining a Flex mobile view-based application

A view-based Flex mobile application provides us with a number of very useful controls and containers that specifically target the mobile application development layout and structure. These include an `ActionBar` along the top of the screen, and the `ViewNavigator` control.

How to do it...

There are two ways to go about creating a Flex mobile view-based application.

When creating a **New Flex Mobile Project** in Flash Builder:

1. Define your **Project Location** and click **Next**.

2. Now simply choose **View-Based Application** in the **Application Template** area and proceed with your project setup:

The second way is to modify an existing Flex project to add certain mobile-related structures:

1. Your Flex project will initially include the following MXML:

```
<?xml version="1.0" encoding="utf-8"?>
<s:Application xmlns:fx="http://ns.adobe.com/mxml/2009"
          xmlns:s="library://ns.adobe.com/flex/spark">
</s:Application>
```

2. We will now modify this in a number of ways. First, change your Application tags to read as ViewNavigatorApplication tags:

```
<?xml version="1.0" encoding="utf-8"?>
<s:ViewNavigatorApplication
       xmlns:fx="http://ns.adobe.com/mxml/2009"
            xmlns:s="library://ns.adobe.com/flex/spark">
</s:ViewNavigatorApplication>
```

3. Create a `View` MXML file within the current project source folder named `MainHomeView.mxml` for this example. In this case, we are creating it within a `views` package in our project structure.It is important to realize that every `ViewNavigatorApplication` includes any number of individual views. A `View` is a type of Flex container that can be managed through the `ViewNavigator` to expose or dismiss various "screens" within a mobile Flex application:

```
<?xml version="1.0" encoding="utf-8"?>
 <s:View xmlns:fx="http://ns.adobe.com/mxml/2009"
     xmlns:s="library://ns.adobe.com/flex/spark"
         title="HomeView">
</s:View>
```

4. Now, we must point to the file we just created as the `firstView` property of our `ViewNavigatorApplication`:

```
<?xml version="1.0" encoding="utf-8"?>
<s:ViewNavigatorApplication
        xmlns:fx="http://ns.adobe.com/mxml/2009"
                xmlns:s="library://ns.adobe.com/flex/spark"
                firstView="views.MainHomeView">
</s:ViewNavigatorApplication>
```

Either of these methods will define a Flex mobile view-based application.

How it works...

What defines whether the `ActionBar` is present within a Flex mobile project is whether or not the application is of type `spark.components.ViewNavigatorApplication` (or `spark.components.TabbedViewNavigatorApplication`). By defining our application as a `ViewNavigatorAppplication`, we have access to all of these mobile specific structures and controls, including the powerful `ViewNavigator` through which we can manage all of our application views.

A View defines a specific "screen" within our application and the user will likely switch between many different views while the application is in use. We can manage all of these views from the `ViewNavigator`, which automatically preserves a view history for us when the application is in use. As a result of this, when the user interacts with the Android back button, previous views can be revisited.

Defining a Flex mobile tabbed application with multiple sections

Setting up a mobile Android project using the Flex framework can be as simple or as complex as we want it to be. Going one step beyond the `ViewNavigatorApplication`, is the `TabbedViewNavigatorApplication`, which includes the ability to have multiple sections of content, each with their own `ViewNavigator` and sets of `Views`. Defining a `TabbedViewNavigatorApplication` will allow us access to the `TabBar`.

How to do it...

There are two ways to go about configuring a Flex mobile tabbed application.

When creating a **New Flex Mobile Project** in Flash Builder:

1. Define your **Project Location** and click **Next >**
2. Now simply choose **Tabbed Application** in the **Application Template** area and proceed with your project setup:

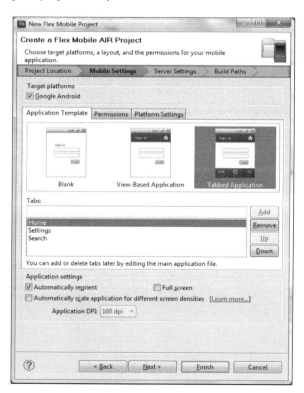

The second way is to modify an existing Flex project to add certain mobile-related structures:

1. Your Flex project will initially include the following MXML:

```
<?xml version="1.0" encoding="utf-8"?>
  <s:Application
          xmlns:fx="http://ns.adobe.com/mxml/2009"
              xmlns:s="library://ns.adobe.com/flex/spark">
  </s:Application>
```

2. We will now modify this in a number of ways. First, change your `Application` tags to read as `TabbedViewNavigatorApplication` tags:

```
<?xml version="1.0" encoding="utf-8"?>
  <s:TabbedViewNavigatorApplication
          xmlns:fx="http://ns.adobe.com/mxml/2009"
              xmlns:s="library://ns.adobe.com/flex/spark">
  </s:TabbedViewNavigatorApplication>
```

3. Create a set of `View` MXML files within the current project source folder. In this case, we are creating them all within a `views` package in our project structure:

TabOne.mxml:

```
<?xml version="1.0" encoding="utf-8"?>
<s:View xmlns:fx="http://ns.adobe.com/mxml/2009"
    xmlns:s="library://ns.adobe.com/flex/spark" title="Tab
             One">
<s:layout>
        <s:VerticalLayout paddingBottom="20" paddingLeft="20"
            paddingRight="20" paddingTop="20"/>
</s:layout>
<s:Label text="Tab View: #1" />
</s:View>
```

TabTwo.mxml:

```
<?xml version="1.0" encoding="utf-8"?>
<s:View xmlns:fx="http://ns.adobe.com/mxml/2009"
    xmlns:s="library://ns.adobe.com/flex/spark" title="Tab
             Two">
<s:layout>
        <s:VerticalLayout paddingBottom="20"
            paddingLeft="20" paddingRight="20"
            paddingTop="20"/>
</s:layout>
<s:Label text="Tab View: #2" />
</s:View>
```

TabThree.mxml:

```xml
<?xml version="1.0" encoding="utf-8"?>
<s:View xmlns:fx="http://ns.adobe.com/mxml/2009"
    xmlns:s="library://ns.adobe.com/flex/spark" title="Tab
        Three">
<s:layout>
    <s:VerticalLayout paddingBottom="20"
        paddingLeft="20" paddingRight="20"
        paddingTop="20"/>
</s:layout>
<s:Label text="Tab View: #3" />
</s:View>
```

4. Now, we must point to the files we just created by nesting a series of `ViewNavigator` declarations within our `TabbedViewNavigatorApplication` structure. Each will point to one of the unique `View` MXML files we have just created:

```xml
<?xml version="1.0" encoding="utf-8"?>
<s:TabbedViewNavigatorApplication
        xmlns:fx="http://ns.adobe.com/mxml/2009"
                xmlns:s="library://ns.adobe.com/flex/spark">
<s:ViewNavigator label="Tab One" width="100%"
    height="100%" firstView="views.TabOne"/>
<s:ViewNavigator label="Tab Two" width="100%"
    height="100%" firstView="views.TabTwo"/>
<s:ViewNavigator label="Tab Three" width="100%"
    height="100%" firstView="views.TabThree"/>
</s:TabbedViewNavigatorApplication>
```

Either of these methods will define a Flex mobile tabbed application:

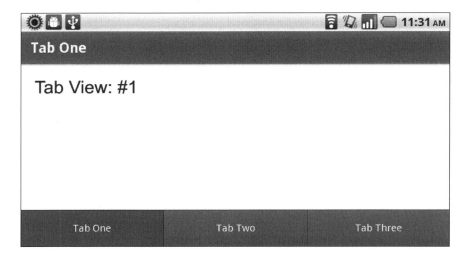

How it works...

What defines whether the `TabBar` is present within a Flex Mobile Project is whether or not the application is of type `spark.components.TabbedViewNavigatorApplication`. When using the more traditional `spark.components.Application` for your Flex mobile project, the `TabBar` and `ViewStack` are no longer present or usable within the project.

There's more...

It is important to note here that when using `TabbedViewNavigator`, each tab has its own exclusive `ViewNavigator` each with its own view stack. The `ViewNavigotor` instances do not have a mechanism to share data with one another unless drawn upon from a separate source, such as a shared data pool, which would be defined by the developer.

Using a splash screen within a Flex mobile application

Adobe AIR for Android is an excellent runtime for building and distributing Android applications, but there are some trade-offs in comparison to native development. Depending upon the size of your application, it may take a few seconds to load everything up for the user. The mobile Flex framework allows us to define a splash screen to let the user know that the application is loading once they launch, and to add an extra bit of flourish to the entire experience.

How to do it...

We will configure our application to display a splash screen while the application loading process takes place:

1. Upon defining our Flex mobile project, we will need to be sure the `ViewNavigatorApplication` or `TabbedViewNavigatorApplication` (depending upon your project) is the currently selected MXML tag and enter **Design** view.

2. Next, we will modify a few settings within the **Common** area of our **Properties** panel. Here, browse to an image file to embed a **Splash image** and set the **Splash scale mode** to **none**, **letterbox**, **stretch**, or **zoom**:

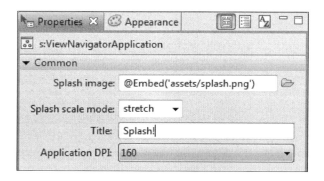

3. Enter **Source view** and the MXML document will appear as follows:

```
<?xml version="1.0" encoding="utf-8"?>
<s:ViewNavigatorApplication
        xmlns:fx="http://ns.adobe.com/mxml/2009"
        xmlns:s="library://ns.adobe.com/flex/spark"
        applicationDPI="240"
        firstView="views.SplashScreenHomeView"
        splashScreenImage="@Embed('assets/splash.png')"
        splashScreenScaleMode="stretch"
        title="Splash!">
</s:ViewNavigatorApplication>
```

4. You can, of course, modify any of the settings we have just configured from here by pointing to another file to embed or changing the scale mode. We will be adding one more property to our main application tag called `splashScreenMinimumDisplayTime` and set its value to the minimum duration, in milliseconds, that we want the splash screen image to display for:

```
<?xml version="1.0" encoding="utf-8"?>
<s:ViewNavigatorApplication
        xmlns:fx="http://ns.adobe.com/mxml/2009"
        xmlns:s="library://ns.adobe.com/flex/spark"
        applicationDPI="240"
        firstView="views.SplashScreenHomeView"
        splashScreenImage="@Embed('AndroidSplash.png')"
        splashScreenScaleMode="stretch"
        splashScreenMinimumDisplayTime="2000"
        title="Splash!">
</s:ViewNavigatorApplication>
```

5. When the user runs the application on their device, they will be presented with a handsome splash screen identifying the application and letting them know that it is now loading:

How it works...

Setting the `splashScreenImage` property on our main application file will allow us to display an embedded custom image to the user while our application is loading. The addition of a `splashScreenMinimumDisplayTime` property allows us to define the minimum length of time (in milliseconds) that our splash screen will display for. If the application takes longer than this defined time, the splash screen will continue to display as needed. The splash screen also can accept a specific scale mode behavior by setting the `splashScreenScaleMode` property:

► Setting `splashScreenScaleMode` to `none` will present our defined image at its native resolution without any modification. This is probably unacceptable as device screen resolutions vary so greatly.

► Setting `splashScreenScaleMode` to `letterbox` will fit the splash image into the frame defined by the device display resolution, but will display empty padding in the areas that the image does not cover.

▶ Setting `splashScreenScaleMode` to `stretch` will stretch the defined image into the frame defined by the device display resolution, filling the entire display area. Some distortion may occur with this setting as the image may be scaled disproportionately.

▶ Setting `splashScreenScaleMode` to `zoom` will fit the splash image into the frame defined by the device display resolution without allowing any padding. It will fill the entire display area by cropping portions of the image from view. This may be undesirable as portions of the image may not be visible to the user.

Example: a 480x800 pixel image will appear as follows when rendered on a device display measuring 320x480:

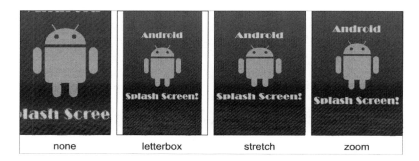

| none | letterbox | stretch | zoom |

Configuring the ActionBar within a Flex mobile project for use with ViewNavigator

The Flex mobile `ViewNavigatorApplication` and `TabbedViewNavigatorApplication` contain a special control called the `ActionBar`, which contains three editable child containers. We can define the contents of these child containers by modifying the MXML in our project documents.

How to do it...

Modify the document MXML to customize our `ActionBar` contents. In this example, we will define some interactive image controls and provide a rich title image across our application `ViewStack`:

1. When we first configure a new Flex mobile project, our main MXML document will appear as follows:

   ```
   <?xml version="1.0" encoding="utf-8"?>
   <s:ViewNavigatorApplication
   xmlns:fx="http://ns.adobe.com/mxml/2009"
   xmlns:s="library://ns.adobe.com/flex/spark"
   ```

```
firstView="views.CustomActionBarHomeView">
</s:ViewNavigatorApplication>
```

2. The `ActionBar` contains three distinct areas within which we can define additional controls, they are the `navigationContent`, `titleContent`, and `actionContent` containers.

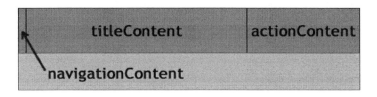

3. We will first define a `navigationContent` node within our main application MXML. Define a Spark `Image` control within, embedding a navigation image that will function as a way for users to get back to the "home" screen of our application:

```
<s:navigationContent>
    <s:Image source="@Embed('images/home.png')"/>
</s:navigationContent>
```

4. Now, define the `titleContent` container and create an `Image` control within it embedding an image used as the title of our application:

```
<s:titleContent>
    <s:Image source="@Embed('images/title.png')"/>
</s:titleContent>
```

5. Finally, define a `actionContent` node and embed another image within it, just as we did for our `navigationContent` container. This will function as a close button:

```
<s:actionContent>
    <s:Image source="@Embed('images/close.png')"/>
</s:actionContent>
```

6. We will then set up a `script` block in our MXML to contain any functions we will be writing:

```
<fx:Script>
    <![CDATA[
    ]]>
</fx:Script>
```

7. Define a method within our script block that will return the user to our initial `View` when the `navigationContent` child `Image` is pressed by invoking the `ViewNavigator.popToFirstView()` method.

```
private function goHome(e:MouseEvent):void {
    navigator.popToFirstView();
}
```

8. Define a second method to exit the application when the `actionContent` child `Image` is pressed by the user:

    ```
    private function closeApp(e:MouseEvent):void {
      NativeApplication.nativeApplication.exit();
    }
    ```

9. Now, we will complete this example by assigning click events to each of our interactive `ActionBarImage` controls, registering them with the methods we created previously:

    ```
    <s:navigationContent>
    <s:Image click="goHome(event)"
            source="@Embed('images/home.png')"/>
    </s:navigationContent>
    <s:actionContent>
    <s:Image click="closeApp(event)"
            source="@Embed('images/close.png')"/>
    </s:actionContent>
    ```

10. We will also define our two `View` mxml files in such a way that these `ActionBar` controls will be clearly functional for this example. The initial `View` will include a Button in order to navigate to the secondary `View` using the `ViewNavigator.push()` method. When invoking this method, we simply need to pass in a reference to the particular the application should enable for the user to interact with. We can optionally pass in a second argument, which contains data to feed the `View`.

11. From the secondary `View`, a user can either exit the application through clicking the `ActionBar` exit `Image`, press the Android back button, or click the `ActionBarhome` `Image` to invoke the `ViewNavigator.popToFirstView()` method and return to the initial application state:

    CustomAction BarHomeView.mxml:

    ```
    <?xml version="1.0" encoding="utf-8"?>
    <s:View xmlns:fx="http://ns.adobe.com/mxml/2009"
        xmlns:s="library://ns.adobe.com/flex/spark" title="Home
            View">
    <s:layout>
        <s:VerticalLayout paddingBottom="20" paddingLeft="20"
            paddingRight="20" paddingTop="20"/>
    </s:layout>
    <fx:Script>
        <![CDATA[
            protected function switchView():void {
    this.navigator.pushView(views.CustomActionBarSecondaryView);
            }
        ]]>
    </fx:Script>
    ```

```
        <s:Label text="Home View: Hit the EXIT icon to exit." />
        <s:Button label="Go to Secondary View"
                click="switchView()"/>
    </s:View>
CustomActionBarSecondaryView.mxml
    <?xml version="1.0" encoding="utf-8"?>
    <s:View xmlns:fx="http://ns.adobe.com/mxml/2009"
        xmlns:s="library://ns.adobe.com/flex/spark"
                title="Secondary View">
    <s:layout>
        <s:VerticalLayout paddingBottom="20" paddingLeft="20"
                paddingRight="20" paddingTop="20"/>
    </s:layout>
    <s:Label text="Secondary View: Hit the HOME icon to pop to
                the first view or the EXIT icon to exit." />
    </s:View>
```

12. When we run the application upon our device, the **ActionBar** will appear as follows:

How it works...

The Flex mobile `ActionBar` is an excellent structural element that can be used across a variety of mobile Android applications. The three container areas; `navigationContent`, `titleContent`, and `actionContent` behave much like any other Flex container. The contents of the `ActionBar` and the functions they perform are really up to the application developer and what makes sense for the target user. We must be sure to consider the amount of space available to us and how this can change across devices.

When dealing with the `ViewNavigator`, there are a number of important methods that mobile developers should be familiar with. We will briefly touch upon them here.

`popToFirstView()` removes all views from the `ViewNavigator` except the bottom view, essentially having the application return to the "home" view. `popView()` pops the current view off the navigation stack, exposing the previous view to the user.

pushView() pushed a new view to the top of the ViewNavigator navigation stack, making it the current view. For this to function, a valid View object reference must be passed in as an argument of this method.

There's more...

We can also manage the view transitions by passing a transition reference through as the final argument in any of the ViewNavigator methods outlined in the previous section. For example, if we wanted to replace the normal sliding transition with a cube flipping up, we could do so through these steps:

1. Import the following classes:

    ```
    import spark.transitions.FlipViewTransition;
    import spark.transitions.FlipViewTransitionMode;
    import spark.transitions.ViewTransitionDirection;
    ```

2. Invoke a method to create our transition and pass it along as an argument of ViewNavigator.popView(). When creating our transition, we can define things such as duration, the direction of movement, and whether the ActionBar control is animated along with the view content or not:

    ```
    protected function removeViews():void {
      var androidTransition:FlipViewTransition =
               new FlipViewTransition();
      androidTransition.duration = 500;
      androidTransition.direction = ViewTransitionDirection.UP;
      androidTransition.transitionControlsWithContent = false;
      androidTransition.mode = FlipViewTransitionMode.CUBE;
      this.navigator.popView(androidTransition);
    }
    ```

There are a number of different transition types for us to explore when developing mobile Flex projects. This is just an example of how to go about using one of them.

Hiding the ActionBar control in a single view for a Flex mobile project

You may want to use the ViewNavigator structure and functionality of the ViewNavigatorApplication container, but simply want to hide the ActionBar in a specific application View.

How to do it...

Set the View `actionBarVisible` property to `true`. The following example shows how to toggle the `ActionBar` off and on for a particular `View` based on a button click:

1. Define a new Flex mobile view-based application:

```
<?xml version="1.0" encoding="utf-8"?>
<s:ViewNavigatorApplication
        xmlns:fx="http://ns.adobe.com/mxml/2009"
                xmlns:s="library://ns.adobe.com/flex/spark"
                firstView="views.MainHomeView">
</s:ViewNavigatorApplication>
```

2. Create a new MXML file called `MainHomeView.mxml` within a `views` package that will define our primary view for this application:

```
<?xml version="1.0" encoding="utf-8"?>
<s:View xmlns:fx="http://ns.adobe.com/mxml/2009"
        xmlns:s="library://ns.adobe.com/flex/spark"
            title="HomeView">
</s:View>
```

3. Define a `Button` component within the MXML file we just created, which constitutes our `ViewNavigatorApplication`first`View`:

```
<s:Button x="10" y="10" label="Toggle"/>
```

4. We will then set up a `script` block in our MXML to contain any functions we will be writing:

```
<fx:Script>
    <![CDATA[
    ]]>
</fx:Script>
```

5. Now, create a function called `toggleActionBar` and within it, we will create an `if` statement checking whether the `actionBarVisible` property of our `View` is `true` or `false`. Depending upon the current `Boolean` value, we will toggle to the opposite value:

```
protected function toggleActionBar():void {
    if(actionBarVisible){
        actionBarVisible = false;
    }else{
        actionBarVisible = true;
    }
}
```

6. Finally, we simply need to create a click event handler on our `Button` component to invoke the function just created:

```
<s:Button x="10" y="10" label="Toggle"
          click="toggleActionBar()"/>
```

7. This `Button` will now toggle the `ActionBar` off and on when toggled:

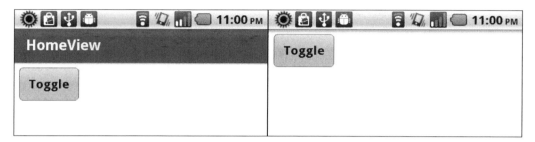

How it works...

Each `View` of your application has an `actionBarVisible` property. Setting `actionBarVisible = false;` will hide the `ActionBar` control for those particular `Views` it is set on. This is really quite flexible, as we can turn the `ActionBar` control on and off as needed, depending upon which `View` we are currently on.

There's more...

The mechanism with which we have removed the `ActionBar` control from our `View` is similar to the one with which we can use to remove the `TabBar` from a `TabbedViewNavigatorApplication` project by setting the following:

```
tabbedNavigator.tabBar.visible = false;
tabbedNavigator.tabBar.includeInLayout = false;
```

7

Native Interaction: StageWebView and URI Handlers

This chapter will cover the following recipes:

- ▶ Opening a website in the default Android browser
- ▶ Rendering a website within an application
- ▶ Managing the StageWebView history
- ▶ Using StageWebView to load ads using ActionScript
- ▶ Using StageWebView to load ads within a Flex mobile project
- ▶ Making a phone call from an application
- ▶ Sending a text message from an application
- ▶ Invoking Google maps from an application
- ▶ Invoking the Android market using application URIs
- ▶ Sending e-mail from an application

Introduction

Traditionally, Flash platform developers have not had access to render HTML websites as part of their applications; that all changes with the introduction of StageWebView in AIR for Android. This chapter includes tips on what makes such a mechanism different from normal display list objects, and how to use it effectively. We will also look at URI handling functions, which allow us to tap into native applications on an Android device such as the web browser, e-mail client, maps, and telephone.

Opening a website in the default Android browser

Similar to desktop Flash and AIR applications, the default system Web browser can be invoked through classes in the `flash.net` package based upon some user interaction. On Android, since all applications take up a full window, we must be extra mindful of any disruption this may cause while the user is interacting with our application. For instance, when the user received a phone call or text message and must exit the application.

How to do it...

Having the application invoke `navigateToURL` and passing in a new `URLRequest` will open the default web browser. In this example, we will open a website once a `TOUCH_TAP` event is detected:

1. First, import the following classes into your project:

   ```
   import flash.display.Sprite;
   import flash.display.StageAlign;
   import flash.display.StageScaleMode;
   import flash.events.TouchEvent;
   import flash.text.TextField;
   import flash.text.TextFormat;
   import flash.net.navigateToURL;
   import flash.net.URLRequest;
   import flash.ui.Multitouch;
   import flash.ui.MultitouchInputMode;
   ```

2. We will now declare a `Sprite` as our interactive element, along with a `TextField` and `TextFormat` pair to serve as a button label:

   ```
   private var fauxButton:Sprite;
   private var traceField:TextField;
   private var traceFormat:TextFormat;
   ```

3. Now, we will continue to set up our `TextField`, apply a `TextFormat` object, and construct a `Sprite` with a simple background fill using the graphics API. The final step in the construction of our button is to add the `TextField` to our `Sprite` and then add the `Sprite` to the `DisplayList`. Here, we create a method to perform all of these actions for us along with some stylistic enhancements:

   ```
   protected function setupTextButton():void {
     traceFormat = new TextFormat();
     traceFormat.bold = true;
     traceFormat.font = "_sans";
     traceFormat.size = 42;
   ```

```
        traceFormat.align = "center";
        traceFormat.color = 0x333333;
        traceField = new TextField();
        traceField.defaultTextFormat = traceFormat;
        traceField.autoSize = "left";
        traceField.selectable = false;
        traceField.mouseEnabled = false;
        traceField.text = "Invoke Browser";
        traceField.x = 30;
        traceField.y = 25;
        fauxButton = new Sprite();
        fauxButton.addChild(traceField);
        fauxButton.graphics.beginFill(0xFFFFFF, 1);
        fauxButton.graphics.drawRect(0, 0, traceField.width+60,
                traceField.height+50);
        fauxButton.graphics.endFill();
        fauxButton.x = (stage.stageWidth/2) - (fauxButton.width/2);
        fauxButton.y = 60;
        addChild(fauxButton);
    }
```

4. If we now run the application on our device, the interactive Sprite should appear as follows:

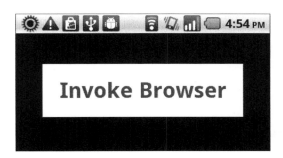

5. We will now assign the Multitouch.inputMode to respond to raw touch events through the MultitouchInputMode.TOUCH_POINT constant. Register an event listener of type TouchEvent.TOUCH_TAP upon the Sprite button. This will detect any touch tap events initiated by the user and invoke a method called onTouchTap, which contains the remainder of our logic:

```
protected function registerListeners():void {
    Multitouch.inputMode = MultitouchInputMode.TOUCH_POINT;
    fauxButton.addEventListener(TouchEvent.TOUCH_TAP, onTouchTap);
}
```

6. Once a touch tap, is detected our `onTouchTap` method will fire, invoking `navigateToURL` and passing in a `URLRequest` containing the HTTP or HTTPS address we want to open up from our application:

```
protected function onTouchTap(e:TouchEvent):void {
  navigateToURL(newURLRequest("http://memoryspiral.com/"));
}
```

7. When we run the application upon our device, a simple touch tap upon our button will invoke the native web browser application and load up our `URL request`:

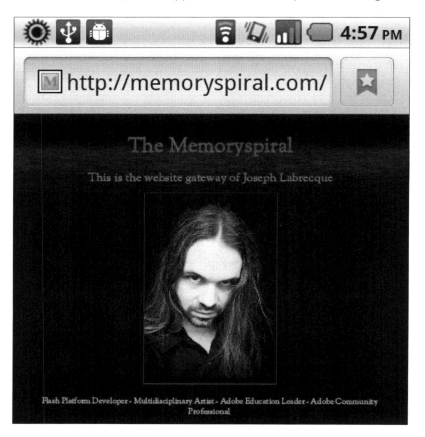

How it works...

When a user of our application touch taps the interactive `Sprite` we've created, they are taken out of our application and into the default Android web browser, as the URL we've supplied is loaded over the network, displaying the requested web site. This is accomplished by passing a `URLRequest` through the `navigateToURL` method, which is very similar to the way we accomplish the same thing with a desktop application.

There's more...

While invoking the Android web browser from within our application can be very useful. It is much more interesting to be able to load web pages into an application without having to jump between applications. The user can, of course, use the Android back button to return to our application from the browser (if it is still open), but there are ways to ensure a more seamless experience. The next few recipes will describe how to accomplish this.

Rendering a website within an application

With Flash content, it is traditionally not possible to display a fully rendered HTML website within an application. Adobe AIR initially changed this by allowing web pages to be loaded into the application on the desktop and interpreted through the internal AIR build of the web kit rendering engine through the desktop only `HTMLLoader` class. On Android, AIR allows us to do similar things through the use of `StageWebView`.

How to do it...

We will construct a new `StageWebView` instance to display a web page within our mobile Android application:

1. First, import the following classes into your project:

   ```
   import flash.display.Sprite;
   import flash.display.StageAlign;
   import flash.display.StageScaleMode;
   import flash.events.Event;
   import flash.events.TouchEvent;
   import flash.geom.Rectangle;
   import flash.media.StageWebView;
   import flash.net.URLRequest;
   import flash.net.navigateToURL;
   import flash.text.TextField;
   import flash.text.TextFormat;
   import flash.ui.Multitouch;
   import flash.ui.MultitouchInputMode;
   ```

2. We will now declare a `Sprite` as our interactive element, along with a `TextField` and `TextFormat` pair to serve as a button label. Additionally, declare a `StageWebView` instance along with a `Rectangle` to define our view port:

   ```
   private var fauxButton:Sprite;
   private var swv:StageWebView;
   private var swvRect:Rectangle;
   private var traceField:TextField;
   private var traceFormat:TextFormat;
   ```

3. Now, we will continue to set up our `TextField`, apply a `TextFormat` object, and construct a `Sprite` with a simple background fill using the graphics API. The final step in the construction of our button is to add the `TextField` to our `Sprite` and then add the `Sprite` to the `DisplayList`. Here, we create a method to perform all of these actions for us along with some stylistic enhancements:

```
protected function setupTextButton():void {
  traceFormat = new TextFormat();
  traceFormat.bold = true;
  traceFormat.font = "_sans";
  traceFormat.size = 42;
  traceFormat.align = "center";
  traceFormat.color = 0x333333;
  traceField = new TextField();
  traceField.defaultTextFormat = traceFormat;
  traceField.autoSize = "none";
  traceField.selectable = false;
  traceField.mouseEnabled = false;
  traceField.text = "Load Website";
  traceField.x = 30;
  traceField.y = 25;
  fauxButton = new Sprite();
  fauxButton.addChild(traceField);
  fauxButton.graphics.beginFill(0xFFFFFF, 1);
  fauxButton.graphics.drawRect(0, 0, traceField.width+60,
          traceField.height+50);
  fauxButton.graphics.endFill();
  fauxButton.x = (stage.stageWidth/2) - (fauxButton.width/2);
  fauxButton.y = 60;
  addChild(fauxButton);
}
```

4. Create a method to construct our `StageWebView` object by defining a new `Rectangle` with the position and size we want the `StageWebView` view port to appear within our application. In this example, we determine the properties of our `Rectangle` based upon the position of the previously created `Sprite`, and the dimensions of the application `Stage`.

5. It is good practice to check whether `StageWebView` is supported by invoking `StageWebView.isSupported` before constructing our `StageWebView` instance. To actually create a `StageWebView` object, we do a simple instantiation and assign the application `stage` to `StageWebView.stage`. Now assign the previously constructed `Rectangle` to the `StageWebView viewport` property:

```
protected function setupStageWebView():void {
```

```
swvRect = new Rectangle(0,fauxButton.y+fauxButton.
          height+40,stage.stageWidth,stage.
          stageHeight-fauxButton.y+fauxButton.height+40);
if(StageWebView.isSupported){
  swv = new StageWebView();
  swv.stage = this.stage;
  swv.viewPort = swvRect;
}
}
```

6. If we now run the application upon our device, the interactive `Sprite` with accompanying `StageWebView` should appear as follows:

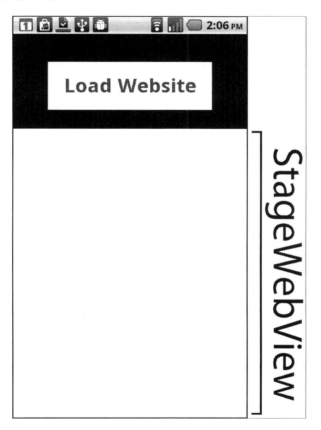

7. We will now assign the `Multitouch.inputMode` to respond to raw touch events through the `MultitouchInputMode.TOUCH_POINT` constant. Register an event listener of type `TouchEvent.TOUCH_TAP` upon the `Sprite` button. This will detect any touch tap events initiated by the user and invoke a method called `onTouchTap`, which will instantiate a page load. We will also register an event of type `Event.COMPLETE` upon our `StageWebView` object to determine when a page load has been completed:

```
protected function registerListeners():void {
   Multitouch.inputMode = MultitouchInputMode.TOUCH_POINT;
   fauxButton.addEventListener(TouchEvent.TOUCH_TAP, onTouchTap);
   swv.addEventListener(Event.COMPLETE, locationChanged);
}
```

8. When a touch tap is detected, our `onTouchTap` method will fire, invoking `navigateToURL`; it will begin to load a web page using `StageWebView.loadURL()`, passing in the page address as a `String` argument:

```
protected function onTouchTap(e:TouchEvent):void {
   swv.loadURL("http://memoryspiral.com/");
}
```

9. Once the page load has been completed, we can gather information about the loaded content, such as the page `title`. In this case, we assign the page `title` to our `TextField` as an example:

```
protected function locationChanged(e:Event):void {
   traceField.text = e.target.title;
}
```

10. The resulting application, once the web page has been completely loaded, will appear as follows:

How it works...

The `StageWebView` class will use whichever web control is default on the host operating system to render any HTML that is displayed in the view port. It is important to note that `StageWebView` is not part of the traditional Flash `DisplayList` and cannot be added to our application in the normal way visual elements are added to the `DisplayList` (through `addChild()`).

As `StageWebView` is not part of the traditional `DisplayList`, we must use an alternative way of defining where it will appear on the `stage` and what space it will occupy. This is done through the use of a `Rectangle` object assigned to the `StageWebView.viewPort` property. The `StageWebView` class also requires a `stage` property to which is assigned the present application `stage`. So long as these two properties are correctly assigned, a viewport will appear within our application.

As `StageWebView` is not a part of the `DisplayList`, we should always call the `dispose()` method upon it once we have finished using it to allow complete removal from our application.

There's more...

As mentioned in the preceding section, AIR for Android will use the native WebKit rendering engine when invoking `StageWebView`. WebKit is used by a number of popular web browsers, including the Android browser, Apple Safari, and Google Chrome. Also of note: WebKit is actually a part of the Adobe AIR desktop runtime. For more information about WebKit, visit `http://www.webkit.org/`.

Managing the StageWebView history

When developing applications for Android, AIR allows us to render complete websites through the use of the`StageWebView` class. We also can tap into the navigation history of our `StageWebView` instance and apply that in different ways within our application.

How to do it...

Once a user has loaded a number of pages within our `StageWebView` instance, we will be able to navigate back and forth through the navigation history:

1. First, import the following classes into your project:

```
import flash.display.Sprite;
import flash.display.StageAlign;
import flash.display.StageScaleMode;
import flash.events.Event;
import flash.events.LocationChangeEvent;
import flash.events.TouchEvent;
import flash.geom.Rectangle;
import flash.media.StageWebView;
import flash.net.URLRequest;
import flash.net.navigateToURL;
import flash.text.TextField;
import flash.text.TextFormat;
import flash.ui.Multitouch;
import flash.ui.MultitouchInputMode;
```

2. We will now declare two `Sprite` objects to act as our interactive elements, along with a `TextField` and `TextFormat` pair to serve as an address indicator. Additionally, declare a `StageWebView` instance along with a `Rectangle` to define our viewport:

```
private var prevButton:Sprite;
private var nextButton:Sprite;
private var swv:StageWebView;
private var swvRect:Rectangle;
private var addressField:TextField;
private var addressFormat:TextFormat;
```

3. Now we will create two methods, which will build our previous and next history controls and add them to the `stage`. Instantiate a new `Sprite` for each and add a unique `name` property, specifying the desired function of the interaction. We will be able to read this later off our `touch tap` event to determine which `Sprite` was tapped. Draw a basic background using the graphics API and perform positioning upon the `stage` before adding each `Sprite` to the `DisplayList`:

```
protected function setupPrevButton():void {
  prevButton = new Sprite();
  prevButton.name = "prev";
  prevButton.graphics.beginFill(0xFFFFFF, 1);
  prevButton.graphics.drawRect(0, 0, 50, 50);
  prevButton.graphics.endFill();
  prevButton.x = 0;
  prevButton.y = 0;
  addChild(prevButton);
}
protected function setupNextButton():void {
  nextButton = new Sprite();
  nextButton.name = "next";
  nextButton.graphics.beginFill(0xFFFFFF, 1);
  nextButton.graphics.drawRect(0, 0, 50, 50);
  nextButton.graphics.endFill();
  nextButton.x = stage.stageWidth - 50;
  nextButton.y = 0;
  addChild(nextButton);
}
```

4. To complete our address indicator, we will continue to set up our `TextField` and apply a `TextFormat` object. In this example, we center the `TextField` upon the `stage` (between our two interactive `Sprites`) to simulate a web browser address bar. Create a method to perform all of these actions along with some stylistic enhancements and assign the default String of **Loading...** to the `TextField` in order to let the user know something is going on.

```
protected function setupAddressBar():void {
  addressFormat = new TextFormat();
  addressFormat.bold = true;
  addressFormat.font = "_sans";
  addressFormat.size = 26;
  addressFormat.align = "center";
  addressFormat.color = 0xFFFFFF;
  addressField = new TextField();
  addressField.defaultTextFormat = addressFormat;
  addressField.autoSize = "left";
  addressField.selectable = false;
  addressField.mouseEnabled = false;
  addressField.text = "Loading...";
  addressField.x = 60;
  addressField.y = 8;
  addChild(addressField);
}
```

5. Create a method to construct our `StageWebView` object by defining a new `Rectangle` with the position and size we want the `StageWebView` to appear within our application. In this example, we determine the properties of our `Rectangle` based upon the position of the previously created `Sprite` and `TextField` objects as well as the dimensions of the application `Stage`.

6. It is good practice to check whether `StageWebView` is supported by invoking `StageWebView. is supported` before constructing our `StageWebView` instance. To actually create a `StageWebView` object, we do a simple instantiation and assign the application `stage` to `StageWebView.stage`. Now assign the previously constructed `Rectangle` to the `StageWebViewviewport` property:

```
protected function setupStageWebView():void {
  swvRect = new  Rectangle(0,addressField.y+addressField.
  height+40,stage.stageWidth ,stage.stageHeight-addressField.
       y+addressField.height+40);
  if(StageWebView.isSupported){
    swv = new StageWebView();
    swv.stage = this.stage;
    swv.viewPort = swvRect;
  }
}
```

7. We will now assign the `Multitouch.inputMode` to respond to raw touch events through the `MultitouchInputMode.TOUCH_POINT` constant. Register an event listener of type `TouchEvent.TOUCH_TAP` upon both of our `Sprite` buttons. This will detect any touch tap events initiated by the user and invoke a method called `onTouchTap`, which will determine whether to go back or forward in the navigation history depending upon which `Sprite` was tapped. We will also register an event of type `LocationChangeEvent.LOCATION_CHANGE` upon our `StageWebView` object to determine when a page load has been completed. Finally, we can invoke `StageWebView.loadURL`, passing in a web address as the only argument. This will begin to load our default location:

```
protected function registerListeners():void {
    Multitouch.inputMode = MultitouchInputMode.TOUCH_POINT;
    prevButton.addEventListener(TouchEvent.TOUCH_TAP, onTouchTap);
    nextButton.addEventListener(TouchEvent.TOUCH_TAP, onTouchTap);
    swv.addEventListener(LocationChangeEvent.LOCATION_CHANGE,
            locationChanged);
    swv.loadURL("http://memoryspiral.com/");
}
```

8. If we were to run the application at this point, we would see all of our interactive elements appear on the stage and the desired Web page would render within our `StageWebView` instance:

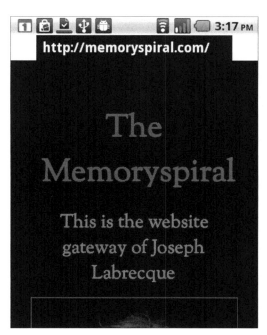

9. As `Sprite` interactions are detected, we determine which particular `Sprite` was tapped by examining the `name` attribute that was provided directly after instantiation. In this way, we know whether to attempt to move forward or backward through the `StageWebView` history through the use of either the `historyBack()` or `historyForward()` methods. In order to detect whether we can actually do so, we can first check to see whether the back or forward history is enabled on the device as shown in the following code snippet:

```
protected function onTouchTap(e:TouchEvent):void {
  switch(e.target.name){
    case "prev":
      if(swv.isHistoryBackEnabled){
        swv.historyBack();
      }
    break;
    case "next":
      if(swv.isHistoryForwardEnabled){
        swv.historyForward();
      }
    break;
  }
}
```

10. As the current location being rendered by our `StageWebView` instance changes, we update our `TextField` with the present URL much in the way a standard web browser address bar would do:

```
protected function locationChanged(e:LocationChangeEvent):void {
  addressField.text = e.location;
}
```

11. The user will now be able to navigate back and forth through the `StageWebView` history as they begin to click on various hyperlinks as shown in the following screenshot:

How it works...

The `StageWebView` class will use whichever web control is default on the host operating system to render any HTML that is displayed in the view port. It is important to note that `StageWebView` is not part of the traditional Flash `DisplayList` and cannot be added to our application in the normal way visual elements are added to the `DisplayList` (through `addChild()`).

To manage the `StageWebView` history, we can use either the `historyBack()` or `historyForward()` methods to navigate along the user history within our application.

Neither of these methods will do anything unless the user has begun clicking on hyperlinks and performing actual navigation within the `StageWebView` instance. We have basically just created our own little web browser.

Using StageWebView to load ads using ActionScript

One of the most sought after features of mobile Android development using the Flash platform has been the ability to include advertisements from services such as Google AdSense or AdMob within applications. This allows developers to distribute their applications for no charge to users, but still receive revenue from advertisements displayed within the application itself.

How to do it...

`StageWebView` opens up a lot of possibilities for mobile application development, one of which is the ability to load HTML-based advertisements in running applications. In the following example, we will examine how simple it is to manage this:

1. First, import the following classes into your project:

   ```
   import flash.display.Sprite;
   import flash.display.StageAlign;
   import flash.display.StageScaleMode;
   import flash.events.TimerEvent;
   import flash.geom.Rectangle;
   import flash.media.StageWebView;
   import flash.utils.Timer;
   ```

2. We will now declare a `StageWebView` instance along with a `Rectangle` to define our viewport. Lastly, set up a `Timer`, which will serve as a mechanism to refresh our ads.

   ```
   private var swv:StageWebView;
   private var swvRect:Rectangle;
   private var adTimer:Timer;
   ```

3. Create a method to construct our `StageWebView` object by defining a new `Rectangle` with the position and size we want the `StageWebView` to appear within our application. It is good practice to check whether `StageWebView` is supported by invoking `StageWebView.isSupported` before constructing our `StageWebView` instance.

4. To actually create a `StageWebView` object, we do a simple instantiation and assign the application `stage` to `StageWebView.stage`. Now assign the previously constructed `Rectangle` to the `StageWebViewviewport` property, and alternatively load up a web page using `loadURL()`, passing in the page address as a `String`:

   ```
   protected function setupStageWebView():void {
   ```

```
swvRect = new Rectangle(0, 0, stage.StageWidth, 70);
if(StageWebView.isSupported){
  swv = new StageWebView();
  swv.stage = this.stage;
  swv.viewPort = swvRect;
  swv.loadURL("http://memoryspiral.com/admob.html");
}
}
```

5. If we have not done so already, in order for this to function correctly, we must set up a web page on our server to interface with the ad service we have chosen. In this example, we are using AdMob (`http://www.admob.com/`) because the ads are tuned for and directed at mobile web and mobile device applications.

6. One important thing here is to be sure and set the `bodymargin` and `padding` to 0 through CSS to avoid any space around our ad. `StageWebView` is essentially just running HTML, so if we don't modify things slightly, the default HTML rendering engine (in the case of Android, this is web Kit) will simply interpret all stylistic elements through its default settings.

7. You will want to replace the `pubid` attribute with your own, or register with a different ad service. Use this snippet as a reference to create your own HTML file to store upon a server and invoke through your particular application as we have done in this example:

```
<html>
 <head>
   <style type="text/css">
   body {
       background-color: #333;
       margin: 0px;
       padding: 0px;
}
   </style>
 </head>
 <body>
 <script type="text/javascript">
   var admob_vars = {pubid: 'xxxxxxxxxx',bgcolor:
             '000000',text: 'FFFFFF',ama: false,test: true};
 </script>
 <script type="text/javascript"
    src="http://mmv.admob.com/static/iphone/iadmob.js"></script>
 </body>
 </html>
```

8. The next step is to set up our `Timer` to switch out ads every 10 seconds. We do this by instantiating a new `Timer` object, and passing 10000 milliseconds (or your preferred amount of time). Now, register an event listener of type `TimerEvent. Timer` to fire off a method of our construction every time the `Timer` hits 10 seconds. To start the `Timer`, we invoke `Timer.start()`:

```
protected function setupTimer():void {
  adTimer = new Timer(10000);
  adTimer.addEventListener(TimerEvent.TIMER, onTimer);
  adTimer.start();
}
```

9. All that remains is to create our `onTimer` method to reload the `StageWebView` instance every time the `Timer` hits 10 seconds. This will make a new call to the web, pulling the HTML down again, thus invoking the ad serving script anew.

```
protected function onTimer(e:TimerEvent):void {
  swv.reload();
}
```

10. The page will refresh every time our `Timer` is fired, revealing a new advertisement in our application:

How it works...

The `StageWebView` class will use whichever web control is default on the host operating system to render any HTML that is displayed in the view port. It is important to note that `StageWebView` is not part of the traditional Flash `DisplayList` and cannot be added to our application in the normal way visual elements are added to the `DisplayList` (through `addChild()`).

To actually render advertisements within the application, we can initially load up a web page using `loadURL()`, passing in the page address as a `String`. This address should point to an HTML document that interfaces with an ad service of our choosing, for which we have previously registered for. Normally, these services simple provide you with a chunk of JavaScript to place into your HTML, which will invoke ads for you upon page load. To refresh our view port and load up a new add, we can simply invoke `StageWebView.reload()`. In the case of our example, we employ a `Timer` to perform this action every 10 seconds.

There's more...

While we decided to use AdMob for this example, a developer can generally include any ad system they prefer. In the following screenshot, I am ingesting ads from Google AdSense in the very same way. You will notice though, that with the normal version of AdSense (when not using mobile content units), the ads do not conform to the screen in an intelligent way. AdMob is tailored for mobile, so works much better in these situations. In the future, there should be plenty of new opportunities in this space beyond the two ad providers mentioned here. We must also keep in mind that these are third-party services, and may change at any time.

Using StageWebView to load ads within a Flex mobile project

As `StageWebView` instances are not part of the `DisplayList`, we could have a perceived problem when it comes to using it within a `ViewNavigatorApplication`. The main problem being that the `StageWebView` will always remain an overlay above all other objects, and that it will not be able to transition along with other items within a particular view. In this recipe, we will examine this and demonstrate some techniques for coping with the inordinate behaviour of the `StageWebView` object.

Getting ready...

For this example, we'll be using Google AdSense **Mobile content | Ad units**. You will need to sign up for an AdSense account at `https://www.google.com/adsense/` and configure a **Mobile content Ad unit**:

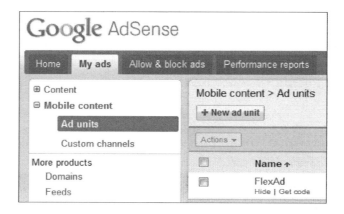

If you already have an AdMob account (or some other service), you can always use that instead, or even a simple ad of your own creation for this demonstration.

How to do it...

We will create a new `ViewNavigatorApplication` with two distinct views, demonstrating how the `StageWebView` exists outside of this structure, how to remove the `StageWebView` from view, and provide reference to an additional ad serving system.

There will be a number of files involved in this example; we will approach their assembly using different sections for clarity.

Creating the HTML file to display our ads

If we have not done so already, in order for this to function correctly, we must set up a web page on our server to interface with Google AdSense. You will want to replace the `client` attribute from the following example with your own. Use this snippet as a reference to create your own HTML file to store upon a server and invoke through your particular application:

```
<html>
<head>
 <style type="text/css">
   body {
   background-color: #333;
   margin: 0px;
```

```
    padding: 0px;
  }
 </style>
</head>
<body>
 <script type="text/javascript"><!--
 // XHTML should not attempt to parse these strings, declare
         them CDATA.
 /* <![CDATA[ */
 window.googleAfmcRequest = {
 client: 'your-id-goes-here',
 format: '320x50_mb',
 output: 'html',
 slotname: '5725525764',
 };
 /* ]]> */
 //--></script>
 <script type="text/javascript" src="http://pagead2.
googlesyndication.com/pagead/show_afmc_ads.js"></script>
</body>
</html>
```

Creating the MXML files for our ViewNavigatorApplication

1. First, we create our main application file with a root node of
   `ViewNavigatorApplication` in order to take advantage of the view-based
   layout it provides. We can set the `applicationDPI`, if need be, and employ the
   `firstView` attribute to reference the initial `View`. We will define this `View` a bit later
   on in the recipe. Before moving on, let's register a method called `init()` to fire once
   our application completes:

   ```
   <?xml version="1.0" encoding="utf-8"?>
   <s:ViewNavigatorApplication xmlns:fx="http://ns.adobe.com/
   mxml/2009"
      xmlns:s="library://ns.adobe.com/flex/spark"
             applicationDPI="160"
      firstView="views.FlexAdsHomeView"
             applicationComplete="init()">
   </s:ViewNavigatorApplication>
   ```

2. Create a script block to hold all of the ActionScript for our application. The code for
   doing so will be defined in another step for clarity.

   ```
   <fx:Script>
       <![CDATA[
       ]]>
   </fx:Script>
   ```

3. Now we will add some functionality to our `ActionBar` by adding two `Button` controls to the `navigationContent` node. Each of these `Button` controls will invoke the `ViewNavigator.pushView()` method. This method accepts a `View` reference as an argument, and when invoked, will bring that `View` to the top of our view stack:

```
<s:navigationContent>
<s:Button label="V1"
        click="navigator.pushView(views.FlexAdsHomeView)"/>
<s:Button label="V2"
        click="navigator.pushView(views.FlexAdsOtherView);"/>
</s:navigationContent>
```

4. Now we will assemble our two views for this example. Place a `Button` control in each `View` along with a `click` event handler, which will invoke a method in our main application file to toggle the ads on and off:

FlexAdsHomeView.mxml

```
<?xml version="1.0" encoding="utf-8"?>
    <s:View xmlns:fx="http://ns.adobe.com/mxml/2009"
    xmlns:s="library://ns.adobe.com/flex/spark"
    title="Primary View" >
    <s:Button y="120" label="Toggle Ads"
            horizontalCenter="0"
            click="this.parentApplication.toggleAds()"/>
</s:View>
```

FlexAdsOtherView.mxml

```
<?xml version="1.0" encoding="utf-8"?>
<s:View xmlns:fx="http://ns.adobe.com/mxml/2009"
        xmlns:s="library://ns.adobe.com/flex/spark"
        title="Secondary View">
<s:Button y="120" label="Toggle Ads" horizontalCenter="0"
        click="this.parentApplication.toggleAds()"/>
</s:View>
```

Generating the ActionScript code to tie it all together

This code will exist within our main application file `script` block, which we had previously defined:

1. First, import the following classes into the project:

```
import flash.events.TimerEvent;
import flash.geom.Rectangle;
import flash.media.StageWebView;
import flash.utils.Timer;
```

2. We will now declare a `StageWebView` instance along with a `Rectangle` to define our view port. Lastly, set up a `Timer`, which will serve as a mechanism to refresh our ads:

```
private var swv:StageWebView;
private var swvRect:Rectangle;
private var adTimer:Timer;
```

3. Set up the initialization function referred to earlier, which will simply invoke the methods we will construct to set up the `StageWebView` instance and our ad refresh `Timer`:

```
protected function init():void {
    setupStageWebView();
    setupTimer();
}
```

4. Create a method to construct our `StageWebView` object by defining a new `Rectangle` with the position and size we want the `StageWebView` to appear within our application. It is good practice to check whether `StageWebView` is supported by invoking `StageWebView.isSupported` before constructing our `StageWebView` instance.

5. To actually create a `StageWebView` object, we do a simple instantiation and assign the application `stage` to `StageWebView.stage`. Now assign the previously constructed `Rectangle` to the `StageWebViewviewport` property, and alternatively load up a web page using `loadURL()`, passing in the page address as a `String`:

```
protected function setupStageWebView():void {
    swvRect = new Rectangle(0, 68, stage.stageWidth, 76);
    if(StageWebView.isSupported){
        swv = new StageWebView();
        swv.stage = this.stage;
        swv.viewPort = swvRect;
        swv.loadURL("http://memoryspiral.com/adsense.html");
    }
}
```

6. To toggle the ads on and off from within the individual views, we simply check whether the `StageWebView.viewPort` is `null` or not and based upon this result, either set it to a `Rectangle` object or assign upon it a value of `null`. If the `viewPort` is `null`, the ad will no longer be visible to the user:

```
public function toggleAds():void {
    if(swv.viewPort != null){
        swv.viewPort = null;
    }else{
        swv.viewPort = swvRect;
    }
}
```

7. The next step is to set up our `Timer` to switch out ads every 8 seconds. We do this by instantiating a new `Timer` object, passing in 8000 milliseconds (or your preferred amount of time). Now, register an event listener of type `TimerEvent.Timer` to fire off a method of our construction every time the `Timer` hits 8 seconds. To start the `Timer`, we invoke `Timer.start()`:

```
protected function setupTimer():void {
   adTimer = new Timer(8000);
   adTimer.addEventListener(TimerEvent.TIMER, onTimer);
   adTimer.start();
}
```

8. All that remains is to create our `onTimer` method to reload the `StageWebView` instance every time the `Timer` hits 10 seconds. This will make a new call to the web, pulling the HTML down again, thus invoking the ad serving script anew:

```
protected function onTimer(e:TimerEvent):void {
   swv.reload();
}
```

9. When the application is run, an ad will immediately be displayed within the `StageWebView` instance and our initial `View` is made present to the user. At this point, the user can interact with the `ActionBar` and switch between each `View`. The `StageWebView` instance will remain in place even though the `View` contents shift as the application `ViewNavigator` shuffles views. At any point, the user can toggle the ads off or on through the `Button` instances in either `View`:

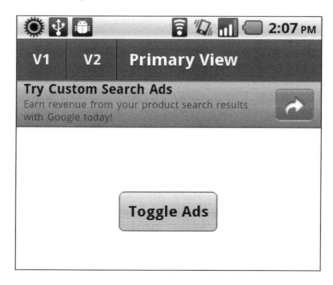

How it works...

Using `StageWebView` within a `ViewNavigatorApplication` may seem troublesome at first, if we keep in mind some of the limitations of this particular object, and manage the `StageWebView` in a mindful way, it isn't that difficult to produce a workable implementation.

There's more...

If ever we want to completely remove a `StageWebView` object from our application, we can invoke `StageWebView.dispose()`, which will remove the `StageWebView` object and allow it to be processed by the garbage collector. Even if we remove a `StageWebView` instance in this way, we can always create a new one, if necessary.

Making a phone call from an application

With all the great features and sheer power of the Android operating system, it is easy to forget that these devices are primarily telephones. In this recipe, we will demonstrate how to invoke the native Android telephone utility from within an application, passing along a phone number to dial.

How to do it...

Having the application invoke `navigateToURL` and passing in a new `URLRequest` with the correct URI of `tel:` will open the default telephone application along with the specified phone number loaded up and ready to be dialed. In this example, we will perform this action once a `TOUCH_TAP` event is detected:

1. First, import the following classes into your project:

```
import flash.display.Sprite;
import flash.display.StageAlign;
import flash.display.StageScaleMode;
import flash.events.TouchEvent;
import flash.text.TextField;
import flash.text.TextFormat;
import flash.net.navigateToURL;
import flash.net.URLRequest;
import flash.ui.Multitouch;
import flash.ui.MultitouchInputMode;
```

2. We will now declare a `Sprite` as our interactive element, along with a `TextField` and `TextFormat` pair to serve as a button label:

```
private var fauxButton:Sprite;
private var traceField:TextField;
private var traceFormat:TextFormat;
```

3. Now, we will continue to set up our `TextField`, apply a `TextFormat` object, and construct a `Sprite` with a simple background fill using the graphics API. The final step in the construction of our button is to add the `TextField` to our `Sprite` and then add the `Sprite` to the `DisplayList`. Here, we create a method to perform all of these actions for us along with some stylistic enhancements:

```
protected function setupTextButton():void {
  traceFormat = new TextFormat();
  traceFormat.bold = true;
  traceFormat.font = "_sans";
  traceFormat.size = 42;
  traceFormat.align = "center";
  traceFormat.color = 0x333333;
  traceField = new TextField();
  traceField.defaultTextFormat = traceFormat;
  traceField.autoSize = "left";
  traceField.selectable = false;
  traceField.mouseEnabled = false;
  traceField.text = "Invoke Phone";
  traceField.x = 30;
  traceField.y = 25;
  fauxButton = new Sprite();
  fauxButton.addChild(traceField);
  fauxButton.graphics.beginFill(0xFFFFFF, 1);
  fauxButton.graphics.drawRect(0, 0, traceField.width+60,
          traceField.height+50);
  fauxButton.graphics.endFill();
  fauxButton.x = (stage.stageWidth/2) - (fauxButton.width/2);
  fauxButton.y = 60;
  addChild(fauxButton);
}
```

4. If we now run the application upon our device, the interactive `Sprite` should appear as the following screenshot:

5. We will now assign the `Multitouch.inputMode` to respond to raw touch events through the `MultitouchInputMode.TOUCH_POINT` constant. Register an event listener of type `TouchEvent.TOUCH_TAP` upon the `Sprite` button. This will detect any touch tap events initiated by the user and invoke a method called `onTouchTap`, which contains the remainder of our logic:

```
protected function registerListeners():void {
  Multitouch.inputMode = MultitouchInputMode.TOUCH_POINT;
  fauxButton.addEventListener(TouchEvent.TOUCH_TAP, onTouchTap);
}
```

6. Once a touch tap is detected, our `onTouchTap` method will fire, invoking `navigateToURL` and passing in a `URLRequest` containing the `tel:` URI prefix followed by the phone number we want to dial from our application:

```
protected function onTouchTap(e:TouchEvent):void {
  navigateToURL(new URLRequest("tel:15555554385"));
}
```

7. When we run the application upon our device, a simple touch tap on our button will invoke the native telephone application along with our specified phone number already entered:

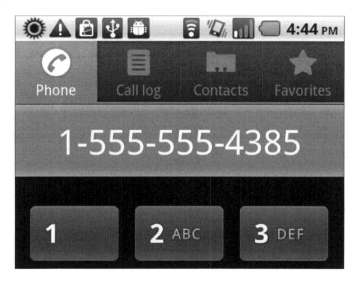

How it works...

When a user of our application touch taps the interactive `Sprite` we've created, they are taken out of our application and into the default Android telephone utility. Along with this invocation is supplied a phone number, which was assigned to this call by passing a `URLRequest` with a `tel:` URI prefix through the `navigateToURL` method. In this way, we can easily allow users of our application access to a phone number without their even having to dial it.

Sending a text message from an application

With Flash on Android, we have the ability to invoke the native Android SMS utility through classes in the `flash.net` package based upon user interaction. We do not have the ability to supply any content for the text message, unfortunately. On Android, since all applications take up a full window, we must be extra mindful of any disruption this may cause while the user is interacting with our application.

How to do it...

Having the application invoke `navigateToURL` and passing in a new `URLRequest` with the correct URI prefix of `sms:` will open the default SMS utility along with the specified phone number loaded up, ready to text. In this example, we will perform this action once a `TOUCH_TAP` event is detected:

1. First, import the following classes into your project:

```
import flash.display.Sprite;
import flash.display.StageAlign;
import flash.display.StageScaleMode;
import flash.events.TouchEvent;
import flash.text.TextField;
import flash.text.TextFormat;
import flash.net.navigateToURL;
import flash.net.URLRequest;
import flash.ui.Multitouch;
import flash.ui.MultitouchInputMode;
```

2. We will now declare a `Sprite` as our interactive element, along with a `TextField` and `TextFormat` pair to serve as a button label:

```
private var fauxButton:Sprite;
private var traceField:TextField;
private var traceFormat:TextFormat;
```

3. Now, we will continue to set up our `TextField`, apply a `TextFormat` object, and construct a `Sprite` with a simple background fill using the graphics API. The final step in the construction of our button is to add the `TextField` to our `Sprite` and then add the `Sprite` to the `DisplayList`. Here, we create a method to perform all of these actions for us along with some stylistic enhancements:

```
protected function setupTextButton():void {
  traceFormat = new TextFormat();
  traceFormat.bold = true;
  traceFormat.font = "_sans";
  traceFormat.size = 42;
  traceFormat.align = "center";
  traceFormat.color = 0x333333;
  traceField = new TextField();
  traceField.defaultTextFormat = traceFormat;
  traceField.autoSize = "left";
  traceField.selectable = false;
  traceField.mouseEnabled = false;
  traceField.text = "Invoke SMS";
  traceField.x = 30;
  traceField.y = 25;
  fauxButton = new Sprite();
  fauxButton.addChild(traceField);
  fauxButton.graphics.beginFill(0xFFFFFF, 1);
  fauxButton.graphics.drawRect(0, 0, traceField.width+60,
          traceField.height+50);
  fauxButton.graphics.endFill();
  fauxButton.x = (stage.stageWidth/2) - (fauxButton.width/2);
  fauxButton.y = 60;
  addChild(fauxButton);
}
```

4. If we now run the application upon our device, the interactive `Sprite` should appear as follows:

5. We will now assign the `Multitouch.inputMode` to respond to raw touch events through the `MultitouchInputMode.TOUCH_POINT` constant. Register an event listener of type `TouchEvent.TOUCH_TAP` upon the `Sprite` button. This will detect any touch tap events initiated by the user and invoke a method called `onTouchTap`, which contains the remainder of our logic:

```
protected function registerListeners():void {
  Multitouch.inputMode = MultitouchInputMode.TOUCH_POINT;
  fauxButton.addEventListener(TouchEvent.TOUCH_TAP, onTouchTap);
}
```

6. Once a touch tap is detected, our `onTouchTap` method will fire, invoking `navigateToURL` and passing in a `URLRequest` containing the `tel:` URI prefix followed by the phone number we want to dial from our application:

```
protected function onTouchTap(e:TouchEvent):void {
  navigateToURL(new URLRequest("sms:15555554385"));
}
```

7. At this point, we will lose application focus and be presented with the Android SMS utility, prepopulated with our desired phone number and ready to compose a text message:

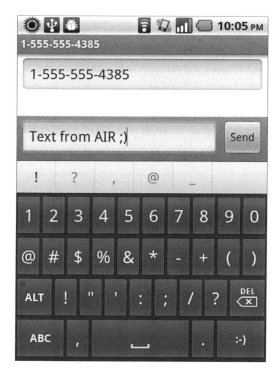

8. Finally, once we hit **Send**, our text message is transmitted to the targeted recipient specified through the phone number used. In this example, it is not a real phone number, of course:

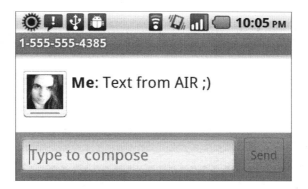

How it works...

When a user of our application touch taps the interactive `Sprite` we've created, they are taken out of our application and into the default Android SMS utility. Along with this invocation is supplied a phone number, which was assigned to this text message by passing a `URLRequest` with a `sms:` URI prefix through the `navigateToURL` method. In this way, we can easily allow users of our application access to a phone number for texting without their even having to input a numeric sequence.

Invoking Google maps from an application

Being that most Android devices are mobile, the ability to tap into some sort of mapping is expected by both developers and users. The Android OS is managed by Google, and the company has a long history of great mapping technologies on the web. This is great for developers because we can piggyback on the very cool Maps application on Android and pass in all sorts of coordinates from our application.

How to do it...

Have the application detect the device geolocation coordinates, invoke `navigateToURL`, and pass in a new `URLRequest` with a correctly formatted URL to access the Android maps application:

1. First, import the following classes into your project:

```
import flash.display.Sprite;
import flash.display.StageAlign;
import flash.display.StageScaleMode;
```

```
import flash.events.TouchEvent;
import flash.events.GeolocationEvent;
import flash.text.TextField;
import flash.text.TextFormat;
import flash.net.navigateToURL;
import flash.net.URLRequest;
import flash.ui.Multitouch;
import flash.ui.MultitouchInputMode;
import flash.sensors.Geolocation;
```

2. We will now declare a `Sprite` as our interactive element, along with a `TextField` and `TextFormat` pair to serve as a button label. We will be employing the `Geolocation` API, and so declare an object for this purpose along with `Number` variables to hold latitude and longitude data values:

```
private var fauxButton:Sprite;
private var traceField:TextField;
private var traceFormat:TextFormat;
private var geo:Geolocation;
private var longitude:Number;
private var latitude:Number;
```

3. Now, we will continue to set up our `TextField`, apply a `TextFormat` object, and construct a `Sprite` with a simple background fill using the graphics API. The final step in the construction of our button is to add the `TextField` to our `Sprite` and then add the `Sprite` to the `DisplayList`. Here, we create a method to perform all of these actions for us, along with some stylistic enhancements:

```
protected function setupTextButton():void {
    traceFormat = new TextFormat();
    traceFormat.bold = true;
    traceFormat.font = "_sans";
    traceFormat.size = 42;
    traceFormat.align = "center";
    traceFormat.color = 0x333333;
    traceField = new TextField();
    traceField.defaultTextFormat = traceFormat;
    traceField.autoSize = "left";
    traceField.selectable = false;
    traceField.mouseEnabled = false;
    traceField.text = "Invoke Maps";
    traceField.x = 30;
    traceField.y = 25;
    fauxButton = new Sprite();
    fauxButton.addChild(traceField);
    fauxButton.graphics.beginFill(0xFFFFFF, 1);
```

```
fauxButton.graphics.drawRect(0, 0, traceField.width+60,
        traceField.height+50);
fauxButton.graphics.endFill();
fauxButton.x = (stage.stageWidth/2) - (fauxButton.width/2);
fauxButton.y = 60;
addChild(fauxButton);
}
```

4. If we now run the application upon our device, the interactive `Sprite` should appear as in the following screenshot:

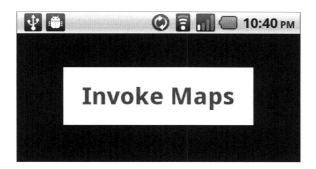

5. We will now assign the `Multitouch.inputMode` to respond to raw touch events through the `MultitouchInputMode.TOUCH_POINT` constant. Register an event listener of type `TouchEvent.TOUCH_TAP` upon the `Sprite` button. This will detect any touch tap events initiated by the user and invoke a method called `onTouchTap`, which contains the remainder of our logic:

```
protected function registerListeners():void {
  Multitouch.inputMode = MultitouchInputMode.TOUCH_POINT;
  fauxButton.addEventListener(TouchEvent.TOUCH_TAP, onTouchTap);
}
```

6. Upon the detection of a touch tap event, we will set up a `Geolocation` object and assign an event listener to it, listening specifically for a `GeolocationEvent.UPDATE` event. We will no longer need to listen for our `TouchEvent.TOUCH_TAP` event, so may remove it to allow for garbage collection:

```
protected function onTouchTap(e:TouchEvent):void {
  fauxButton.removeEventListener(TouchEvent.TOUCH_TAP,
          onTouchTap);
  geo = newGeolocation();
  geo.addEventListener(GeolocationEvent.UPDATE, onGeoEvent);
}
```

7. Once `Geolocation` data is gathered and reported back to our application, the `onGeoEvent` method will fire, providing us with the `longitude` and `latitude` data we need to pass in to the native Android maps application.

8. To complete our sequence, we will invoke `navigateToURL` and pass in a `URLRequest` containing the `http://maps.google.com/` URL followed by a query string containing the `latitude` and `longitude` values from our `Geolocation` update event data. Since we now have all the data we need, remove the `GeolocationEvent.UPDATE` event listener:

```
protected function onGeoEvent(e:GeolocationEvent):void {
  geo.removeEventListener(GeolocationEvent.UPDATE, onGeoEvent);
  longitude = e.longitude;
  latitude = e.latitude;
  navigateToURL(new URLRequest("http://maps.google.com/?q="+
              String(latitude)+", "+String(longitude)));
}
```

9. As the URI prefix used in this example is simply `http://`, a model dialog will appear over our application, asking whether we would like to open the `URLRequest` using the **Browser** or **Maps** application. We will choose **Maps**. Selecting the **Use by default for this action** checkbox will prevent this dialog from appearing in the future:

10. Finally, the **Maps** application will appear and present the user with a view based upon the detected latitude and longitude Geolocation coordinates that our application was able to detect:

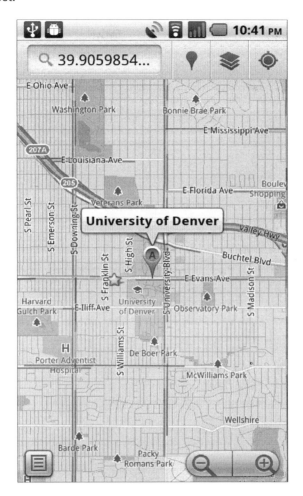

How it works...

When a user of our application touch taps the interactive `Sprite` we've created, we configure a `Geolocation` object to listen for location data. Once this data is acquired, we can then pass a `URLRequest` with the `http://` URI prefix through the `navigateToURL` method to summon `maps.google.com`. We also append a query string formed from the collected `Geolocation` latitude and longitude data, informing the **Maps** application the exact coordinates to navigate to on our map.

There's more...

An alternative to detecting `Geolocation` data from device sensors would be to store a variety of coordinates within the application and then present the user with a number of choices. This would be useful for a specialized restaurant application, allowing users to easily view locations on a map, for instance.

Invoking the Android Market using application URIs

The Android Market is unique to the Android platform and there is a dedicated application which allows users to easily search for, find, and install applications on their devices. Android allows a developer to tap into the Market application by passing in certain search terms.

How to do it...

We will build a small application to invoke `navigateToURL` and pass a predefined search term through a `URLRequest` object with the `market:` URI prefix. This will open the Android Market application and have it perform a search for us. In this example, we will open a new request once a `TOUCH_TAP` event is detected:

1. First, import the following classes into your project:

```
import flash.display.Sprite;
import flash.display.StageAlign;
import flash.display.StageScaleMode;
import flash.events.TouchEvent;
import flash.text.TextField;
import flash.text.TextFormat;
import flash.net.navigateToURL;
import flash.net.URLRequest;
import flash.ui.Multitouch;
import flash.ui.MultitouchInputMode;
```

2. We will now declare a `Sprite` as our interactive element, along with a `TextField` and `TextFormat` pair to serve as a button label:

```
private var fauxButton:Sprite;
private var traceField:TextField;
private var traceFormat:TextFormat;
```

3. Now, we will continue to set up our `TextField`, apply a `TextFormat` object, and construct a `Sprite` with a simple background fill using the graphics API. The final step in the construction of our button is to add the `TextField` to our `Sprite` and then add the `Sprite` to the `DisplayList`. Here, we create a method to perform all of these actions for us along with some stylistic enhancements:

```
protected function setupTextButton():void {
  traceFormat = new TextFormat();
  traceFormat.bold = true;
  traceFormat.font = "_sans";
  traceFormat.size = 42;
  traceFormat.align = "center";
  traceFormat.color = 0x333333;
  traceField = new TextField();
  traceField.defaultTextFormat = traceFormat;
  traceField.autoSize = "left";
  traceField.selectable = false;
  traceField.mouseEnabled = false;
  traceField.text = "Invoke Market";
  traceField.x = 30;
  traceField.y = 25;
  fauxButton = new Sprite();
  fauxButton.addChild(traceField);
  fauxButton.graphics.beginFill(0xFFFFFF, 1);
  fauxButton.graphics.drawRect(0, 0, traceField.width+60,
          traceField.height+50);
  fauxButton.graphics.endFill();
  fauxButton.x = (stage.stageWidth/2) - (fauxButton.width/2);
  fauxButton.y = 60;
  addChild(fauxButton);
}
```

4. If we now run the application upon our device, the interactive `Sprite` should appear as shown in the following screenshot:

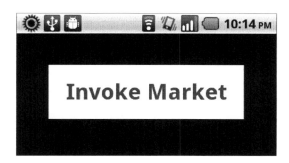

5. We will now assign the `Multitouch.inputMode` to respond to raw touch events through the `MultitouchInputMode.TOUCH_POINT` constant. Register an event listener of type `TouchEvent.TOUCH_TAP` upon the `Sprite` button. This will detect any touch tap events initiated by the user and invoke a method called `onTouchTap`, which contains the remainder of our logic.

```
protected function registerListeners():void {
  Multitouch.inputMode = MultitouchInputMode.TOUCH_POINT;
  fauxButton.addEventListener(TouchEvent.TOUCH_TAP, onTouchTap);
}
```

6. Once a touch tap is detected, our `onTouchTap` method will fire, invoking `navigateToURL` and passing in a `URLRequest` with a URI prefix of `market:` containing the search terms we want to have the application perform against the Market inventory:

```
protected function onTouchTap(e:TouchEvent):void {
  navigateToURL(new URLRequest("market://search?q=Fractured
          Vision Media, LLC"));
}
```

7. When we run the application upon our device, a simple touch tap upon our button will invoke the Android Market application and perform a search for the terms that we've passed over from our application:

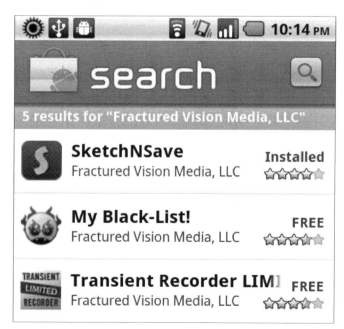

How it works...

When a user of our application touch taps the interactive `Sprite` we've created, they are taken out of our application and into the Android Market application, where a search is instantly performed against the search terms specified in our request. The Android Market application will reveal to the user whatever applications it finds in the current inventory. For instance, passing in the exact title of our application will allow a user to manually check for updates from within the application. Passing in our company or developer name will bring up all of the applications we have made available for the user to browse.

If further specificity is required, there are additional search queries that can be performed.

To search for a specific application, we can use the format:

```
navigateToURL(new URLRequest("market://search?q=pname:air.com.
fracturedvisionmedia.SketchNSave"));v
```

To search for a specific publisher, we use the following (notice we are escaping quotes by using the "\" character in our query string):

```
navigateToURL(new URLRequest("market://search?q=pub:\"Fractured
Vision Media, LLC\""));
```

Sending e-mail from an application

Similar to desktop Flash and AIR applications, the default system e-mail client can be invoked through classes in the `flash.net` package based upon some user interaction. On Android, since all applications take up a full window, we must be extra mindful of any disruption this may cause while the user is interacting with our application.

How to do it...

Having the application invoke `navigateToURL` and passing an e-mail address through a new `URLRequest` with the `mailto:` URI prefix will open the default e-mail utility. In this example, we will open a new e-mail once a `TOUCH_TAP` event is detected:

1. First, import the following classes into your project:

```
import flash.display.Sprite;
import flash.display.StageAlign;
import flash.display.StageScaleMode;
import flash.events.TouchEvent;
import flash.text.TextField;
import flash.text.TextFormat;
import flash.net.navigateToURL;
import flash.net.URLRequest;
```

```
import flash.ui.Multitouch;
import flash.ui.MultitouchInputMode;
```

2. We will now declare a `Sprite` as our interactive element, along with a `TextField` and `TextFormat` pair to serve as a button label:

```
private var fauxButton:Sprite;
private var traceField:TextField;
private var traceFormat:TextFormat;
```

3. Now, we will continue to set up our `TextField`, apply a `TextFormat` object, and construct a `Sprite` with a simple background fill using the graphics API. The final step in the construction of our button is to add the `TextField` to our `Sprite` and then add the `Sprite` to the `DisplayList`. Here, we create a method to perform all of these actions for us along with some stylistic enhancements:

```
protected function setupTextButton():void {
  traceFormat = new TextFormat();
  traceFormat.bold = true;
  traceFormat.font = "_sans";
  traceFormat.size = 42;
  traceFormat.align = "center";
  traceFormat.color = 0x333333;
  traceField = new TextField();
  traceField.defaultTextFormat = traceFormat;
  traceField.autoSize = "left";
  traceField.selectable = false;
  traceField.mouseEnabled = false;
  traceField.text = "Invoke Email";
  traceField.x = 30;
  traceField.y = 25;
  fauxButton = new Sprite();
  fauxButton.addChild(traceField);
  fauxButton.graphics.beginFill(0xFFFFFF, 1);
  fauxButton.graphics.drawRect(0, 0, traceField.width+60,
            traceField.height+50);
  fauxButton.graphics.endFill();
  fauxButton.x = (stage.stageWidth/2) - (fauxButton.width/2);
  fauxButton.y = 60;
  addChild(fauxButton);
}
```

4. If we now run the application upon our device, the interactive `Sprite` should appear as follows:

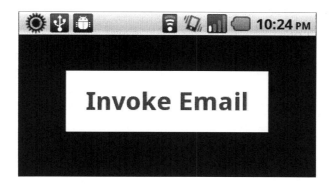

5. We will now assign the `Multitouch.inputMode` to respond to raw touch events through the `MultitouchInputMode.TOUCH_POINT` constant. Register an event listener of type `TouchEvent.TOUCH_TAP` upon the `Sprite` button. This will detect any touch tap events initiated by the user and invoke a method called `onTouchTap`, which contains the remainder of our logic:

```
protected function registerListeners():void {
  Multitouch.inputMode = MultitouchInputMode.TOUCH_POINT;
  fauxButton.addEventListener(TouchEvent.TOUCH_TAP, onTouchTap);
}
```

6. Once a touch tap is detected, our `onTouchTap` method will fire, invoking `navigateToURL` and passing in a `URLRequest` with a URI prefix of `mailto:` containing the e-mail address we want to open up from our application, along with a subject parameter, if desired:

```
protected function onTouchTap(e:TouchEvent):void {
  navigateToURL(new URLRequest("mailto:info@fracturedvisionmedia.
      com?subject=Email%20From%20Adobe%20AIR%20on%20Android!"));
}
```

7. When we run the application on our device, a simple touch tap upon our button will invoke the native e-mail client and populate it with the values that we've passed over from our application.

How it works...

When a user of our application touch taps the interactive Sprite we've created, they are taken out of our application and into the default Android e-mail client. This is accomplished by passing the desired e-mail address through a URLRequest with a URI prefix of mailto: along with a set of appended parameters through the navigateToURL method, which is very similar to the way we accomplish the same thing with a desktop or web application.

There's more...

Of course, we could always write an application that handles e-mail internally, just as we would on a web application. So long as we have access to a server with e-mail capability; this may be preferred for some applications.

8
Abundant Access: File System and Local Database

This chapter will cover the following recipes:

- ▶ Opening a local file from device storage
- ▶ Saving a file to device storage
- ▶ Saving data across sessions through Local Shared Object
- ▶ Storing application state automatically by using Flex
- ▶ Creating a local SQLite database
- ▶ Providing a default application database
- ▶ Automating database tasks with FlexORM

Introduction

Many file system attributes are shared between desktop and mobile, yet there are specific use cases on Android devices for handling application state preservation in case of session interruption, or to simply preserve data across sessions. This chapter will cover tips for loading and saving individual files, creating and managing local databases, dealing with local shared objects, and preserving navigation state using the mobile Flex framework.

Opening a local file from device storage

Oftentimes, we may want to read certain files from the application storage or from some other location on our Android device. In the following example, we will perform this action upon a simple text file, but this can also be used to read in all sorts of files from image data to encoded MP3 audio bytes.

How to do it...

Employ a variety of classes within the `flash.filesystem` package to open local file data within an application:

1. First, we will need to import the following classes:

```
import flash.display.Sprite;
import flash.display.StageAlign;
import flash.display.StageScaleMode;
import flash.events.Event;
import flash.filesystem.File;
import flash.filesystem.FileMode;
import flash.filesystem.FileStream;
import flash.text.TextField;
import flash.text.TextFormat;
```

2. We will now go about defining a set of constants and variables to be used throughout the application. Initialize a `String` constant to retain the file path, which will be used within the example. We will also require a `File` and accompanying `FileStream` in order to open the text file within our application, along with a `TextField` and `TextFormat` pair to serve as our final output display:

```
private const PATH:String = "android.txt";
private var file:File;
private var stream:FileStream;
private var traceField:TextField;
private var traceFormat:TextFormat;
```

3. Now, we will continue to set up our `TextField`, apply a `TextFormat`, and add it to the `DisplayList`. Here, we create a method to perform all of these actions for us:

```
protected function setupTextField():void {
  traceFormat = new TextFormat();
  traceFormat.bold = true;
  traceFormat.font = "_sans";
  traceFormat.size = 24;
  traceFormat.align = "center";
  traceFormat.color = 0xCCCCCC;
```

```
traceField = new TextField();
traceField.defaultTextFormat = traceFormat;
traceField.selectable = false;
traceField.multiline = true;
traceField.wordWrap = true;
traceField.mouseEnabled = false;
traceField.x = 20;
traceField.y = 20;
traceField.width = stage.stageWidth-40;
traceField.height = stage.stageHeight-40;
addChild(traceField);
}
```

4. To actually open the file within our application, we will first instantiate our
    `File` object and assign it to the current application directory through `File.`
    `applicationDirectory`. We can then specify a file within that location by passing
    in the constant, which declares it through the `File.resolvePath()` method.

5. The second portion of this process involves instantiating a `FileStream`, which
    will allow us to perform the remainder of our processes. Register an event listener
    of type `Event.COMPLETE` upon the `FileStream`. Finally, invoke `FileStream.`
    `openAsync()` passing in the previously defined `File` as the first parameter followed
    by the `FileMode`. We are going to simply read in the bytes of this file, so use
    `FileMode.READ`:

```
protected function beginFileOpen():void {
  file = new File();
  file = File.applicationDirectory;
  file = file.resolvePath(path);
  stream = new FileStream();
  stream.addEventListener(Event.COMPLETE, fileOpened);
  stream.openAsync(file, FileMode.READ);
}
```

6. Once the `FileStream` has completed its work, our `fileOpened` method will
    fire, allowing us to read in the `File` bytes as plain text (specified by `File.`
    `systemCharset`) and assign the text to our `TextField`. Whenever we are finished
    working with a `FileStream` object, we must invoke `close()` upon it:

```
protected function fileOpened(e:Event):void {
  traceField.text =
  stream.readMultiByte(stream.bytesAvailable, File.systemCharset);
  stream.close();
}
```

7. When we compile and run our application upon a device, it should appear as follows:

How it works...

We can open a file within our application by creating a `File` reference and opening that reference through a `FileStream`. Once the process is complete, we can then work with the contents of the file itself, either through direct assignment or through the processing of the bytes within. In this example, we are reading in the contents of a text file and outputting that to a basic `TextField` in our application. The `FileStream` class has many different methods and properties, which can be used more or less effectively on different file types and processes. For example, we use the `FileStream.openAsync()` method here to actually open the `FileStream`. We could have also used use the `FileStream.open()` method just as well, but using `openAsync()` will allow us to employ an event listener so that we can react to the data that is loaded with confidence. The important thing is to read up on these through the documentation and use what is best for your particular situation.

There are a number of static properties that we can leverage with the `flash.filesystem.File` class for quick access to a variety of storage locations. These are listed as follows:

 ▶ `File.applicationStorageDirectory`: Unique application storage directory [read/write]

 ▶ `File.applicationDirectory`: Application installation directory [read only]

 ▶ `File.desktopDirectory`: Maps to the SD card root[read/write]

 ▶ `File.documentsDirectory`: Maps to the SD card root[read/write]

 ▶ `File.userDirectory`: Maps to the SD card root[read/write]

For a comprehensive look at the `File` class, please refer to the Adobe LiveDocs:

```
http://help.adobe.com/en_US/FlashPlatform/reference/actionscript/3/
flash/filesystem/File.html
```

While we are opening a text file in this example, any file can be opened and processed in a similar fashion. However, reading the bytes of a complex file type can be incredibly difficult if you do not have a good background on how such things work, and for larger files, the process can be slow on mobile devices due to the amount of processing you may be performing upon the loaded bytes.

Saving a file to device storage

There are a number of ways in which we can save data from an application to local device storage. Audio, images, and text data can all be created by the user and saved to either an application-defined location, or the user can be allowed to choose, which specific location to store the file upon within an Android device. In this example, we will demonstrate this through the generation of a simple text file.

How to do it...

We will allow the user to select the location and name of a basic text file that they will generate within our application and save to their Android device:

1. First, we will need to import the following classes:

```
import flash.display.Sprite;
import flash.display.StageAlign;
import flash.display.StageScaleMode;
import flash.events.Event;
import flash.events.TouchEvent;
import flash.filesystem.File;
import flash.text.TextField;
import flash.text.TextFormat;
import flash.ui.Multitouch;
import flash.ui.MultitouchInputMode;
```

2. We will need to declare a number of objects for use within this application. A `String` constant will serve to define our file name. Next, we declare a `File` object, which will be used eventually to save our text file to disk. A `TextField` and `TextFormat` pair will relay text messages onto the device display. Finally, declare a `Sprite` as our interactive element, along with an additional `TextField` and `TextFormat` pair to serve as a button label:

```
private const FILE_NAME:String = "airandroid.txt";
private var file:File;
private var traceField:TextField;
private var traceFormat:TextFormat;
```

```
private var fauxButton:Sprite;
private var buttonField:TextField;
private var buttonFormat:TextFormat;
```

3. Now, we will continue to set up our `TextField`, apply a `TextFormat`, and add it to the `DisplayList`. Here, we create a method to perform all of these actions for us. Be sure to set the `TextField.type` to `input` in order to allow the user to type!

```
protected function setupTextField():void {
    traceFormat = new TextFormat();
    traceFormat.bold = true;
    traceFormat.font = "_sans";
    traceFormat.size = 44;
    traceFormat.align = "center";
    traceFormat.color = 0x000000;
    traceField = new TextField();
    traceField.defaultTextFormat = traceFormat;
    traceField.type = "input";
    traceField.border = true;
    traceField.multiline = true;
    traceField.wordWrap = true;
    traceField.background = true;
    traceField.border = true;
    traceField.x = 20;
    traceField.y = 20;
    traceField.width = stage.stageWidth-40;
    traceField.height = 250;
    addChild(traceField);
}
```

4. Now; we will continue to set up our `TextField`, apply a `TextFormat` object, and construct a `Sprite` with a simple background fill using the graphics API. The final step in the construction of our button is to add the `TextField` to our `Sprite` and then add the `Sprite` to the `DisplayList`. Here, we create a method to perform all of these actions for us along with some stylistic enhancements:

```
protected function setupTextButton():void {
    buttonFormat = new TextFormat();
    buttonFormat.bold = true;
    buttonFormat.font = "_sans";
    buttonFormat.size = 42;
    buttonFormat.align = "center";
    buttonFormat.color = 0x333333;
    buttonField = new TextField();
    buttonField.defaultTextFormat = buttonFormat;
    buttonField.autoSize = "left";
```

```
    buttonField.selectable = false;
    buttonField.mouseEnabled = false;
    buttonField.text = "Save as File";
    buttonField.x = 30;
    buttonField.y = 25;
    fauxButton = new Sprite();
    fauxButton.addChild(buttonField);
    fauxButton.graphics.beginFill(0xFFFFFF, 1);
    fauxButton.graphics.drawRect(0, 0, buttonField.width+60,
            buttonField.height+50);
    fauxButton.graphics.endFill();
    fauxButton.x = (stage.stageWidth/2) (fauxButton.width/2);
    fauxButton.y = traceField.y+traceField.height+40;
    addChild(fauxButton);
}
```

5. If we run our application, we can see how everything lays out on the display. We can also, at this point, freely edit the `TextField`, which serves as input for our text file:

6. We will now assign the `Multitouch.inputMode` to respond to raw touch events through the `MultitouchInputMode.TOUCH_POINT` constant. Register an event listener of type `TouchEvent.TOUCH_TAP` upon the `Sprite` button. This will detect any touch tap events initiated by the user and invoke a method called `onTouchTap`, which contains the remainder of our logic:

```
protected function registerListeners():void {
  Multitouch.inputMode = MultitouchInputMode.TOUCH_POINT;
  fauxButton.addEventListener(TouchEvent.TOUCH_TAP, onTouchTap);
}
```

7. As the user interacts with the application and performs a touch tap upon the button to save any text input as a file, the following method is fired. Within this function, we first create a new `File` object and register an event listener of type `Event.COMPLETE` before invoking `File.save()`. The `File.Save()` method expects two arguments, the contents of the file to create, and the name of the file:

```
protected function onTouchTap(e:TouchEvent):void {
  file = new File();
  file.addEventListener(Event.COMPLETE, fileSaved);
  file.save(traceField.text, FILE_NAME);
}
```

8. Once the user inputs some text and hits the button to save it as a file, Android will produce an overlay requesting confirmation to perform the save. The user, at this point, can rename the file or save to an alternate location. By default, the file is saved to the root of the device SD card. If we want to avoid a save dialog, we can employ a `flash.filesystem.FileStream` class to do so:

9. Once the save has completed successfully, we can remove our event listeners, clear out the input `TextField` and change the button label `TextField` to let the user know everything has saved correctly:

```
protected function fileSaved(e:Event):void {
  fauxButton.removeEventListener(TouchEvent.TOUCH_TAP,
          onTouchTap);
  file.removeEventListener(Event.COMPLETE, fileSaved);
  traceField.text = "";
  buttonField.text = "File Saved!";
}
```

10. The following image illustrates what the user will see upon a successful save:

11. The user can now use a file browser or some other application to open the text file within the default Android text viewer, as seen in the following screenshot:

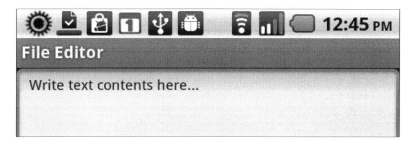

How it works...

Writing a plain text file to the device storage is fairly straightforward. The process involves creating a `File` object and then invoking the `save()` method upon that object. Using this method, we pass over the contents of the file to save, along with the desired file name. Note that while we are passing over simple text in this case, we can also save bytes in the form of audio files or images. If we require more control over the entire process, we can also use a `FileStream` object to set various encodings and write the bytes in a greater variety of ways. Using a `FileStream` will also allow us to append a previously created file with new information, and avoids the save dialog seen in this example.

There's more...

You will need to provide any application which writes local files access to write to the local file system through the Android manifest file. For more information on this, see *Chapter 9, Manifest Assurance: Security and Android Permissions*.

Saving data across sessions through local shared object

Shared objects have been used for years in browser-based Flash applications. They are sometimes referred to as "Flash Cookies" or "Super Cookies" and do provide much of the same functionality as normal browser-based cookies, but are tailored more to the Flash environment. Normally explicit permissions are needed to save such data using a Flash application on the web; however, using AIR frees us of many of these restrictions.

How to do it...

Create a local `SharedObject` to preserve specific application data across sessions. We will use an interactive `Sprite` to illustrate this visually:

1. First, we will need to import the following classes:

    ```
    import flash.display.Sprite;
    import flash.display.StageAlign;
    import flash.display.StageScaleMode;
    import flash.events.Event;
    import flash.events.TouchEvent;
    import flash.geom.Point;
    import flash.net.SharedObject;
    import flash.net.SharedObjectFlushStatus;
    import flash.text.TextField;
    import flash.text.TextFormat;
    ```

```
import flash.ui.Multitouch;
import flash.ui.MultitouchInputMode;
```

2. Then we will need to declare a number of objects for use within this application. Declare a `SharedObject`, which will be used to preserve session data. The `Point` object will be used to write coordinates onto the `SharedObject`. A `Sprite` will serve as the user interaction element and visual reference for this example. Finally, declare a `TextField` and `TextFormat` pair to relay text messages onto the device display:

```
private var airSO:SharedObject;
private var ballPoint:Point;
private var ball:Sprite;
private var traceField:TextField;
private var traceFormat:TextFormat;
```

3. Now, we will continue to set up our `TextField`, apply a `TextFormat`, and add it to the `DisplayList`. Here, we create a method to perform all of these actions for us:

```
protected function setupTextField():void {
    traceFormat = new TextFormat();
    traceFormat.bold = true;
    traceFormat.font = "_sans";
    traceFormat.size = 24;
    traceFormat.align = "center";
    traceFormat.color = 0xCCCCCC;
    traceField = new TextField();
    traceField.defaultTextFormat = traceFormat;
    traceField.selectable = false;
    traceField.multiline = true;
    traceField.wordWrap = true;
    traceField.mouseEnabled = false;
    traceField.x = 20;
    traceField.y = 20;
    traceField.width = stage.stageWidth-40;
    traceField.height = stage.stageHeight-40;
    addChild(traceField);
}
```

4. We will need to set up an interactive object for the user to move around based on touch. The coordinates of this object will eventually be preserved across application sessions. Let's create a basic circular `Sprite` with the graphics API:

```
protected function setupBall():void {
    ball = new Sprite();
    ball.graphics.beginFill(0xFFFFFF);
    ball.graphics.drawCircle(0, 0, 60);
    ball.graphics.endFill();
```

```
    ball.x = stage.stageWidth/2;
    ball.y = 260;
    addChild(ball);
}
```

5. Before moving too far into this example, we must perform some actions upon the `SharedObject` we've declared. First, invoke `SharedObject.getLocal("airandroid")` upon our `SharedObject` instance. This will read in the `SharedObject` called `airandroid`, if it exists. If the `SharedObject` does not yet exist, this invocation will create it for us.

6. Now we can check to see whether the `ballPoint` object exists within the `SharedObject` `data` property. If so, this means we have gone through and completed a session previously and can assign the `ballPoint` x and y properties to our `ballSprite`:

```
protected function setupSharedObject():void {
  airSO = SharedObject.getLocal("airandroid");
  if(airSO.data.ballPoint != undefined){
    ball.x = airSO.data.ballPoint.x;
    ball.y = airSO.data.ballPoint.y;
    traceField.text = "Existing Shared Object!";
  }else{
    traceField.text = "No Shared Object Found!";
  }
}
```

7. When we run the application for the first time, we are told that no shared object is detected and the ball is placed in the default position:

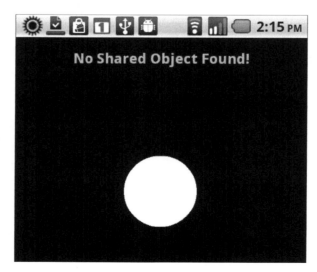

8. We will now assign the `Multitouch.inputMode` to respond to raw touch events through the `MultitouchInputMode.TOUCH_POINT` constant. Register two event listeners of type `TouchEvent.TOUCH_MOVE` and `TouchEvent.TOUCH_END` upon the circular `Sprite`. This will detect any touch events initiated by the user and invoke certain methods to deal with each:

```
protected function registerListeners():void {
  Multitouch.inputMode = MultitouchInputMode.TOUCH_POINT;
  ball.addEventListener(TouchEvent.TOUCH_MOVE, onTouchMove);
  ball.addEventListener(TouchEvent.TOUCH_END, onTouchEnd);
}
```

9. As `TouchEvent.TOUCH_MOVE` events are detected upon our `Sprite`, the `onTouchMove` method fires, allowing us to change the x and y coordinates of the `Sprite` to allow the user to drag it around the `Stage`:

```
protected function onTouchMove(e:TouchEvent):void {
  ball.x = e.stageX;
  ball.y = e.stageY;
}
```

10. When our application detects a `TouchEvent.TOUCH_END` event upon the `Sprite` object, we will use this opportunity to wrap the `Sprite` x and y coordinates in a `Point` object, and assign it to our `SharedObject`. To perform this action, we first assign the `Sprite` coordinates to our `Point` object, which is then assigned to our `SharedObjectdata` property.

11. In order to write the `SharedObject` to the local file system, we must invoke `SharedObject.flush()`. We can assign the `flush()` commands return value to a `String` in order to monitor and respond to its status. In this example, we simply use a switch/case statement to check `SharedObjectFlushStatus` and write a message into our `TextField`, letting the user know what is happening:

```
protected function onTouchEnd(e:Event):void {
  ballPoint = new Point(ball.x, ball.y);
airSO.data.ballPoint = ballPoint;
  var flushStatus:String;
  flushStatus = airSO.flush();
  if(flushStatus != null) {
    switch(flushStatus) {
      case SharedObjectFlushStatus.FLUSHED:
      traceField.text = "Ball location x:" + ball.x +
      "/y:" + ball.y + " saved!";
      break;
      default:
      traceField.text = "There was a problem :(";
      break;
    }
  }
}
```

12. The user can now interact with the ball by touching and moving it around the display. When the user stops interacting with the ball, these coordinates are saved to our local shared object:

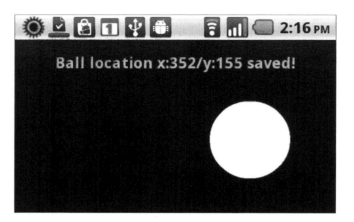

 If the user exists and at some future time opens the application again, the local shared object is read in and the ball is repositioned based upon this preserved data. In order to truly test this upon a device, a developer will need to kill the application using the application management features under the Android **Settings** menu, or employ a third party "task killer" to ensure the application is completely stopped.

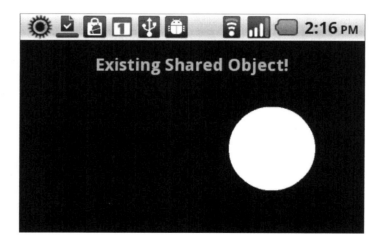

How it works...

A `SharedObject` in Flash is a lot like the cookie implementation used in web browsers. It was initially implemented in browser-based Flash to allow for a similar experience when developers wanted to preserve small pieces of data across user sessions. Luckily, this also works in AIR and cam be used as simple storage within our Android applications.

To read a `SharedObject`, simply invoke the `getLocal()` method upon it, passing in the name of the `SharedObject` we wish to retrieve. To save a `SharedObject`, we assign it with new data and invoke the `flush()` method, which saves the new information to disk.

There's more...

We use a local `SharedObject` in this instance, but could also save such data to a local or remote database, a text or XML file, or even use a remote `SharedObject` depending upon our needs.

Storing application state automatically by using Flex

While there are many times in which we will need to store specific application parameters in the case that our session is interrupted by other device functions (such as an incoming phone call), the mobile Flex framework does provide a good level of session preservation, which can be handled automatically for us.

How to do it...

Instruct Flex to preserve application state for us automatically by enabling `persistNavigatorState`:

1. We will first set up a new mobile Flex project with two views, these we simply call `first` and `second`. Our initial `ViewNavigatorApplication` file will appear as such:

    ```
    <?xml version="1.0" encoding="utf-8"?>
    <s:ViewNavigatorApplication xmlns:fx="http://ns.adobe.com/mxml/
            2009"
        xmlns:s="library://ns.adobe.com/flex/spark"
            firstView="views.first">
    </s:ViewNavigatorApplication>
    ```

2. Add a button to our `first` view that will enable us to push the `second` view from there:

```
<s:Button label="Engage Second State"
        click="navigator.pushView(views.second);"/>
```

3. Add a button to our `second` view allowing us to return to the `first` view. Now we can navigate back and forth, building up our `ViewNavigator` history:

```
<s:Button label="Engage First State"
        click="navigator.pushView(views.first)"/>
```

4. In order to allow Flex to preserve both our `ViewNavigator` history and retain our current place within that history in the event that our session is interrupted, we will modify the `ViewNavigatorApplication` to include an attribute called `persistNavigatorState` and we will set this to `true`. Let's also declare a `creationComplete` event, which will invoke a function called `init()`. We will use this to set up some additional functionality:

```
<?xml version="1.0" encoding="utf-8"?>
<s:ViewNavigatorApplication xmlns:fx="http://ns.adobe.com/
mxml/2009"
    xmlns:s="library://ns.adobe.com/flex/spark" firstView="views.
first"
  persistNavigatorState="true" creationComplete="init()">
</s:ViewNavigatorApplication>
```

5. Create a `Script` tag within the MXML and import the `FlexEvent` class:

```
<fx:Script>
    <![CDATA[
        import mx.events.FlexEvent;
    ]]>
</fx:Script>
```

6. Now, we must declare our `init()` method, which will be invoked upon `creationComplete`. Within this method, we will register an event listener of type `FlexEvent.NAVIGATOR_STATE_SAVING` on our application:

```
public function init():void {
  this.addEventListener(FlexEvent.NAVIGATOR_STATE_SAVING,
          stateSaving);

}
```

7. Whenever our application begins to save the application state upon application exit through the Flex persistence manager, our `stateSaving` method will fire, allowing us to perform additional actions, or even invoke `preventDefault()` upon the `FlexEvent` to allow our own logic to take command before exiting. In development and testing, we can easily place a breakpoint within this method in order to introspect our application state.

```
protected function stateSaving(e:FlexEvent):void {
  // Interception Code
}
```

8. When we compile and run our application, it will appear as shown in the next screenshot. Flipping from our first to second view and back a number of times will populate the application `ViewNavigator` history:

9. If our application session is interrupted by a phone call, or some other event, the navigation history and current view will be preserved. When the application is run again, the user will be able to continue exactly where the interruption occurred:

How it works...

When using the mobile Flex framework, we have the option of enabling `persistNavigatorState` within the application. This will automatically preserve our `ViewNavigator` history, as well as remember which view we were interacting with upon application session interruption. It does this by saving session information to a local Shared Object on the device. The data which is saved includes information about the application version number, the full navigation stack, and the current navigation view.

Additionally, we can intercept the `FlexEvent.NAVIGATOR_STATE_SAVING` event when the application begins to exit and perform our own desired actions in its place, such as saving critical application data to the file system, a Local Shared Object, or even an SQLite database.

Creating a local SQLite database

Adobe AIR has had support for embedded SQLite databases from the beginning. This is one of the best ways of storing structured information within our Android applications. SQLite is a software library that implements a self-contained, serverless, zero-configuration, transactional SQL database engine. The database files it creates are simply individual `.db` files, which can be transported across a network, copied, and deleted just like any other file type.

How to do it...

We will create a mobile application along with a local SQLite database, which can employ the SQL query language to allow the user access to add new records and run a simple query based upon these entries:

1. First, import the following classes necessary for this example:

```
import flash.data.SQLConnection;
import flash.data.SQLStatement;
import flash.data.SQLResult;
import flash.display.Sprite;
import flash.display.StageAlign;
import flash.display.StageScaleMode;
import flash.events.Event;
import flash.events.TouchEvent;
import flash.filesystem.File;
import flash.text.TextField;
import flash.text.TextFormat;
import flash.ui.Multitouch;
import flash.ui.MultitouchInputMode;
```

2. We will need to declare a number of objects for use within this application. A `SQLConnection` will allow us to interact with a local SQLite database. The first `TextField` and `TextFormat` pair will serve as an input field for the user to type into. Another `TextField` and `TextFormat` pair will relay text messages onto the device display. Finally, declare a `Sprite` as our interactive element, along with a final `TextField` and `TextFormat` pair to serve as a button label:

```
private var sqlConnection:SQLConnection;
private var itemField:TextField;
private var itemFormat:TextFormat;
private var fauxButton:Sprite;
```

```
private var buttonField:TextField;
private var buttonFormat:TextFormat;
private var traceField:TextField;
private var traceFormat:TextFormat;
```

3. Now, we will continue to set up our `TextField`, apply a `TextFormat`, and add it to the `DisplayList`. Here, we create a method to perform all of these actions for us. Be sure to set the `TextField.type` to `input` in order to allow the user to type!

```
protected function setupTextField():void {
  itemFormat = new TextFormat();
  itemFormat.bold = true;
  itemFormat.font = "_sans";
  itemFormat.size = 44;
  itemFormat.align = "center";
  itemFormat.color = 0x000000;
  itemField = new TextField();
  itemField.defaultTextFormat = itemFormat;
  itemField.type = "input";
  itemField.border = true;
  itemField.multiline = true;
  itemField.wordWrap = true;
  itemField.background = true;
  itemField.border = true;
  itemField.x = 20;
  itemField.y = 20;
  itemField.width = stage.stageWidth-40;
  itemField.height = 60;
  addChild(itemField);
}
```

4. For our interactive `Sprite`, we will set up a `TextField`, apply a `TextFormat` object, and construct a `Sprite` with a simple background fill using the graphics API. The final step in the construction of our button is to add the `TextField` to our `Sprite` and then add the `Sprite` to the `DisplayList`. Here, we create a method to perform all of these actions for us along with some stylistic enhancements:

```
protected function setupTextButton():void {
  buttonFormat = new TextFormat();
  buttonFormat.bold = true;
  buttonFormat.font = "_sans";
  buttonFormat.size = 42;
  buttonFormat.align = "center";
  buttonFormat.color = 0x333333;
  buttonField = new TextField();
  buttonField.defaultTextFormat = buttonFormat;
```

```
    buttonField.autoSize = "left";
    buttonField.selectable = false;
    buttonField.mouseEnabled = false;
    buttonField.text = "Insert to DB";
    buttonField.x = 30;
    buttonField.y = 25;
    fauxButton = new Sprite();
    fauxButton.addChild(buttonField);
    fauxButton.graphics.beginFill(0xFFFFFF, 1);
    fauxButton.graphics.drawRect(0, 0, buttonField.width+60,
            buttonField.height+50);
    fauxButton.graphics.endFill();
    fauxButton.x = (stage.stageWidth/2) - (fauxButton.width/2);
    fauxButton.y = itemField.y+itemField.height+40;
    addChild(fauxButton);
}
```

5. Our final visual element involves another `TextField` and `TextFormat` pair to display database records upon the device:

```
protected function setupTraceField():void {
    traceFormat = new TextFormat();
    traceFormat.bold = true;
    traceFormat.font = "_sans";
    traceFormat.size = 24;
    traceFormat.align = "left";
    traceFormat.color = 0xCCCCCC;
    traceField = new TextField();
    traceField.defaultTextFormat = traceFormat;
    traceField.selectable = false;
    traceField.multiline = true;
    traceField.wordWrap = true;
    traceField.mouseEnabled = false;
    traceField.x = 20;
    traceField.y = fauxButton.y+fauxButton.height+40;
    traceField.width = stage.stageWidth-40;
    traceField.height =stage.stageHeight - traceField.y;
    addChild(traceField);
}
```

6. We will now assign the `Multitouch.inputMode` to respond to raw touch events through the `MultitouchInputMode.TOUCH_POINT` constant. Register an event listener of type `TouchEvent.TOUCH_TAP` upon the `Sprite` button. This will detect any touch tap events initiated by the user and invoke a method called `onTouchTap` to perform additional actions.

```
protected function registerListeners():void {
  Multitouch.inputMode = MultitouchInputMode.TOUCH_POINT;
  fauxButton.addEventListener(TouchEvent.TOUCH_TAP, insertDBItem);
}
```

7. To create the application database, we must first initialize our `SQLConnection` object and pass a `File.db` reference into the `SQLConnection.open()` method to establish the connection. If the database file does not exist, it will be automatically created. In order to write SQL syntax to interact with our database, we must initialize a `SQLStatement` object and assign our established `SQLConnection` to the `SQLStatement.sqlConnection` property. At this point, we can pass in a `String` of SQL statements into the `SQLStatement.text` property and invoke `SQLConnection.execute()` to actually execute the statement. This syntax will create a table within our database with two columns, `name` and `time`. If the table already exists, the statement will be ignored:

```
protected function createDB():void {
  sqlConnection = new SQLConnection();
  sqlConnection.open(File.applicationStorageDirectory.
    resolvePath("airandroid.db"));
  var sqlStatement:SQLStatement = new SQLStatement();
  sqlStatement.sqlConnection = sqlConnection;
  sqlStatement.text = "CREATE TABLE IF NOT EXISTS items
        (name TEXT, time TEXT)";
  sqlStatement.execute();
  getDBItems();
}
```

8. To retrieve existing records from the database, we will again initialize a `SQLStatement` and assign the established `SQLConnection` to the `SQLStatement.sqlConnection` property. We will then pass in a `String` of SQL statements into the `SQLStatement.text` property and invoke `SQLConnection.execute()` to retrieve all records from the database.

9. To write out the returned data to a `TextField`, we simply initialize a new `Array` to contain the returned records by assigning the `data` property (which is itself an `Array`) of `SQLStatement.getResult()` to the `Array`. Now create a `for` loop to parse the results, outputting the various properties assigned to each record to our `TextField`. This visually exposes the query results on an Android device:

```
protected function getDBItems():void {
  traceField.text = "";
  var sqlStatement:SQLStatement = new SQLStatement();
  sqlStatement.sqlConnection = sqlConnection;
  sqlStatement.text = "SELECT * FROM items";
  sqlStatement.execute();
  var sqlArray:Array = new Array();
```

```
var sqlResult:SQLResult = sqlStatement.getResult();
if(sqlResult.data != null){
sqlArray = sqlResult.data;
}
var itemCount:int = sqlArray.length;
for(var i:int=0; i<itemCount; i++){
traceField.appendText("NAME: " + sqlArray[i].name + "\n");
traceField.appendText("DATE: " + sqlArray[i].time + "\n");
traceField.appendText("\n");
}
}
```

10. The final method we need to write will allow the user to insert records to the database. A lot of this is very similar to how we have established and executed `SQLStatement` objects in the past two methods. An insertion, however, can be a bit more complex and structured, so we are making use of the inbuilt `SQLStatement.parametersArray` in assigning values to our record. For the `name` value, we read from the input `TextField` value provided by the user. In order to generate a timestamp to populate the value of `time`, we instantiate a new `Date` object and invoke `toUTCString()`. Following the execution of this fully-formed statement, we invoke `getDBItems()` once again to return the new database results, letting the user see immediately that the record has been inserted correctly:

```
protected function insertDBItem(e:TouchEvent):void {
  var date:Date = new Date();
  var sqlStatement:SQLStatement = new SQLStatement();
  sqlStatement.sqlConnection = sqlConnection;
  sqlStatement.text = "INSERT into items values(:name, :time)";
  sqlStatement.parameters[":name"] = itemField.text;
  sqlStatement.parameters[":time"] = date.toUTCString();
  sqlStatement.execute();
  getDBItems();
  itemField.text = "";
}
```

11. Running the application on our Android device allows us to input a name using the native virtual keyboard touch tap the **Insert to DB** button, which will create a new entry in our database consisting of the input text and current timestamp.

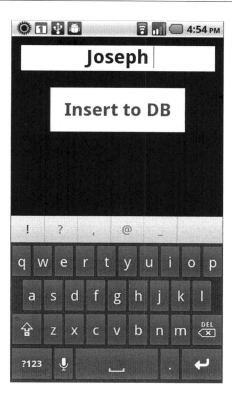

12. Each time we enter a new name into the application, the new entry is inserted and a query is made to trace all entries out into the `TextField`, along with the timestamp from when they were inserted:

How it works...

SQLite is a local, self-contained database, which can be used within AIR for Android applications for a variety of tasks, ranging from simple to complex. In order to use this functionality, we must establish a `SQLConnection` to a local `.db` file on the device. Once this connection is established, we can use a set of `SQLStatements` to perform table creation and management tasks, selection, insertion, and deletion queries through standard SQL syntax. In this example, a user can insert records and perform a general selection query upon a database file within the application storage directory.

In this demonstration, we make use of `flash.data.SQLStatement` to perform both `INSERT` and `SELECT` operations. For further exploration of this, and related classes, we refer you to the Adobe LiveDocs:

```
http://help.adobe.com/en_US/FlashPlatform/reference/actionscript/3/
flash/data/SQLStatement.html
```

Providing a default application database

Allowing the user to add and remove items from an application database, directly or indirectly, can be very useful in all sorts of scenarios. Perhaps though, we want to start the user out with a standard data set, or maybe provide some default settings for the user to manipulate down the road? These scenarios call for the ability of the application to provide itself with a default database. In this recipe, we will demonstrate how to handle this intelligently through the file system.

Getting ready...

In this recipe, we will be bundling an already established SQLite database file within our application directory. If you do not have access to a SQLite database file already, you can either use some of the other recipes in this chapter to generate one, else use any one of a variety of other freely available mechanisms for creating these portable little database files.

How to do it...

We will package a default SQLite database along with our application, check to see whether a user defined database exists, and provide the user with our default if need be:

1. First, import the following classes necessary for this example:

```
import flash.data.SQLConnection;
import flash.data.SQLStatement;
import flash.display.Sprite;
```

```
import flash.display.StageAlign;
import flash.display.StageScaleMode;
import flash.filesystem.File;
import flash.text.TextField;
import flash.text.TextFormat;
```

2. We will need to declare a few objects for use within this application. A `SQLConnection` will allow us to interact with a local SQLite database and a `TextField` and `TextFormat` pair will relay text messages onto the device display:

```
private var sqlConnection:SQLConnection;
private var traceField:TextField;
private var traceFormat:TextFormat;
```

3. Now, we will set up our `TextField`, apply a `TextFormat`, and add it to the `DisplayList` along with some stylistic enhancements. Here, we create a method to perform all of these actions for us:

```
protected function setupTraceField():void {
    traceFormat = new TextFormat();
    traceFormat.bold = true;
    traceFormat.font = "_sans";
    traceFormat.size = 24;
    traceFormat.align = "left";
    traceFormat.color = 0xCCCCCC;
    traceField = new TextField();
    traceField.defaultTextFormat = traceFormat;
    traceField.selectable = false;
    traceField.multiline = true;
    traceField.wordWrap = true;
    traceField.mouseEnabled = false;
    traceField.x = 20;
    traceField.y = 20;
    traceField.width = stage.stageWidth-40;
    traceField.height = stage.stageHeight-40;
    addChild(traceField);
}
```

4. This method will fire as soon as the `TextField` has been established, as we will be outputting messages to this visual element as each step in the copy process is completed.

5. The first thing to do is establish whether or not an application database exists, as this will determine whether or not we need to copy the default database over. To do this, we will instantiate a new `File` object and reference a file called `products.db` within the application installation directory. If this file does not exist, we must create another `File` object, referencing the file name and location we wish to copy the file to.

6. Once this is established, use the `File.copyTo()` method upon the source `File`, passing in the destination `File`. If all goes well, you should now have an exact copy of the default database within the application storage directory:

```
protected function checkDefaultDB():void {
  traceField.appendText("Checking if DB exists...\n\n");
  var dbFile:File = File.applicationStorageDirectory;
  dbFile = dbFile.resolvePath("products.db");
  if(dbFile.exists){
    traceField.appendText("Application DB Okay!\n\n");
  }else{
    traceField.appendText("Application DB Missing!\n\n");
    traceField.appendText("Copying Default DB...\n\n");
    var sourceFile:File = File.applicationDirectory;
    sourceFile = sourceFile.resolvePath("default.db");
    var destination:File = File.applicationStorageDirectory;
    destination = destination.resolvePath("products.db");
    sourceFile.copyTo(destination, true);
    traceField.appendText("Database Copy Completed!\n\n");
  }
  connectDB();
}
```

7. To open the application database, we must first initialize our `SQLConnection` object and pass a `File.db` reference into the `SQLConnection.open()` method to establish the connection. Now that we have a connection to the newly copied database, we invoke the `getDBItems()` method to retrieve the records for display:

```
protected function connectDB():void {
  sqlConnection = new SQLConnection();
  sqlConnection.open(File.applicationStorageDirectory.
        resolvePath("products.db"));
  getDBItems();
}
```

8. To retrieve all of the records from the copied database, we will initialize a `SQLStatement` and assign the established `SQLConnection` to the `SQLStatement.sqlConnection` property. We will then pass in a `String` of SQL statements into the `SQLStatement.text` property and invoke `SQLConnection.execute()` to retrieve all records from the database.

9. To write out the returned data to a `TextField`, we simply initialize a new `Array` to contain the returned records by assigning the `data` property (which is itself an `Array`) of `SQLStatement.getResult()` to the `Array`. Now create a `for` loop to parse the results, outputting the various properties assigned to each record to our `TextField`. This visually exposes the query results on an Android device:

```
protected function getDBItems():void {
    traceField.appendText("Gathering items from application DB...\
            n\n");
    var sqlStatement:SQLStatement = new SQLStatement();
    sqlStatement.sqlConnection = sqlConnection;
    sqlStatement.text = "SELECT * FROM Products";
    sqlStatement.execute();
    var sqlArray:Array = sqlStatement.getResult().data;
    var itemCount:int = sqlArray.length;
    traceField.appendText("Database Contains:\n");
    for(var i:int=0; i<itemCount; i++){
    traceField.appendText("PRODUCT: " + sqlArray[i].ProductName +
            "\n");
    }
}
```

10. The first time the application is run, a database is not found within the application storage directory. The default database is then copied into the expected position and then records are retrieved and displayed for the user to view:

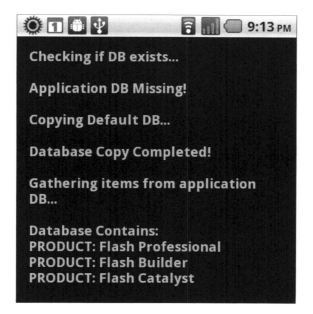

11. If the user runs this application subsequent times, the database is now in the expected location and the application simply performs a query and displays the records without any need to copy files from one location to another:

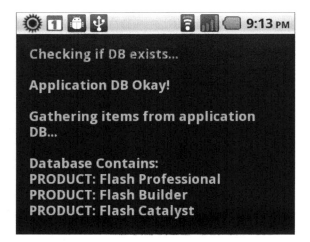

How it works...

In this recipe, we use a combination of `File` and `SQLConnection/SQLStatement` objects to determine whether or not a database exists, followed by either a simple query and record display, or a more involved file copy from the application install directory into the application storage directory using `File.copyTo()`. This method will copy a file reference, which is passed in as an initial argument into the specified location. There are many other similar methods for file manipulation. We will list some of these as follows:

- `File.copyTo()`: Copies the file or directory to a new location
- `File.moveTo()`: Moves the file or directory to a new location
- `File.deleteFile()`XE "default application database:File.deleteFile() method" : Deletes the specified file
- `File.createDirectory()`: Creates a directory as well as any needed parent directories
- `File.deleteDirectory()`: Deletes the specified directory

For a comprehensive look at the `File` class, please refer to the Adobe LiveDocs:

```
http://help.adobe.com/en_US/FlashPlatform/reference/actionscript/3/
flash/filesystem/File.html
```

The database file, being just a regular file, can easily be manipulated through ActionScript just like any other file. It is important though to have a fair understanding of which directories the application does or does not have permission to write to, in such a case. For instance, `File.applicationDirectory` is read only. We cannot write files to this directory.

If you require a tool to create or manage SQLite database files, you may be interested in a software project such as SQLite Database browser, freely downloaded from `http://sqlitebrowser.sourceforge.net/`.

Automating database tasks with FlexORM

While we certainly do have full control over application databases through supported SQLite syntax, there are libraries of code to make things a bit easier. One such library is called **FlexORM**, and as the name suggests, it can only be used within a Flex project so pure ActionScript is out.

FlexORM is an Object Relational Mapping framework, which avoids having the developer write any database code or SQL for a project. Objects are made to be persistent, and any database transitions are handled by the framework itself, behind the scenes.

Getting ready...

When preparing this application example, you will want to take some additional steps to get ready as there is some setup involved in regard to acquiring the FlexORM library and setting it up within a project:

1. First, we must open a web browser and go to `http://flexorm.riaforge.org/` the project page for FlexORM.

2. Download the files either through the `ZIP` package at the bottom of the screen, or through the SVN repository.

3. Once the files are on your system, we will want to navigate to **trunk | flexorm | src** and grab everything under **src**. This is the package we must import into Flash Builder in order to use FlexORM.

4. Create a new Mobile Flex Project and drag the files from **src** under the Flex project **src** folder. We can now begin to use **FlexORM** within our application.

5. Your project will look very similar to the one shown in the following screenshot:

How to do it...

Using the **FlexORM** framework, we will define a persistent object structure and manage the creation and deletion of object entries through a simple Flex mobile project:

1. The first thing we will do is create a class within a `vo` [Value Object] package called `Product`. This will serve as the declaration of our bindable object and is a reflection of what we will be inserting and reading from our database. Using metadata specific to **FlexORM,** we declare a table called `Products` with an ID column named `id` and an additional column called `ProductName`. These objects act as interfaces to our actual table structure and allow us to manage SQL commands through a familiar object-oriented paradigm:

```
package vo {
 [Bindable]
 [Table(name="Products")]
 public class Product {
  [Id]public var id:int;
  [Column]public var ProductName:String;
 }
}
```

2. The next step will be to write a `ViewNavigatorApplication` MXML file to serve as our main application file. We can include both a `firstView` attribute pointing to a specific `View`, and an `applicationComplete` attribute, which will invoke an initialization function for us:

```
<?xml version="1.0" encoding="utf-8"?>
  <s:ViewNavigatorApplication xmlns:fx=
          "http://ns.adobe.com/mxml/2009"
xmlns:s="library://ns.adobe.com/flex/spark"
      firstView="views.FlexORMHomeView"
          applicationComplete="init()">
</s:ViewNavigatorApplication>
```

3. Now we will declare a `Script` block and perform a set of imports, which are necessary for this portion of our application. All we need from **FlexORM** is the `EntityManager`. This is what is used to read from and write to our database. We must also import our `vo` object class for use with **FlexORM**, along with `ArrayCollection` to hold any records that are produced:

```
<fx:Script>
<![CDATA[
import nz.co.codec.flexorm.EntityManager;
import vo.Product;
import mx.collections.ArrayCollection;
]]>
</fx:Script>
```

4. Here, we will instantiate both the `EntityManager` and the `ArrayCollection` for use in the application. Invoking `EntityManager.getInstance()` will allow us to begin using **FlexORM**:

```
protected var entityManager:EntityManager =
  EntityManager.getInstance();
  [Bindable] public var productArrayCollection:ArrayCollection;
```

5. We must define the initialization method referred to in our `ViewNavigatorApplication` tag. Within this method, use the `File` class to refer to the database file to create within the application storage directory. Create a new `SQLConnection` and open the previously defined `File` reference with it. The `SQLConnection` can now be bound to the `sqlConnection` property of our `EntityManager`, allowing us to interact with the database using **FlexORM**:

```
protected function init():void {
  var databaseFile:File =
  File.applicationStorageDirectory.resolvePath("products.db");
  var connection:SQLConnection = new SQLConnection();
  connection.open(databaseFile);
  entityManager.sqlConnection = connection;
  loadProducts();
}
```

6. This method can be invoked whenever we want to refresh our collection from the database. Simply invoking `findAll()` upon the `EntityManager` and passing in the class name we want to retrieve from will return all the records from the table bound to that class:

```
protected function loadProducts():void {
  productArrayCollection = entityManager.findAll(Product);
  productArrayCollection.refresh();
}
```

7. We will need to set up methods to insert and delete records from the application database. To save a record, we create an object based upon the class corresponding to the table we wish to save to. Now, we will assign properties to this class based upon the fields we are writing values to for this insertion. Invoking `EntityManager.save()` while passing in this object will instruct **FlexORM** to insert a new record into the database:

```
public function saveProduct(e:String):void {
  var ProductEntry:Product = new Product();
  ProductEntry.ProductName = e;
  entityManager.save(ProductEntry);
  loadProducts();
}
```

8. Deleting a record from the database is just as simple. Invoke `EntityManager.remove()` while passing along the object within our collection, which corresponds to the specific record to remove from our database will ensure that **FlexORM** deletes the true record for us:

```
public function deleteProduct(index:int):void {
  entityManager.remove(productArrayCollection.getItemAt(index));
  loadProducts();
}
```

9. Now to construct our application view. Create a new `View` MXML file with whatever properties suits your specific project view. In this case, we are assigning it with a `VerticalLayout` with some generous padding:

```
<?xml version="1.0" encoding="utf-8"?>
<s:View xmlns:fx="http://ns.adobe.com/mxml/2009"
xmlns:s="library://ns.adobe.com/flex/spark" title="Product
Catalog">
  <s:layout>
  <s:VerticalLayout gap="20" paddingBottom="20" paddingLeft="20"
paddingRight="20" paddingTop="20"/>
  </s:layout>
</s:View>
```

10. The controls in our application which a user is able to interact with will consist of a `TextInput` to type in, a `Button` to submit from, and a `List` to display all of our database records. We will invoke a function called `addProduct()` on button click, and another function called `removeProduct()`, which is tied to our list change event. The final modification will be to bind our `ListdataProvider` to the defined `productArrayCollection` within our main MXML file.

 We are using `parentApplication` as a convenience in this example. Depending upon the structure of your application, you may not want to do this, as it creates an oftentimes unwanted relationship between the application and its various modules.

```
<s:TextInput id="entry" width="100%"/>
<s:Button click="addProduct(event)" width="100%"
       label="Insert New Product"/>
<s:List id="productList" change="removeProduct(event)"
 dataProvider="{this.parentApplication.productArrayCollection}"
    labelField="ProductName" width="100%"
       height="100%"></s:List>
```

11. Create a `Script` block and import the `IndexChangeEvent` class needed for our `List` change event to properly fire:

```
<fx:Script>
<![CDATA[
import spark.events.IndexChangeEvent;
]]>
</fx:Script>
```

12. Now all that is left to do is to create some local functions to pass along information to our main MXML file and perform local cleanup duty. First we create the method for our `Button` click event, which passes data along to the `saveProduct()` method we created previously. We will pass along the entered text and then clear out our `TextInput` to allow for further records to be defined:

```
protected function addProduct(e:MouseEvent):void {
  this.parentApplication.saveProduct(entry.text);
  entry.text = "";
}
```

13. Finally, write the function to handle removal of records based upon change events generated from the `List`. Any index change detected upon the `List` will pass index data along to the `deleteProduct()` method we created previously. We then set our `ListselectedIndex` to -1, signifying that no items are selected:

```
protected function removeProduct(e:IndexChangeEvent):void {
  this.parentApplication.deleteProduct(e.newIndex);
```

```
        productList.selectedIndex = -1;
    }
```

14. When the user runs our application upon a device, they are able to type in data through the native Android virtual keyboard. Tapping the **Insert New Product** button will add their information to the database:

15. The user will be able to add multiple records to the database and they will immediately appear within the List control. Tapping an item within the List will cause a change event to fire and consequently remove the corresponding record from the application database:

How it works...

FlexORM takes some initial setup to get the framework functioning in a way that is beneficial for us when developing an application, but once everything is in place, it can be a huge time saver with less complex databases. Whereas SQL is nothing at all such as ActionScript in syntax or usage. FlexORM provides an interface through which we can manage database records in an object-oriented manner through the use of the same language we are using for the rest of our application, ActionScript!

There is more...

FlexORM is great for simple transactions, but does not fully support everything that SQLite offers. For example, we cannot create and manage an encrypted database using FlexORM. For such specific activities, it is best to write your queries by hand.

9
Manifest Assurance: Security and Android Permissions

This chapter will cover the following recipes:

- ▶ Setting application permissions with the Android Manifest file
- ▶ Preventing the device screen from dimming
- ▶ Establishing Android Custom URI Schemes
- ▶ Anticipating Android Compatibility Filtering
- ▶ Instructing an Application to be installed to Device SDCard
- ▶ Encrypting a Local SQLite Database

Introduction

Android has in place a very specific permissions and security system based around manifest file declarations which allow or restrict applications from accessing various device capabilities. This chapter will detail how to enable your Flash Platform applications to correctly identify the permissions needed to take advantage of the Android Market filtering, apply local application database encryption, and other useful tidbits!

Setting application permissions with the Android Manifest file

When users choose to install an application on Android, they are always presented with a warning about which permissions the application will have within their particular system. From Internet access to full Geolocation, Camera, or External Storage permissions; the user is explicitly told what rights the application will have on their system. If it seems as though the application is asking for more permissions than necessary, the user will usually refuse the install and look for another application to perform the task they need. It is very important to only require the permissions your application truly needs, or else users might be suspicious of you and the applications you make available.

How to do it...

There are three ways in which we can modify the `Android Manifest` file to set application permissions for compiling our application with Adobe AIR.

Using Flash Professional:

Within an AIR for Android project, open the **Properties** panel and click the little wrench icon next to **Player** selection:

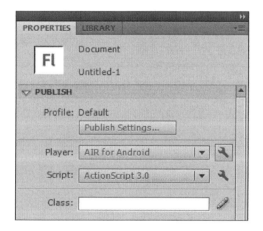

The **AIR for Android Settings** dialog window will appear. You will be presented with a list of permissions to either enable or disable for your application. Check only the ones your application will need and click **OK** when finished.

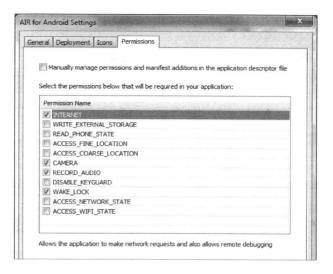

Using Flash Builder:

1. When first setting up your AIR for Android project in Flash Builder, define everything required in the **Project Location** area, and click **Next**.

2. You are now in the **Mobile Settings** area of the **New Flex Mobile Project** dialog. Click the **Permissions** tab, making sure that **Google Android** is the selected platform. You will be presented with a list of permissions to either enable or disable for your application. Check only the ones your application will need and continue along with your project setup:

3. To modify any of these permissions after you've begun developing the application, simply open the AIR descriptor file and edit it as is detailed in the following sections.

Using a simple text editor:

1. Find the AIR Descriptor File in your project. It is normally named something like `{MyProject}-app.xml` as it resides at the project root.

2. Browse the file for a node named `<android>` within this node will be another called `<manifestAdditions>`which holds a child node called `<manifest>`. This section of the document contains everything we need to set permissions for our Android application.

3. All we need to do is either comment out or remove those particular permissions that our application does not require. For instance, this application needs Internet, External Storage, and Camera access. Every other permission node is commented out using the standard XML comment syntax of `<!-- {comment here} -->`:

```
<uses-permission name="android.permission.INTERNET"/>
        <uses-permission name="android.permission.WRITE_EXTERNAL_
STORAGE"/>
        <!--<uses-permission name="android.permission.READ_PHONE_
STATE"/>-->
        <!--<uses-permission name="android.permission.ACCESS_FINE_
LOCATION"/>-->
        <!--<uses-permission name="android.permission.DISABLE_
KEYGUARD"/>-->
        <!--<uses-permission name="android.permission.WAKE_LOCK"/>--
>
        <uses-permission name="android.permission.CAMERA"/>
        <!--<uses-permission name="android.permission.RECORD_
AUDIO"/>-->
        <!--<uses-permission name="android.permission.ACCESS_
NETWORK_STATE"/>-->
        <!--<uses-permission name="android.permission.ACCESS_WIFI_
STATE"/>-->
```

How it works...

The permissions you define within the AIR descriptor file will be used to create an Android Manifest file to be packaged within the `.apk` produced by the tool used to compile the project. These permissions restrict and enable the application, once installed on a user's device, and also alert the user as to which activities and resources the application will be given access to prior to installation. It is very important to provide only the permissions necessary for an application to perform the expected tasks once installed upon a device.

The following is a list of the possible permissions for the Android manifest document:

- ▶ ACCESS_COARSE_LOCATION: Allows the Geoloctaion class to access WIFI and triangulated cell tower location data.

- ▶ ACCESS_FINE_LOCATION: Allows the Geolocation class to make use of the device GPS sensor.

- ▶ ACCESS_NETWORK_STATE: Allows an application to access the network state through the NetworkInfo class.

- ▶ ACCESS_WIFI_STATE: Allows and application to access the WIFI state through the NetworkInfo class.

- ▶ CAMERA: Allows an application to access the device camera.

- ▶ INTERNET: Allows the application to access the Internet and perform data transfer requests.

- ▶ READ_PHONE_STATE: Allows the application to mute audio when a phone call is in effect.

- ▶ RECORD_AUDIO: Allows microphone access to the application to record or monitor audio data.

- ▶ WAKE_LOCK: Allows the application to prevent the device from going to sleep using the SystemIdleMode class. (Must be used alongside DISABLE_KEYGUARD.)

- ▶ DISABLE_KEYGUARD: Allows the application to prevent the device from going to sleep using the SystemIdleMode class. (Must be used alongside WAKE_LOCK.)

- ▶ WRITE_EXTERNAL_STORAGE: Allows the application to write to external memory. This memory is normally stored as a device SD card.

Preventing the device screen from dimming

The Android operating system will dim, and eventually turn off the device screen after a certain amount of time has passed. It does this to preserve battery life, as the display is the primary power drain on a device. For most applications, if a user is interacting with the interface, that interaction will prevent the screen from dimming. However, if your application does not involve user interaction for lengthy periods of time, yet the user is looking at or reading something upon the display, it would make sense to prevent the screen from dimming.

How to do it...

There are two settings in the AIR descriptor file that can be changed to ensure the screen does not dim. We will also modify properties of our application to complete this recipe:

1. Find the AIR descriptor file in your project. It is normally named something like `{MyProject}-app.xml` as it resides at the project root.

2. Browse the file for a node named `<android>` within this node will be another called `<manifestAdditions>`, which holds a child node called `<manifest>`. This section of the document contains everything we need to set permissions for our Android application.

3. All we need to do is make sure the following two nodes are present within this section of the descriptor file. Note that enabling both of these permissions is required to allow application control over the system through the `SystemIdleMode` class. Uncomment them if necessary.

   ```
   <uses-permission android:name="android.permission.WAKE_LOCK" />
   <uses-permission android:name="android.permission.DISABLE_
   KEYGUARD" />
   ```

4. Within our application, we will import the following classes:

   ```
   import flash.desktop.NativeApplication;
   import flash.desktop.SystemIdleMode;
   import flash.display.Sprite;
   import flash.display.StageAlign;
   import flash.display.StageScaleMode;
   import flash.text.TextField;
   import flash.text.TextFormat;
   ```

5. Declare a `TextField` and `TextFormat` pair to trace out messages to the user:

   ```
   private var traceField:TextField;
   private var traceFormat:TextFormat;
   ```

6. Now, we will set the system idle mode for our application by assigning the `SystemIdleMode.KEEP_AWAKE` constant to the `NativeApplication.nativeApplication.systemIdleMode` property:

   ```
   protected function setIdleMode():void {
     NativeApplication.nativeApplication.systemIdleMode =
         SystemIdleMode.KEEP_AWAKE;
   }
   ```

7. We will, at this point, continue to set up our `TextField`, apply a `TextFormat`, and add it to the `DisplayList`. Here, we create a method to perform all of these actions for us:

```
protected function setupTraceField():void {
  traceFormat = new TextFormat();
  traceFormat.bold = true;
  traceFormat.font = "_sans";
  traceFormat.size = 24;
  traceFormat.align = "left";
  traceFormat.color = 0xCCCCCC;
  traceField = new TextField();
  traceField.defaultTextFormat = traceFormat;
  traceField.selectable = false;
  traceField.multiline = true;
  traceField.wordWrap = true;
  traceField.mouseEnabled = false;
  traceField.x = 20;
  traceField.y = 20
  traceField.width = stage.stageWidth-40;
  traceField.height = stage.stageHeight - traceField.y;
  addChild(traceField);
}
```

8. Here, we simply output the currently assigned system idle mode String to our `TextField`, letting the user know that the device will not be going to sleep:

```
protected function checkIdleMode():void {
  traceField.text = "System Idle Mode: " + NativeApplication.
      nativeApplication.systemIdleMode;
}
```

9. When the application is run on a device, the **System Idle Mode** will be set and the results traced out to our display. The user can leave the device unattended for as long as necessary and the screen will not dim or lock. In the following example, this application was allowed to run for five minutes without user intervention:

How it works...

There are two things that must be done in order to get this to work correctly and both are absolutely necessary. First, we have to be sure the application has correct permissions through the Android Manifest file. Allowing the application permissions for WAKE_LOCK and DISABLE_KEYGUARD within the AIR descriptor file will do this for us. The second part involves setting the NativeApplication.systemIdleMode property to keepAwake. This is best accomplished through use of the SystemIdleMode.KEEP_AWAKE constant. Ensuring that these conditions are met will enable the application to keep the device display lit and prevent Android from locking the device after it has been idle.

See also...

In this recipe, we have edited the AIR descriptor file through a basic text editor. For other ways of setting these permissions in a variety of environments, refer to the previous recipe.

Establishing Android custom URI schemes

Android exposes a number of useful URI protocols to AIR for standard operations such as mapping, sms, and telephone. Defining a custom URI for our application allows it to be invoked from anywhere on the system: through the web browser, email, or even a native application. Custom URIs provides an alternative method of invoking an AIR application.

How to do it...

We will create an application that can be opened from the device web browser using a custom URI. We define the URI intent settings through modification of the AIR descriptor file:

1. Find the AIR descriptor file in your project. It is normally named something like {MyProject}-app.xml as it resides at the project root.

2. Browse the file for a node named <android>; within this node will be another called <manifestAdditions>, which holds a child node called <manifest>. This section of the document contains everything we need to set permissions for our Android application.

3. We will now add the highlighted <intent-filter> node to our descriptor file. The portion of the intent which defines our URI is <data android:scheme="fvm"/>. This will enable our application to use the fvm:// URI. Note that "fvm" is being used for this example; when authoring an application based on such an example, we are free to change this value to whatever is suited to a particular application:

```
<application android:enabled="true">
<activity android:excludeFromRecents="false">
<intent-filter>
<action android:name="android.intent.action.MAIN"/>
<category android:name="android.intent.category.LAUNCHER"/>
</intent-filter>
<intent-filter>
<action android:name="android.intent.action.VIEW"/>
<category android:name="android.intent.category.BROWSABLE"/>
<category android:name="android.intent.category.DEFAULT"/>
<data android:scheme="fvm"/>
</intent-filter>
</activity>
</application>
```

4. Within our application, we will import the following classes:

```
import flash.desktop.NativeApplication;
import flash.display.Sprite;
import flash.display.StageAlign;
import flash.display.StageScaleMode;
import flash.events.InvokeEvent;
import flash.text.TextField;
import flash.text.TextFormat;
```

5. Declare a TextField and TextFormat pair to trace out messages to the user:

```
private var traceField:TextField;
private var traceFormat:TextFormat;
```

6. We will, at this point, continue to set up our `TextField`, apply a `TextFormat`, and add it to the `DisplayList`. Here, we create a method to perform all of these actions for us:

```
protected function setupTraceField():void {
  traceFormat = new TextFormat();
  traceFormat.bold = true;
  traceFormat.font = "_sans";
  traceFormat.size = 24;
  traceFormat.align = "left";
  traceFormat.color = 0xCCCCCC;
  traceField = new TextField();
  traceField.defaultTextFormat = traceFormat;
  traceField.selectable = false;
  traceField.multiline = true;
  traceField.wordWrap = true;
  traceField.mouseEnabled = false;
  traceField.x = 20;
  traceField.y = 40;
  traceField.width = stage.stageWidth-40;
  traceField.height =stage.stageHeight - traceField.y;
  addChild(traceField);
}
```

7. Register an event listener of type InvokeEvent.INVOKE upon the NativeApplication. This will detect any application invocation events initiated by the user employing our defined URI:

```
protected function registerListeners():void {
  NativeApplication.nativeApplication.
        addEventListener(InvokeEvent.INVOKE, onInvoke);
}
```

8. When the application is opened from our URI, the following method will be processed. We can gather a certain amount of information from our invoke event, such as the `reason` property. This property will have a value of either `"login"` or `"standard"`. If the application is launched automatically at system login, the value will read `"login"`. In the case of URI invocation, it will read `"standard"`. We can also access the `currentDirectory`. The app may have been invoked from within the file system, or access any `arguments` passed through the URI. Note that in the case of a URI invocation from a web browser, as we have here, the `arguments` property will only contain the full URL from the selected link. This is a way in which we can pass in data to our application at launch.

```
protected function onInvoke(e:InvokeEvent):void {
  traceField.text = "";
```

```
traceField.text = "Invoke Reason: " + e.reason + "\n";
   traceField.appendText("Directory URL: " + e.currentDirectory.
   url + "\n\n");
var args:Array = e.arguments;
if (arguments.length > 0) {
traceField.appendText("Message: " + args.toString() + "\n");
}
}
```

9. For this example, let us set up a simple web page which includes a link with our defined `fvm://` URI:`<a href="fvm://arg1=Hello&arg2=AIRAndroid">O pen AIR Android App!</a>`. If a user has the application already installed and clicks this link, the application should open as our URI intent is registered on the device:

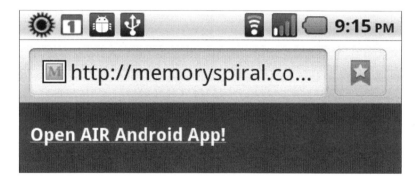

10. Once the user clicks upon the link which uses our defined URI, the AIR application will open and detect an `InvokeEvent`, which displays the following information upon the device display. We can see here that the directory URL is empty, as the application was not invoked from within the device file system:

How it works...

When we define the URI intent within our application descriptor file, this gets compiled into the Android manifest file along with our application. Installing this application on a device informs the operating system of the URI intent we have defined. This makes the OS aware of that specific URI and instructs it to open the application when that URI is encountered. We can place the URI in a number of different locations, including native Android applications upon the system. This allows native applications to open AIR for Android applications. In the earlier example, we embed the URI within HTML and use the Android web browser to open our application.

See also...

For more on working with URI protocols in AIR for Android, have a look through *Chapter 7, Native Interaction: StageWebView and URI Handlers*.

Anticipating Android Compatibility Filtering

Depending upon which APIs is used in a particular application, some Android devices may not be able to provide access to expected sensors or hardware hooks. If a user downloads an application which does not work as expected, that user will become frustrated and will most likely provide us with a poor rating and perhaps even a nasty comment. Luckily, there is a bit of filtering that the Android Market can perform, on our behalf, to ensure that only devices which support our application will be served the option to download and install it.

How to do it...

Modify the Android Manifest file to specify which particular features are required by our application:

1. Find the AIR descriptor file in your project. It is normally named something like `{MyProject}-app.xml` as it resides at the project root.

2. Browse the file for a node named `<android>`; within this node will be another called `<manifestAdditions>`, which holds a child node called `<manifest>`. This section of the document will contain everything we need to declare compatibility for our Android application.

3. We will add certain tags based upon our needs. See the following information layout to determine what you should add within the manifest node for a particular feature dependency. Setting `android:required="false"` makes a feature optional.

When using features of the Android camera:

```
<uses-feature android:name="android.hardware.camera"
android:required="false"/>


<uses-feature android:name="android.hardware.camera.autofocus"
android:required="false"/>


<uses-feature android:name="android.hardware.camera.flash"
android:required="false"/>
```

When using features of the Android microphone:

```
<uses-feature android:name="android.hardware.microphone"
android:required="false"/>
```

When using the Geolocation Sensor:

```
<uses-feature android:name="android.hardware.location"
android:required="false"/>
<uses-feature android:name="android.hardware.location.network"
android:required="false"/>
<uses-feature android:name="android.hardware.location.gps"
android:required="false"/>
```

When using the Accelerometer Sensor:

```
<uses-feature android:name="android.hardware.accelerometer"
android:required="false"/>
```

How it works...

By specifying certain required or optional features of the camera and microphone, we can ensure that only users whose devices meet these specific requirements will be presented with the option to download and install our application. We make these specifications known through the modification of the Android manifest file through additions to our AIR description file as demonstrated in this recipe. Compiling our application with these modifications will ensure that these specifications are encoded along with our .APK and exposed through the Android Market once our application is published.

See also...

For more on working with the camera and microphone in AIR for Android, have a look at *Chapter 4, Visual and Audio Input: Camera and Microphone Access.*

Instructing an application to be installed to Device SDCard

By slightly modifying the Android manifest instructions within our AIR application descriptor file, we can inform the device operating system that our application should, if possible, be installed on the external SD card rather than internal storage. This will help reserve internal device storage for the operating system and associated files.

How to do it...

Modify the Android Manifest file to determine installation location options:

1. Find the AIR Descriptor File in your project. It is normally named something like `{MyProject}-app.xml`and resides at the project root.

2. Browse the file for a node named `<android>`; within this node will be another called `<manifestAdditions>`, which holds a child node called `<manifest>`.

3. We will add the `installLocation` attribute to our `<manifest>` node. To set the application to install at the discretion of Android:

   ```
   <manifest android:installLocation="auto"/>
   ```

4. To set the application to prefer the device SD card:

   ```
   <manifest android:installLocation="preferExternal"/>
   ```

 There is no guarantee that setting `installLocation="preferExternal` will actually install the application to the device SD card.

The user can also move the application, if allowed, via the following steps:

1. First, navigate to the **application management** screen on the device where our AIR application is installed. The location of this screen on most Android devices is **Settings | Applications | Manage Applications**. Now choose an AIR application you have created from this screen.

2. To move the application to the device SD card, simply click the button labeled **Move to SD card**:

How it works...

It is a good idea to allow the user some degree of choice as to where they can install their application. On Android, there are only two options: the device storage area or external SD card. Taking into consideration that most devices have a lot more storage on the SD card than internal; it is probably best to prefer the SD card by setting `android:installLocation= "preferExternal"` on our manifest node within the AIR descriptor file. While there is no guarantee that Android will use the external SD card when installing our application, this will at least let the system know that location is preferred. Whether or not Android is able to install applications to external storage has mostly to do with the operating system version. Generally, if the device can install and run the AIR for Android runtime, it should have the capability to do this.

As we've seen earlier, the user can always move the application from internal storage to external storage and back again if they wish. Also of note: the application storage directory, local shared objects, and any temporary files are still written to internal storage even when the application is installed on the device SD card. If we intend to save lots of data with our application, then we will use `File.documents` directory or `File.user` directory to store this data onto the external SD card.

See also...

For more on working with the local file system, have a look through *Chapter 8, Abundant Access: File System and Local Database.*

Encrypting a local SQLite database

Normally, a local SQLite database does not require any security or encryption. However, if our application contains sensitive data stored within the local application database files, we would want to ensure that an intruder or thief cannot access this information. Thankfully, we can encrypt the databases available to us on AIR for Android to ensure that even if a user's device is lost or stolen, their private information remains secure.

Getting ready...

In order to properly encrypt a database file, we will need to use an encryption library. In this example, we will use the as3crypto package available at `http://code.google.com/p/as3crypto/`. Download the `.SWC` to follow along with this example.

We need to make the `.SWC` available within our project. Depending upon the tool being used, the procedure to do this does vary.

Instructions to include a .SWC package into a Flash Builder project

1. Within your project, select the **File** menu and choose **Properties**.

2. In the left column, click **ActionScript Build Path** and choose the **Library path** tab. Locate the button labeled **Add SWC...** within this screen and click it.

3. A dialog window will appear. Choose the **Browse to SWC** option, locate the `.SWC` containing our encryption library, and hit **OK**.

4. The encryption library will now appear within the **Build path libraries** section of this screen. Verify that this is correct and exit out of the **Properties** window. The encryption library is now ready to be used within our mobile Android project.

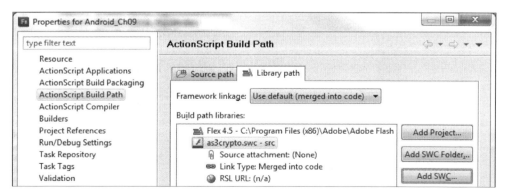

Instructions to include a .SWC package into a Flash Professional project

1. Within your Flash project, navigate to the **Properties** panel and click the little wrench icon next to the **Script** selection box:

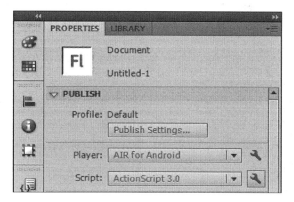

2. This will open the **Advanced ActionScript 3.0 Settings** dialog window. Choose the **Library path** tab. Locate the **Browse to SWC file** icon within this screen and click it. It appears as a white and red box and is the only icon which is not grayscale upon this screen:

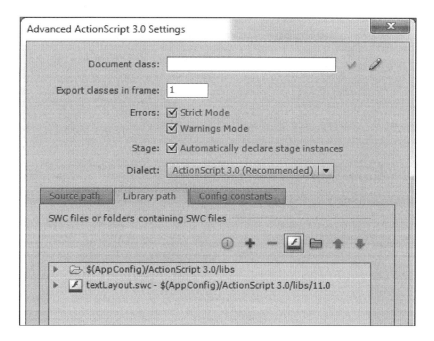

3. A **file browse** dialog window will appear. Locate the .SWC containing our encryption library, and hit **OK**.

4. The encryption library will now appear within the **Library path** section of this screen. Verify that this is correct and exit out of the **Advanced ActionScript 3.0 Settings** window. The encryption library is now ready to be used within our mobile Android project:

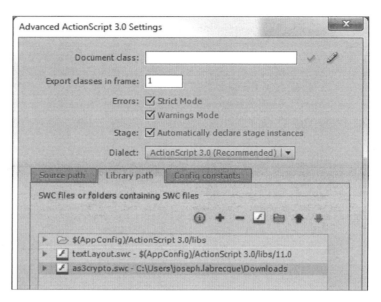

How to do it...

In order to encrypt an application database, we will declare a password and encrypt it using an external encryption library. This will be used when creating and opening our database connection:

1. Within our application, we will import the following classes. Be sure to import the MD5 class or an equivalent for proper key encryption:

```
import com.hurlant.crypto.hash.MD5;
import flash.data.SQLConnection;
import flash.data.SQLMode;
import flash.data.SQLStatement;
import flash.display.Sprite;
import flash.display.StageAlign;
import flash.display.StageScaleMode;
import flash.events.SQLEvent;
import flash.filesystem.File;
import flash.text.TextField;
```

```
import flash.text.TextFormat;
import flash.utils.ByteArray;
```

2. We must now declare a number of objects for use within this application. A `String` constant will hold our plain text password for later encryption. Normally, this would be supplied by the user and is hard-coded here for simplicity. We will need a `SQLConnection` to create or open our database file along with a set of `ByteArray` objects and a `MD5` object to perform the actual encryption. Finally, we declare a `TextField` and `TextFormat` pair to trace out messages to the user:

```
private const pass:String = "AIR@ndr0idIsKo0l";
private var sqlConnection:SQLConnection;
private var encryptionPass:ByteArray;
private var encryptionKey:ByteArray;
private var md5:MD5;
private var traceField:TextField;
private var traceFormat:TextFormat;
```

3. We will, at this point, continue to set up our `TextField`, apply a `TextFormat`, and add it to the `DisplayList` for textual output. Here, we create a method to perform all of these actions for us:

```
protected function setupTraceField():void {
    traceFormat = new TextFormat();
    traceFormat.bold = true;
    traceFormat.font = "_sans";
    traceFormat.size = 24;
    traceFormat.align = "left";
    traceFormat.color = 0xCCCCCC;
    traceField = new TextField();
    traceField.defaultTextFormat = traceFormat;
    traceField.selectable = false;
    traceField.multiline = true;
    traceField.wordWrap = true;
    traceField.mouseEnabled = false;
    traceField.x = 20;
    traceField.y = 40;
    traceField.width = stage.stageWidth-40;
    traceField.height =stage.stageHeight - traceField.y;
    addChild(traceField);
}
```

4. To perform the encryption of our database, we will first instantiate a `ByteArray` and invoke the `writeUTFBytes()` method, passing in our predefined password constant. This will write our `String` to the byte stream.

5. Now, instantiate a new `MD5` object along with another `ByteArray`, assigning the `ByteArray` to the result of the `MD5.hash()` method, passing in the previous `ByteArray` holding the password bytes.

6. Instantiate an `SQLConnection` and register an event listener of type `SQLEvent.OPEN`. This will fire an event once the database is either created or opened successfully.

7. Finally, invoke the `SQLConnection.open()` method, passing in the path to the database as a `File` object, the open mode constant of `SQLMode.CREATE`, an auto-compact `Boolean`, default page size of 1024, and most importantly for this example, our MD5-encrypted `ByteArray`:

```
protected function encryptDB():void {
    encryptionPass = new ByteArray();
    encryptionPass.writeUTFBytes(pass);

    md5 = new MD5();
    encryptionKey = new ByteArray();
    encryptionKey = md5.hash(encryptionPass);

    sqlConnection = new SQLConnection();
    sqlConnection.addEventListener(SQLEvent.OPEN, dbOpened);
    sqlConnection.open(File.applicationStorageDirectory.
        resolvePath("encrypted.db"), SQLMode.CREATE, false, 1024,
        encryptionKey);
}
```

8. So long as the database is created (or opened) successfully along with valid encryption, the following method will fire, outputting information about the encrypted database to our display:

```
protected function dbOpened(e:SQLEvent):void {
    traceField.appendText("Encrypted DB Created!\n\n");
    traceField.appendText("Pass: " + pass + "\n\n");
    traceField.appendText("Key: " + encryptionKey.toString());
}
```

9. When the application is run on our Android device, it will appear as follows. As the key is a truly MD5-encrypted `ByteArray`, it appears as garbled characters in the `TextField`, for it is no longer a plain text `String`:

How it works...

If an application requires encryption on a database, the encryption key must be applied when our database is created. Implementing the `SQLConnection.open()` or `SQLConnection.openAsync()` methods require us to pass in an encrypted `ByteArray` key created using `as3Crypto` or a similar encryption library. If we ever need to modify the encryption key, we can use the `SQLConnection.reencrypt()` to do so, generating the key in the same manner as demonstrated in this recipe. Note that a valid encryption key must be 16 bytes in length.

See also...

For more on working with local databases in AIR for Android, have a look through *Chapter 8, Abundant Access: File System and Local Database.*

10
Avoiding Problems: Debugging and Resource Considerations

This chapter will cover the following recipes:

- ▶ Debugging an application with Flash Professional
- ▶ Debugging an application with Flash Builder
- ▶ Rendering application Elements using the Device GPU
- ▶ Automating application Shutdown upon Device Interruption Events
- ▶ Exiting your application with the Device Back Button
- ▶ Monitoring Memory Usage and Frame Rate in an Application

Introduction

Being that Android is a mobile operating system, it presents a new set of specific challenges in regard to optimizing both for performance and user experience. This is something Flash Platform developers must take into consideration when developing applications with AIR for Android and mobile Flash Player. This chapter will provide an overview of debugging and optimization techniques along with user experience tweaks to make our AIR for Android applications behave as nicely as possible.

Debugging an application with Flash Professional

Debugging AIR for Android applications using Flash Professional is very similar to debugging desktop AIR or Flash projects, with some notable exceptions.

Getting ready...

Be sure your AIR for Android project is open in Flash Professional and that your Player is AIR for Android. This can be verified through the **Properties** panel:

How to do it...

Use the mobile debug launcher or debug on the device itself through USB:

1. In the application menu, choose **Debug** and hover over the option labeled **Debug Movie**. This will cause a submenu of debug options to appear:

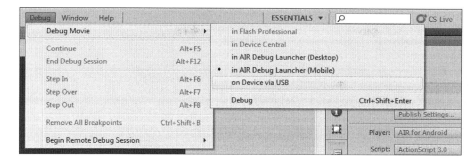

2. When choosing to debug **in AIR Debug Launcher (Mobile)**, Flash Professional will switch to the full Debug Console and launch the application within the device debugger. This is useful for performing quick debugging of your application when multi-touch, accelerometer, or other device-specific inputs and sensors are not involved. Breakpoints, trace statements, and other debug tools will function exactly the same as within a normal desktop project.

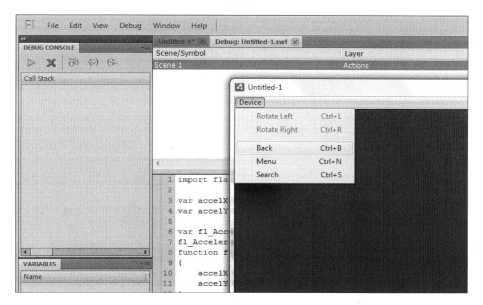

3. Once we have performed our preliminary tests in the debug player and are ready to debug on the device through USB, we can switch to that option in the **Debug** menu. If we have never configured the AIR for Android Settings for this project, a dialog window will appear, allowing us to do so. This window should not appear during subsequent debug sessions. Be sure to choose the **Debug** option under **Android deployment type** and have the **Install and Launch** options selected in the **After publishing** section.

4. You will notice there are fields for determining a certificate to sign your application at this point. To learn more about the code-signing process, please refer to *Chapter 11, Final Considerations: Application Compilation and Distribution*.

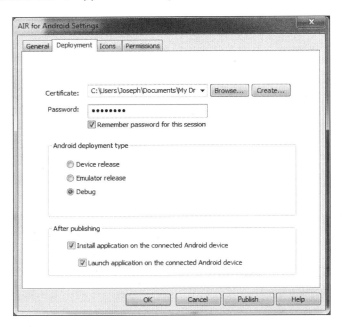

5. After initiating a debug session to deploy on our device, Flash Professional will take a few seconds to compile and deploy the application. As the application begins to load upon the device, AIR will launch a small dialog letting us know that it is attempting to connect to the debugger on our computer. Once this connection occurs, the window will go away and our full application will launch, allowing us to test and debug as normal.

How it works...

Debugging applications through breakpoints and variable inspection is on par with the course when developing applications using any Flash Platform technology. With AIR for Android, we are dealing with external hardware and a few extra steps must be taken to ensure that we are able to debug within our normal environment, while also interacting with an application running on a real device. This recipe demonstrates the steps necessary to get this all functioning within our present workflow.

See also...

For more information about project setup using Flash Professional, you may refer to *Chapter 1, Getting Ready to Work with Android: Development Environment and Project Setup.*

Debugging an application with Flash Builder

The ability to define debug configurations in Flash Builder is an excellent workflow improvement that we should take advantage of when setting up a new mobile project or preparing to test a project we have been working on for some time. We are able to set up multiple configurations for the same project using the Flash Builder **Debug Configurations** panel.

How to do it...

We are going to explore the **Debug Configurations** panel to configure a custom set of launch settings for our mobile project:

1. Select a mobile project and click the arrow next to the **Debug** button in the Flash Builder toolbar. Choose the **Debug Configurations...** option from this menu. The Debug Configurations dialog window will open up:

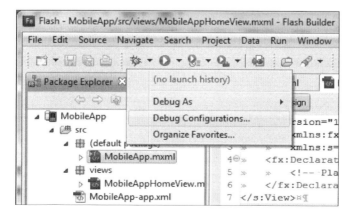

2. Double click on the left-hand menu entry labeled **MobileApp** to edit the particular settings for this selected project. From this window, we can select another project to configure, specify the default `Application` file for the project, set a `Target` platform (Google Android, in our case), and configure a `Launch` method. If debugging on the desktop, we can also select from a variety of device profiles and even configure our own. In the next screenshot , we have chosen to debug using the dimensions and resolution present on the Motorola Droid:

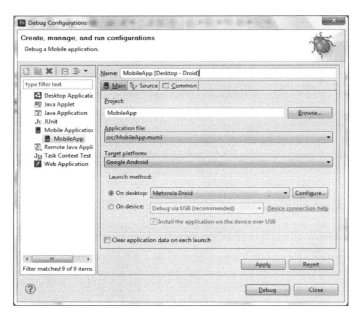

3. If it is necessary to define additional devices, we can click the **Configure...** button to launch the **Device Configurations** screen, which allows us to Import device profiles, or even add our own:

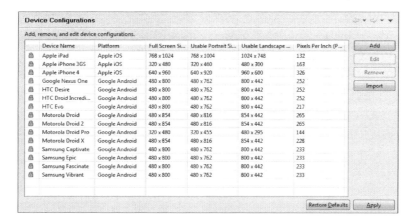

	Device Name	Platform	Full Screen Si...	Usable Portrait Si...	Usable Landscape ...	Pixels Per Inch (P...	
🔒	Apple iPad	Apple iOS	768 x 1024	768 x 1004	1024 x 748	132	Add
🔒	Apple iPhone 3GS	Apple iOS	320 x 480	320 x 460	480 x 300	163	Edit
🔒	Apple iPhone 4	Apple iOS	640 x 960	640 x 920	960 x 600	326	Remove
🔒	Google Nexus One	Google Android	480 x 800	480 x 762	800 x 442	252	Import
🔒	HTC Desire	Google Android	480 x 800	480 x 762	800 x 442	252	
🔒	HTC Droid Incredi...	Google Android	480 x 800	480 x 762	800 x 442	252	
🔒	HTC Evo	Google Android	480 x 800	480 x 762	800 x 442	217	
🔒	Motorola Droid	Google Android	480 x 854	480 x 816	854 x 442	265	
🔒	Motorola Droid 2	Google Android	480 x 854	480 x 816	854 x 442	265	
🔒	Motorola Droid Pro	Google Android	320 x 480	320 x 455	480 x 295	144	
🔒	Motorola Droid X	Google Android	480 x 854	480 x 816	854 x 442	228	
🔒	Samsung Captivate	Google Android	480 x 800	480 x 762	800 x 442	233	
🔒	Samsung Epic	Google Android	480 x 800	480 x 762	800 x 442	233	
🔒	Samsung Fascinate	Google Android	480 x 800	480 x 762	800 x 442	233	
🔒	Samsung Vibrant	Google Android	480 x 800	480 x 762	800 x 442	233	

4. When adding a custom device profile, we are given options for specifying width and height of our display along with supported pixels per inch. Google Android has a standard platform UI that can differ between devices depending upon how much customization the manufacturer performs over the standard display elements. The notifications bar, for instance, always appears unless the device is in full screen mode. If the notifications bar was taller or shorter on a specific device, we can account for it here.

 While resolution and PPI can be simulated here, unless the development machine has a multi-touch interface, we will have to test any touch or gesture input on an actual device. Of course, device performance is not part of the simulation either.

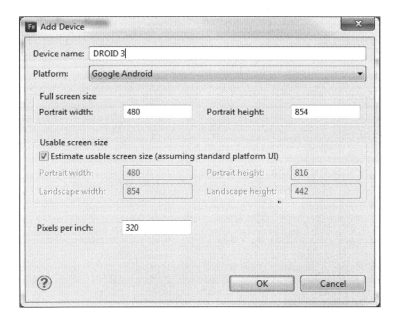

5. When choosing to debug on actual physical hardware, we can choose to debug on a device through USB or over a wireless network. USB debugging is often the more direct way and is recommended for most situations. Within the following screenshot, you can see that we have now defined one configuration for desktop debug and one for debugging on a USB-connected device:

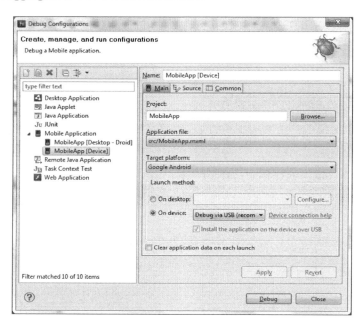

6. When finished, click **Apply** and then **Close**. We can now access any of the defined configurations from the Flash Builder debug icon or the project context menu:

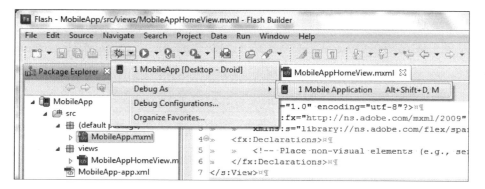

7. Once we choose to launch a debug session for our project, it will open within the Flash Builder mobile debug player when debugging on the desktop, or in the case of USB device debug; it will be compiled, pushed to the device, and installed. For a device debug session, AIR will launch a small dialog letting us know that it is attempting to connect to the debugger on our computer. Once this connection occurs, the window will go away and our full application will launch, allowing us to test and debug as normal.

How it works...

If you choose to launch on desktop, you will be able to debug locally within Flash Builder. You can also emulate a variety of Android devices by choosing from a set of profiles. If you wish to create your own profile, you can do so by clicking the **Configure** button.

When choosing to launch on a device, you also have the option of debugging on the device, through Flash Builder. This is, by far, the best way of debugging your mobile application, because it is tested on true Android hardware.

See also...

For more information about project setup using Flash Builder, you may refer to *Chapter 1, Getting Ready to Work with Android: Development Environment and Project Setup.*

Rendering application elements using the device GPU

While older Android devices must rely on the CPU for everything being rendered within a mobile Adobe AIR project, many of the newer devices on the market have full support for Graphics Processing Unit (GPU) rendering and providing necessary hooks for our applications to take advantage of this. This recipe will demonstrate the necessary steps we must take to enable GPU acceleration upon application elements.

How to do it...

We will modify settings in the AIR descriptor file and enable `DisplayObject` instances to take advantage of these modifications:

1. Locate the AIR descriptor file in your project. It is normally named something like `{MyProject}-app.xml` and resides at the project root.

2. Browse the file for a node named `<initialWindow>` near the beginning of this document. This node contains many default settings dealing with the visual aspects of our application window.

3. We now must locate the child node named `<renderMode>`. If this node does not exist, we can easily add it here. The `renderMode` value determines whether the application will use the CPU or GPU for rendering content. There are three possible values for application `renderMode`:

   - **AUTO**: The application will attempt to use the device GPU to render visual display objects:

     ```
     <renderMode>auto</renderMode>
     ```

   - **GPU**: The application will be locked to GPU mode. If the device does not support GPU rendering within Adobe AIR, problems will ensue:

     ```
     <renderMode>gpu</renderMode>
     ```

   - **CPU**: The application will use the device CPU for rendering all visual display objects. This is the safest setting, but provides the fewest benefits:

     ```
     <renderMode>cpu</renderMode>
     ```

4. Now, whenever we want to take advantage of this with `DisplayObject` instances within our application, we must set both the `DisplayObject` instances `cacheAsBitmap` property to `true` and assign the `cacheAsBitmapMatrix` property to a new Matrix object. This will enable 2D content rendering for these individual objects through the device GPU. When using objects in 2.5D space, they will automatically be rendered using the GPU and do not require these additional settings.

```
displayObject.cacheAsBitmap = true;
displayObject.cacheAsBitmapMatrix =new Matrix();
```

How it works...

Setting the application `renderMode` within the AIR descriptor file to `gpu` will force the application to render visual objects using the GPU. However, individual objects not being rendered in 2.5D space will require that both the `cacheAsBitmap` property be set to `true` and the `cacheAsBitmapMatix` property be assigned to a Matrix object. When setting `renderMode` to `auto`, the application will attempt to render these objects through the GPU, and will fall back to CPU rendering if GPU acceleration is not supported on a particular device. We can also set the `renderMode` to `cpu`, which simply renders everything through the CPU, bypassing any GPU rendering altogether.

When used appropriately, setting the application `renderMode` can greatly speed up visual object rendering within an application. It is important to realize that many devices will not have full GPU support available through AIR for Android, in which case forcing GPU may actually be quite problematic for the application and may even render it unusable on particular devices. There are also a number of limitations present when using the GPU. For instance: filters, PixelBender blends, and a variety of standard blend modes are not supported.

There's more...

If using Flash Professional, we can also set the `Render` mode through the AIR for **Android Settings** panel. This is accessible through the **Properties** panel. Click the little wrench icon next to **Player selection** to configure these settings.

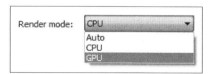

Automating application shutdown upon device interruption events

When an application is running on an Android device, there is a good chance that a user session can be interrupted by a telephone call, or some other unforeseen event. When a situation like this occurs, we should consider whether it may be appropriate to exit the application and free up system resources for other tasks.

How to do it...

We will listen to the application to fire a deactivate event and exit the application in response:

1. To begin, we will need to import the following classes into our application:

    ```
    import flash.desktop.NativeApplication:
    import flash.display.Sprite;
    import flash.display.StageAlign;
    import flash.display.StageScaleMode;
    import flash.events.Event;
    ```

2. We must register an event listener of type `Event.DEACTIVATE` upon our `NativeApplication.nativeApplication` object. This event will fire in response to the application losing focus on the device in the event of a telephone call or some other interruption:

    ```
    protected function registerListeners():void {
      NativeApplication.nativeApplication.addEventListener(Event.
          DEACTIVATE, appDeactivate);
    }
    ```

3. Within the following function, we will invoke the `exit()` method upon the `NativeApplication.nativeApplication` object, closing the application completely. This will free up resources for other device applications:

    ```
    protected function appDeactivate(e:Event):void {
      NativeApplication.nativeApplication.exit();
    }
    ```

How it works...

We want to be good stewards of the resources set aside for our application to run while active on a user's device. An effective way to do this is to make sure to release any memory that our application is using when not in an active state. Listening for a deactivate event will allow us to know when some other application receives focus. At this point, we can exit the application completely which frees up the resources being used for whatever the user is currently doing.

See also...

Before actually exiting the application, we have a chance to preserve any session data through local shared objects or local databases. For more information on how to do this, take a look at *Chapter 8, Abundant Access: File System and Local Database*.

Exiting your application with the device back button

Android devices generally have a set of four soft-keys along one side of the device which are always present to the user. Two of these keys involve navigation—the back and home keys. When a user activates an event such as when pressing the back button, we should consider whether it may be appropriate to fully exit the application and free up system resources for other tasks.

 The home button will always return the user to the Android desktop, thus deactivating our application. To see how to close an application in such an event, refer the previous recipe.

How to do it...

We will listen to the dedicated Android back button to be pressed and exit the application in response:

1. To begin, we will need to import the following classes into our application.

    ```
    import flash.desktop.NativeApplication;
    import flash.display.Sprite;
    import flash.display.StageAlign;
    import flash.display.StageScaleMode;
    import flash.events.KeyboardEvent;
    import flash.ui.Keyboard;
    ```

2. We must register an event listener of type `KeyboardEvent.KEY_DOWN` upon our `NativeApplication.nativeApplication` object. This event will fire in response to the user activating the dedicated Android back key:

    ```
    protected function registerListeners():void {
      NativeApplication.nativeApplication.
          addEventListener(KeyboardEvent.KEY_DOWN, onBackPressed);
    }
    ```

In the event of the back key being pressed by the user, we will invoke the `exit()` method upon the `NativeApplication.nativeApplication` object, closing the application completely. This will free up resources for other device applications:

```
protected function onBackPressed(e:KeyboardEvent):void {
  if(e.keyCode == Keyboard.BACK){
    NativeApplication.nativeApplication.exit();
  }
}
```

How it works...

We want to be good stewards of the resources set aside for our application to run while active on a user's device. An effective way to do this is to make sure to release any memory that our application is using when not in an active state. One way of doing this is to listen for keyboard events and intercepting a back key press. At this point, we can exit the application completely which frees up the resources being used for whatever the user is currently doing.

Depending upon the current state of our application, we can choose whether it is appropriate to exit the application or simply return to some previous state. When performing such actions within a Flex-based mobile project, we would probably only exit the application if our current view was the initial view within our application `ViewNavigator`.

There's more...

It is also possible to prevent the Android back button from doing anything at all by using `KeyboardEvent.preventDefault()`:

```
protected function onBackPressed(e:KeyboardEvent):void {
  if(e.keyCode == Keyboard.BACK){
    KeyboardEvent.preventDefault();
  }
}
```

See also...

Note that before actually exiting the application, we have a chance to preserve any session data through local shared objects or local databases. For more information on how to do this, take a look at *Chapter 8, Abundant Access: File System and Local Database.*

Monitoring memory usage and frame rate in an application

Android devices generally have a lot less memory and much less CPU power than a traditional desktop or laptop machine. We have to be very careful when building Android applications so as not to create something so power-hungry, that the frame rate drops to unacceptable levels or the application becomes unresponsive. To assist us in troubleshooting and monitoring these issues, we can keep track of the memory consumption and calculated frame rate of the running application which should respond accordingly.

How to do it...

We can monitor many system properties through use of the `flash.system` package along with the `flash.utils.getTimer` class for calculating the present application frame rate:

1. To begin, we will need to import the following classes into our application:

```
import flash.display.Sprite;
import flash.display.StageAlign;
import flash.display.StageScaleMode;
import flash.events.Event;
import flash.system.Capabilities;
import flash.system.System;
import flash.text.TextField;
import flash.text.TextFormat;
import flash.utils.getTimer;
```

2. We need to declare a set of `Number` objects to hold persistent timing values in order to calculate the application frame rate. Also, declare a `TextField` and `TextFormat` pair to trace out this and other device messages to the user:

```
private var prevTime:Number;
private var numFrames:Number;
private var frameRate:Number;
private var traceField:TextField;
private var traceFormat:TextFormat;
```

3. We will, at this point, continue to set up our `TextField`, apply a `TextFormat`, and add it to the `DisplayList`. Here, we create a method to perform all of these actions for us:

```
protected function setupTraceField():void {
  traceFormat = new TextFormat();
  traceFormat.bold = true;
  traceFormat.font = "_sans";
  traceFormat.size = 24;
  traceFormat.align = "left";
  traceFormat.color = 0xCCCCCC;
  traceField = new TextField();
  traceField.defaultTextFormat = traceFormat;
  traceField.selectable = false;
  traceField.multiline = true;
  traceField.wordWrap = true;
  traceField.mouseEnabled = false;
  traceField.x = 20;
  traceField.y = 40;
  traceField.width = stage.stageWidth-40;
```

```
    traceField.height = stage.stageHeight - traceField.y;
    addChild(traceField);
}
```

4. The next step entails creation of the mechanism which handles our frame rate calculation. We will set the `prevTimeNumber` to the current elapsed milliseconds as the application has been initialized. We'll also set the `numFrames` variable to `0` for the moment. This provides us with a base set of numbers to work off. Finally, we register an event listener of type `Event.ENTER_FRAME` upon our application to periodically perform new frame rate calculations for us:

```
protected function registerListeners():void {
  prevTime = getTimer();
  numFrames = 0;
  this.addEventListener(Event.ENTER_FRAME, onEnterFrame);
}
```

5. This lengthy method will refresh everything within our `TextField`, every time a frame is entered. First, we will write out some information about the CPU architecture, manufacturer, and the memory available to our application. The memory is the important bit in this step.

6. To calculate the running frame rate, we will first increment our frame counter and once again gather the number of milliseconds elapsed from the initialization of our application. The previous reading of this can be then subtracted, giving us the time that has elapsed since this function last ran.

7. If the time elapsed is over 1000, a second has transpired and we can then perform some calculations to determine our actual frames per second. We will retrieve the frames per minute by dividing the number of frames we are dealing with in this cycle by the variable holding our previous time, multiplied by 1000. Setting the previous time variable to the present time elapsed, and resetting our frame count to `0`, will begin a new cycle:

```
protected function onEnterFrame(e:Event):void {
  traceField.text = "CPU Arch: " + Capabilities.cpuArchitecture +
"\n";
  traceField.appendText("Manufacturer: " + Capabilities.
      manufacturer + "\n");
  traceField.appendText("OS: " + Capabilities.os + "\n\n");
  traceField.appendText("Free Memory: " + System.freeMemory +
      "\n");
  traceField.appendText("Total Memory: " + System.totalMemory +
      "\n\n");
  numFrames++;
  var timeNow:Number = getTimer();
  var timePast:Number = timeNow - prevTime;
```

```
if(timePast > 1000){
  var fpm:Number = numFrames/timePast;
  frameRate = Math.floor(fpm * 1000);
  prevTime = timeNow;
  numFrames = 0;
}

traceField.appendText("Framerate: " + frameRate);
}
```

8. When we run the application upon a device, we can see the CPU and OS information, along with memory usage and the calculated frame rate:

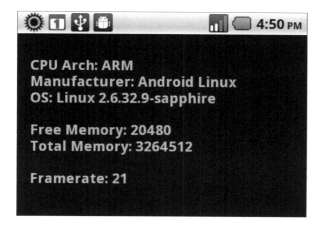

How it works...

There is a wealth of information which can be accessed through the Capabilities and System classes regarding CPU and memory use. We can gather additional information about the current frame rate by calculating actual FPS based upon data gathered from the `getTimer()` utility method. Using all of this together will provide us with a reasonable set of data to determine how well our application is running upon a particular device. We can then use this data to make smart decisions while the application is running by modifying application properties, changing the way we are rendering content, or even alerting the user that there may be a problem.

There's more...

If the frame rate becomes too sluggish, we may want to consider lowering the frame rate or even dropping the rendering quality of our application to improve performance. This can be done using the following code snippets:

```
this.stage.frameRate = 10;
this.stage.quality = StageQuality.LOW;
```

See also...

We can also recommend the use of a package like Hi-ReS-Stats which can be downloaded from https://github.com/mrdoob/Hi-ReS-Stats and used on mobile Android applications to monitor resource usage. Usage of this class will produce a graph overlay within our application to monitor application performance.

11
Final Considerations: Application Compilation and Distribution

This chapter will cover the following recipes:

- ▶ Generating a code-signing certificate using Flash Professional
- ▶ Generating a code-signing certificate using Flash Builder
- ▶ Generating a code-signing certificate using FDT
- ▶ Generating a code-signing certificate using the AIR Developer Tool
- ▶ Preparing Icon Files for distribution
- ▶ Compiling an application using Flash Professional
- ▶ Compiling an application using Flash Builder
- ▶ Compiling an application using FDT
- ▶ Compiling an application using the AIR Developer Tool
- ▶ Submitting an application to the Android Market

Introduction

When deploying a mobile Flash application (.swf) to the Web, the process is very similar to what it is on desktop; embed your .swf into an HTML container, and you are done. Deploying an AIR application to the Android Market, however, is quite a different experience. In this chapter, we will discover how to prepare an application for distribution to the Android Market, the generation of appropriate code signing certificates, and details around the compilation and submission process.

Generating a code-signing certificate using Flash Professional

Applications distributed on the Android Market are required to have been digitally signed with a 25 year code signing certificate. There are a number of different ways we can go about generating a code signing certificate for Android applications. We will demonstrate how to generate such a certificate using Flash Professional within this recipe.

How to do it...

In Flash Professional, perform the following actions to create a self-signed digital certificate:

1. With a project open which targets **AIR for Android**, open the **Properties** panel and click the little wrench icon beside the **Player selection** box. This will open the **AIR for Android Settings** dialog:

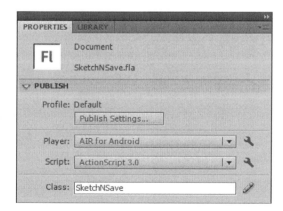

2. Within the **AIR for Android Settings** dialog, click the **Create...** button to open the **Create Self-Signed Digital Certificate** dialog window:

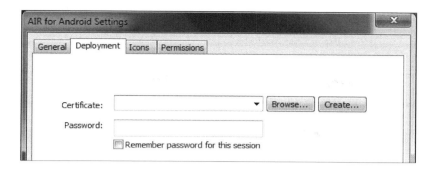

3. Now that the **Create Self-Signed Digital Certificate** dialog is before us, we will enter the required information and choose a name and location for the certificate. When everything has been entered properly, we will click **OK** to have Flash Professional generate the certificate. Be sure to enter 25 years in the **Validity period** input for Android:

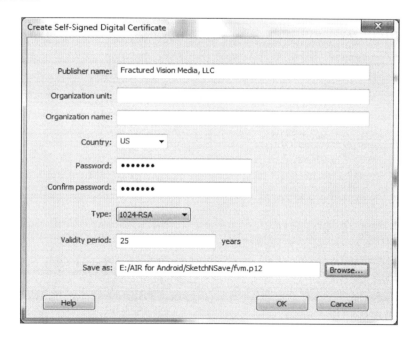

How it works...

By generating a valid digital code signing certificate, we are able to correctly sign our Android application for submission to the Android Market. Flash Professional provides a simple way to generate the appropriate certificate type and apply it to our applications for distribution.

Generating a code-signing certificate using Flash Builder

Applications distributed on the Android Market are required to have been digitally signed with a 25 year code signing certificate. There are a number of different ways we can go about generating a code signing certificate for Android applications. We will demonstrate how to generate such a certificate using Flash Builder within this recipe.

How to do it...

In Flash Builder, perform the following actions to create a self-signed digital certificate:

1. With a mobile project selected in the **Package Explorer**, enter the **File** menu and select **Properties**. The **Properties** dialog will appear for this project.

2. Within the **Properties** dialog, scroll down the **Flex Build Packaging** or **ActionScript Build Packaging** item (depending upon the type of project selected) and choose **Google Android**. With the **Digital Signature** tab selected, click the **Create...** button to open the **Create Self-Signed Digital Certificate** dialog:

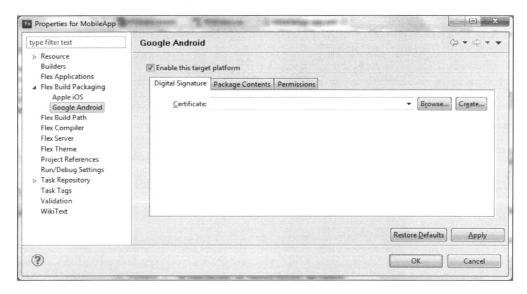

3. All that is now needed is to enter the required information and choose a name and location for the certificate. When everything has been entered properly, we will click **OK** to have Flash Builder generate the certificate:

How it works...

By generating a valid digital code signing certificate, we are able to correctly sign our Android application for submission to the Android Market. Flash Professional provides a simple way to generate the appropriate certificate type and apply it to our applications for distribution.

Generating a code-signing certificate using FDT

Applications distributed on the Android Market are required to have been digitally signed with a 25 year code signing certificate. There are a number of different ways we can go about generating a code signing certificate for Android applications. We will demonstrate how to generate such a certificate using PowerFlasher FDT within this recipe.

How to do it...

In FDT, perform the following actions to create a self-signed digital certificate:

1. Click upon the small arrow next to the **Run** icon in the top menu and choose
    Run Configurations... from the sub menu that appears. This will open the **Run
    Configurations** dialog:

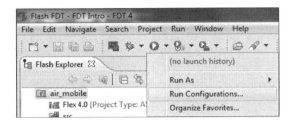

2. With the **Run Configurations** dialog window now open, double-click the **FDT
    AIR Application Release** menu item to create a new configuration. Choose the
    Certificate tab and to enter the required information, choosing a name and location
    for the certificate. Once everything has been entered properly, we will click **Create
    Certificate** to have FDT generate the certificate for us:

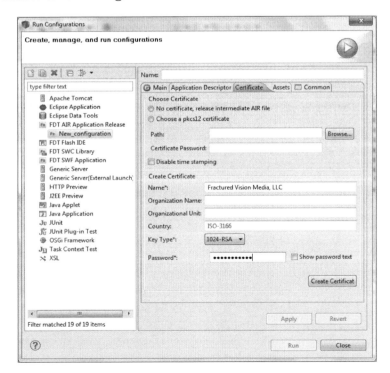

How it works...

By generating a valid digital code signing certificate, we are able to correctly sign our Android application for submission to the Android Market. FDT provides a simple way to generate the appropriate certificate type and apply it to our applications for distribution.

Generating a code-signing certificate using the AIR Developer Tool

Applications distributed on the Android Market are required to have been digitally signed with a 25 year code signing certificate. There are a number of different ways we can go about generating a code signing certificate for Android applications. We will demonstrate how to generate such a certificate using ADT command line tool within this recipe.

Getting ready...

For steps on configuring ADT within your particular environment, take a look at *Chapter 1, Getting Ready to Work with Android: Development Environment and Project Setup.*

How to do it...

Using the ADT command line tool, perform the following actions to create a self-signed digital certificate:

1. For this example, we will assume the following:

   ```
   Publisher Name:    "Joseph Labrecque"
   Validity Period:     25 (years)
   Key Type:      1024-RSA
   PFX File:      C:\Users\Joseph\Documents\airandroid.p12
   Password:      airAndroidPass
   ```

2. Open a command prompt or terminal (depending upon the operating system) and type in the command string to generate our certificate:

   ```
   adt -certificate -cn "Joseph Labrecque" -validityPeriod 25 1024-
   RSA C:\Users\Joseph\Documents\airandroid.p12 airAndroidPass
   ```

3. The ADT utility will now process the command and complete the certificate generation process. If there is a problem with our command, ADT will print out error messages here, letting us know something went wrong:

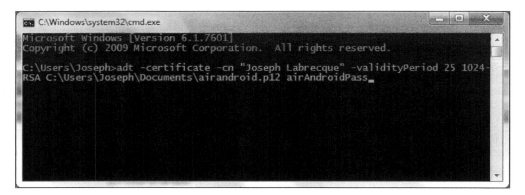

4. We can now browse to the location specified within the command string to locate our newly created certificate and can use this to sign our AIR for Android applications:

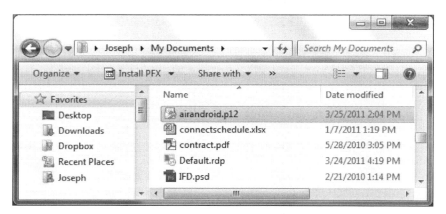

How it works...

By generating a valid digital code signing certificate, we are able to correctly sign our Android application for submission to the Android Market. Using the ADT tools bundled with the AIR SDK, we can generate the appropriate certificate type for distribution.

Preparing icon files for distribution

When we compile an application for distribution in the Android Market, we must include a set of standard icon images along with our application. The locations for these icons are defined within our AIR application descriptor file. Android expects a set of three icons: 36x36, 48x48, and 72x72. Each icon is used for a different screen density and should all be included as standard PNG files.

How to do it...

Depending on which tool is being used, this task can be approached in different ways. We will demonstrate how to include these icons within an application with Flash Professional CS5.5 and through direct modification of the AIR application descriptor file.

Using Flash Professional CS5.5

1. With a project open which targets **AIR for Android**, open the **Properties** panel and click the little wrench icon beside the **Player selection** box. This will open the **AIR for Android Settings** dialog:

2. Within the **AIR for Android Settings** dialog, click the **Icon** tab. To specify specific icons for our project, we simply need to select each icon entry in the list and to browse to locate a file to be used for each one through use of the folder and magnifying glass icon:

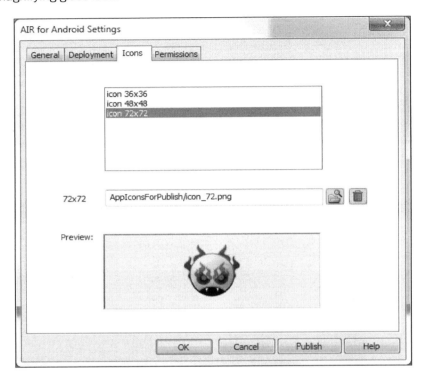

Direct modification of the AIR descriptor file

1. Locate the AIR descriptor file in your project. It is normally named something like {MyProject}-app.xml and resides at the project root.

2. Browse the file for a node named <icon>within this document. This node contains many default settings dealing with the visual aspects of our application window. If it has been commented out, we must uncomment it before proceeding.

3. We now must now make sure that the following three child nodes exist within the <icon> node. Be sure that the paths to our icon files are correct. If they are not correct, the compiler will let us know once we attempt to compile this application:

```
<image36x36>assets/icon_36.png</image36x36>
<image48x48>assets/icon_48.png</image48x48>
<image72x72>assets/icon_72.png</image72x72>
```

As an example, here is a set of three icons that are valid for use in an Android application, along with their pixel measurements:

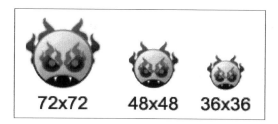

How it works...

Including a set of icons within an Android application package is essential when distributing the application through the Android Market. It also adds an easily recognizable visual cue for the user once the application is installed upon a device. Take some time to come up with a set of icons that really reflect the application they will represent.

There's more...

If the application is to be published onto the Android Market, there are also a variety of other images that we will need to produce to properly brand our application. Check the Android Market for details on what images are currently required at `https://market.android.com/`.

Compiling an application using Flash Professional

Compiling a project to an Android release version `.apk` file is the final step before distributing an application to the Android Market or some other channel. There are many methods of doing this depending upon what tool is being used. In this recipe, we will use the tools available within Flash Professional to compile and package our application.

How to do it...

To compile an `.apk` from Flash Professional, we will take the following steps:

1. With a project open which targets **AIR for Android**, open the **Properties** panel and click the **Publish Settings...** button. This will open the **Publish Settings** dialog:

2. We can look over our settings here and even simply click **Publish** if we know for certain everything is configured appropriately. To verify all of the settings are in place to publish to Android, click the little wrench icon for our **Player selection** box, which should be set to **AIR for Android**. This will provide access to the **AIR for Android Settings** dialog:

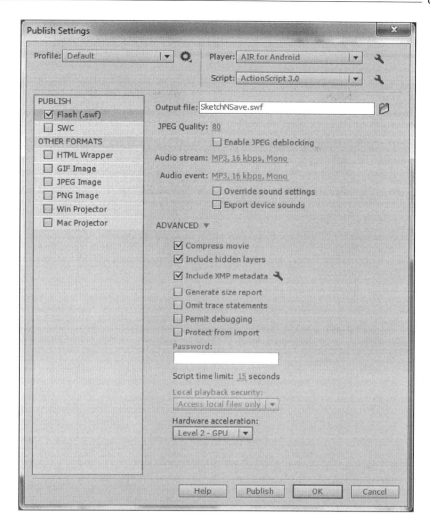

3. With the **AIR for Android Settings** dialog now open, we can go about verifying our **specific configuration** options before deciding to publish. The **General** tab contains a number of important inputs including the path to the generated `.apk` file, the application name, version, ID, and other required configuration settings. We can also choose to include files other than the compiled `.swf` and AIR descriptor file, such as external image assets. The **Icons** tab allows us to include icon files with a basic GUI, and the **Permissions** tab will allow us to set application permissions specific to Android.

These settings all modify the application descriptor file, which in turn generates the Android manifest document. We can think of these settings as a GUI for these files.

4. As a final step, click on the **Deployment** tab:

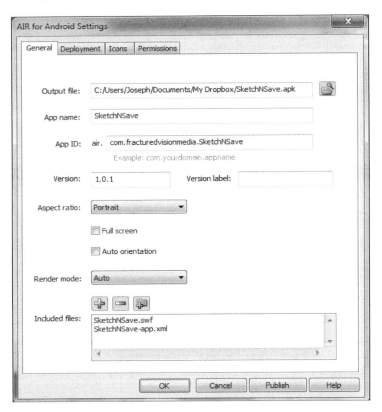

5. Within the **Deployment** tab exists a setting for deployment type and the chance to sign our application with a self-signed certificate. This is very important because the Android Market will not accept unsigned applications or applications which to not fulfill the requirements set for by Android Market terms.

6. Be sure to provide both App name, used to identify the application by a user once installed upon a device, and a unique App ID. The App ID is very important, as this is the primary identifier for your application within the Android Market. It must be unique in order for application updates to function correctly and it is recommended that developers take special care to use reverse domain notation to retain this uniqueness.

7. We will need to be sure that the Get AIR runtime from selection indicates the particular distribution market we are targeting. For the general Android Market, we choose Google Android Market. This dialog also provides us with the option of compiling an application build for different purposes through the Android deployment type settings:

   ❑ **Device release**: This is the option we will need to select when we want to distribute our application through the Android Market

   ❑ **Emulator release**: Generates a release compatible with the Android SDK emulator and the emulator build of the AIR runtime

   ❑ **Debug**: This option generates a release specifically for debugging the application

8. Once we are satisfied with all of our configuration settings, we can exit back out to the **Publish Settings** dialog and hit **Publish**, or simply click the **Publish** button here. We can also publish using traditional methods available in Flash Professional, so long as we've previously gone through these configuration steps.

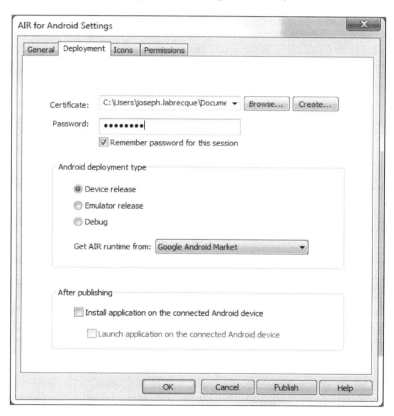

We now have a fully compiled, validly signed `.apk` file ready for distribution.

How it works...

The configuration settings we change through the Flash Professional GUI dialogs are actually modifying the AIR descriptor file behind-the-scenes. Once we choose to publish our application, Flash Professional will use this file to compile and package everything into a valid .apk ready for distribution on the Android Market.

Compiling an application using Flash Builder

Compiling a project to an Android release version .apk file is the final step before distributing an application over the Android Market or some other channel. There are many methods of doing this depending upon what tool is being used. In this recipe, we will use the tools available within Flash Builder to compile and package our application.

How to do it...

To compile an .apk from Flash Builder, take the following steps:

1. Within a mobile ActionScript or Flex project, navigate to the Flash Builder menu and choose the **Project** menu item. This will reveal a submenu with a number of options. From this menu, choose **Export Release Build...** opening the **Export Release Build** dialog window:

2. Within this window, we are given the option to specify the project and specific application within that project we wish to perform a release build upon, decide which platforms to target, specify the path, and filename of our build, and choose what sort of application to export as. For Android, we will choose **Signed packages** for each target platform. So long as we have selected **Google Android** as a target platform, this will open the **Packaging** Settings dialog once we click **Next**:

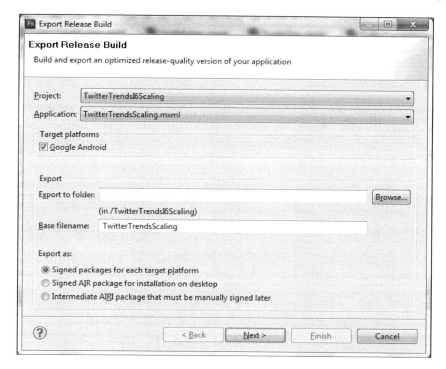

3. Now, we are able to configure some advanced properties for the build. Click on the **Package Contents** tab to verify that all required files are to be included in the build. If we want to package additional files, or even exclude certain assets, we can do so through use of the checkboxes aside each item. Click the **Digital Signature** tab to continue:

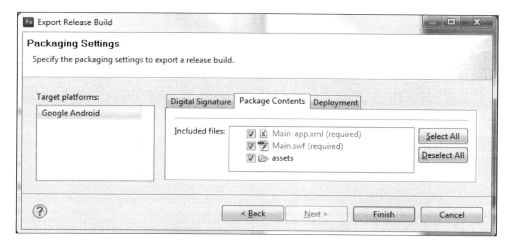

4. The final task will be to choose a signing certificate in order to digitally sign our application for distribution on the Android Market. Select a certificate and type in the associated password. Clicking **Finish** will perform the build and save a compiled .apk into the location we had previously chosen. If we wish, we can include external files through the **Package Contents** tab and choose to deploy to any connected devices through the **Deployment** tab:

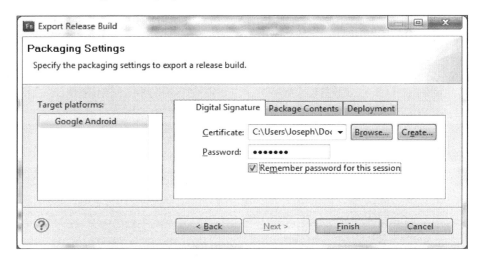

We now have a fully compiled, validly signed .apk file ready for distribution.

How it works...

Flash Builder provides the concept of a target platform when exporting the release build of a project. If we choose Google Android for a target platform, we are given additional options specific to Android that we can modify based on the needs of our particular project. The additional dialog elements allow us to compile and package everything into a valid .apk ready for distribution on the Android Market.

Compiling an application when using FDT

Compiling a project to an Android release version .apk file is the final step before distributing an application over the Android Market or some alternate channel. There are many methods of doing this depending upon what tool is being used. In this recipe, we will discuss three popular methods available to us when using Powerflasher FDT to compile and package our application.

How to do it...

As of this writing, FDT does not support working with AIR for Android in a direct way. There are, however, three main methods in which FDT users can compile their projects for Android distribution.

Using a mobile project template

The FDT community has produced a number of mobile project templates that support AIR for Android. These templates work with the new template system used by all FDT projects and add varying levels of functionality to the workflow. Most of these also include ANT scripts, which compile an .apk using the AIR Developer Tool.

Using ANT

This is by far the most flexible method of compiling a project for Android, as it is actually IDE-agnostic and can be used by anyone. ANT comes packaged along with a standard installation of FDT and many starter scripts deploying AIR for Android can be found online through the community. To get started using ANT with FDT, have a look at `http://fdt.powerflasher.com/docs/FDT_Ant_Tasks`.

Using ADT through CLI

The most basic method is to simply develop a mobile project using FDT and then package it as an .apk using the AIR Developer Tool through command line interface. The next recipe actually details how this is accomplished.

How it works...

Whichever method is chosen, the goal is the same—compile and package everything into a valid .apk ready for distribution on the Android Market. One of the strengths of FDT is that it does not restrict developers to do things in one specific way. When producing release builds for Android, we have many choices with which to do so.

Compiling an application using the AIR Developer Tool

Compiling a project to an Android release version .apk file is the final step before distributing an application over the Android Market or some other channel. There are many methods of doing this depending upon what tool is being used. In this recipe, we will use the **AIR Developer Tool** (**ADT**) command line utility to compile and package our application.

How to do it...

To compile an `.apk` from a mobile AIR project using the ADT command line tools, we will take the following steps:

1. For this example, we will assume the following:

   ❑ **Certificate**: android.p12

   ❑ **Desired APK**: `mobileAIR.apk`

   ❑ **AIR Descriptor**: `mobileAIR\src\mobileAIR-app.xml`

   ❑ **SWF File**: `mobileAIR\src\mobileAIR.swf`

2. Open a command prompt or terminal (depending upon the operating system) and type in the command string to generate our certificate. In this case, we will set the target type to `.apk` for a release build. We could also set this to apk-debug for a debug build, or apk-emulator for installation on an emulator:

   ```
   -package -target apk -storetype pkcs12 -keystore android.p12
   mobileAIR.apkmobileAIR\src\mobileAIR-app.xml mobileAIR\src\
   mobileAIR.swf
   ```

3. Any other files such as assets or icons can be included after the .swf entry, delimited by whitespaces:

   ```
   -package -target apk -storetype pkcs12 -keystore android.p12
   mobileAIR.apkmobileAIR\src\mobileAIR-app.xml mobileAIR\src\
   mobileAIR.swf mobileAIR\src\assets\icon_32.pngmobileAIR\src\
   assets\icon_36.pngmobileAIR\src\assets\icon_72.png
   ```

4. The ADT utility will now process the command and complete the `.apk` compilation process. If there is a problem with our command, ADT will print out error messages here, letting us know something went wrong. Normally, if something does go wrong, it will be a problem with the AIR descriptor file or an incorrect file path to an expected input file.

5. We can now browse to the result location specified within the command string to locate our newly created `.apk` file, which can be installed directly upon an Android device or distributed through the Android Market:

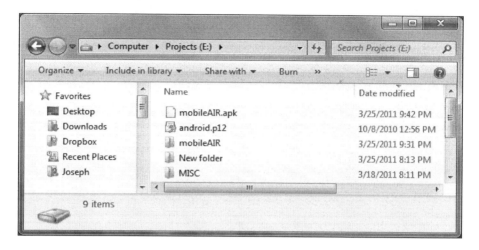

We now have a fully compiled, validly signed `.apk` file ready for distribution.

How it works...

Assuming we have configured our application properly, ADT will compile, sign, and package all of our project files into an `.apk` for us. ADT has many different utilities and configuration options available to perform many actions upon a project. Have a look at `http://help.adobe.com/en_US/air/build/` and click **AIR Developer Tool** (**ADT**) in the menu for full documentation.

See also...

For steps on configuring ADT within your particular environment, take a look at *Chapter 1, Getting Ready to Work with Android*: *Development Environment and Project Setup*.

Submitting an application to the Android Market

Google makes it very easy to register as an Android Developer and publish applications to the Android Market. This recipe will detail the steps necessary to do so, after compiling a completed `.apk`.

Getting ready...

Before a developer is able to submit anything to the Android Market, a developer account must be created. The process can be completed in minutes, is simple, and inexpensive.

To register as an Android developer:

1. Use a web browser and go to `http://market.android.com/publish/signup`.
2. Sign in with your Google Account (or create a new account).
3. Complete the registration form and pay the one time setup fee of $25.
4. Congratulations on becoming an Android Developer!

How to do it...

1. Upload a compiled and signed `.apk` file to the Android Market for worldwide distribution.
2. Sign in to the Android Market at `https://market.android.com/publish/` using your Android Developer credentials.
3. Click on the button in the lower right that says **Upload Application**:

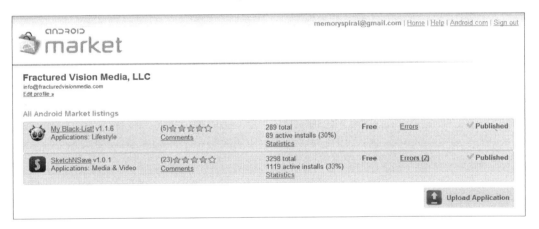

4. We are now presented with a rather lengthy form which allows us to include all sorts of information about our application. We can categorize our application, add descriptive and promotional text, update release notes, and choose whether we will charge users for the application or allow free downloads. If we decide to require payment, we must first establish a Google Merchant account from the provided link on this page.

5. In addition to textual entries and other input choices, we also have the opportunity to upload a wide variety of images which will represent our application in the Android Market. Specific image attributes are detailed within this form:

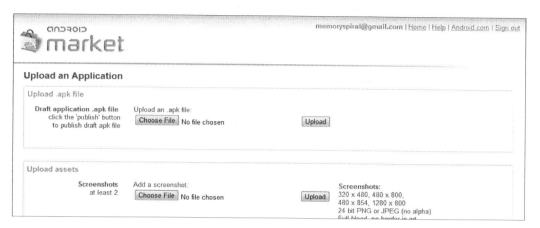

6. At the bottom of this page are three buttons. We can click **Save** to save our application profile for later editing. Clicking the **Delete** button will allow us to remove an application from the Android Market completely. To publish our application, we will click the **Publish** button.

 Once you publish an application, this button will read as **Unpublish**, and the **Delete** button will no longer appear as an option if users have installed the application.

The application has now been published to the Android Market and is available to millions of users worldwide.

How it works...

Uploading and publishing an application to the Android Market will allow users to download and install the application. We have full control over the application description, versioning information, and associated image assets. We are also able to track rating and comments from the developer area, as well as manage a merchant account, if necessary to our application. Publication to the Android Market is immediate. There is no approval and disapproval process like there is with other application marketplaces.

There's more...

Updating an application to a new version is much simpler than setting up an entirely new application:

1. Once in the Android Market, click the name of an existing application. This will allow you to edit any of the images or text associated with it.

2. To actually publish a new version of the application, we must click the link [Upload Upgrade]. This will cause a new set of form controls to appear.

3. Click **Choose File** and browse for the new .apk file. Now click **Upload** to submit the file to Google servers.

4. The new file will be parsed for versioning information and to verify the contents are valid. Any changes to the version number, application icon, requested permissions, and so forth will be reflected in the draft.

5. The version number defined within the application descriptor file must be of a higher version than that of the previously submitted build in order to have a valid upgrade. We can also perform additional edits to the general application information on this page, if necessary. Clicking **Publish** at the bottom of the page will make the new version immediately available in the Android Market.

Index

Thank you for buying
Flash Development for Android Cookbook

About Packt Publishing

Packt, pronounced 'packed', published its first book "*Mastering phpMyAdmin for Effective MySQL Management*" in April 2004 and subsequently continued to specialize in publishing highly focused books on specific technologies and solutions.

Our books and publications share the experiences of your fellow IT professionals in adapting and customizing today's systems, applications, and frameworks. Our solution based books give you the knowledge and power to customize the software and technologies you're using to get the job done. Packt books are more specific and less general than the IT books you have seen in the past. Our unique business model allows us to bring you more focused information, giving you more of what you need to know, and less of what you don't.

Packt is a modern, yet unique publishing company, which focuses on producing quality, cutting-edge books for communities of developers, administrators, and newbies alike. For more information, please visit our website: www.packtpub.com.

Writing for Packt

We welcome all inquiries from people who are interested in authoring. Book proposals should be sent to author@packtpub.com. If your book idea is still at an early stage and you would like to discuss it first before writing a formal book proposal, contact us; one of our commissioning editors will get in touch with you.

We're not just looking for published authors; if you have strong technical skills but no writing experience, our experienced editors can help you develop a writing career, or simply get some additional reward for your expertise.

Android User Interface Development: Beginner's Guide

ISBN: 978-1-849514-48-4   Paperback: 304 pages

Quickly design and develop compelling user interfaces for your Android applications

1. Leverage the Android platform's flexibility and power to design impactful user-interfaces

2. Build compelling, user-friendly applications that will look great on any Android device

3. Make your application stand out from the rest with styles and themes

4. A practical Beginner's Guide to take you step-by-step through the process of developing user interfaces to get your applications noticed!

Flash Multiplayer Virtual Worlds

ISBN: 978-1-849690-36-2   Paperback: 412 pages

Build immersive, full-featured interactive worlds for games, online communities, and more

1. Build virtual worlds in Flash and enhance them with avatars, non player characters, quests, and by adding social network community

2. Design, present, and integrate the quests to the virtual worlds

3. Create a whiteboard that every connected user can draw on

4. A practical guide filled with real-world examples of building virtual worlds

Please check **www.PacktPub.com** for information on our titles

Flash 10 Multiplayer Game Essentials

ISBN: 978-1-847196-60-6   Paperback: 336 pages

Create exciting real-time multiplayer games using Flash

1. A complete end-to-end guide for creating fully featured multiplayer games

2. The author's experience in the gaming industry enables him to share insights on multiplayer game development

3. Walk-though several real-time multiplayer game implementations

4. Packed with illustrations and code snippets with supporting explanations for ease of understandingl

Cocos2d for iPhone 0.99 Beginner's Guide

ISBN: 978-1-849513-16-6   Paperback: 368 pages

Make mind-blowing 2D games for iPhone with this fast, flexible, and easy-to-use framework!

1. A cool guide to learning cocos2d with iPhone to get you into the iPhone game industry quickly

2. Learn all the aspects of cocos2d while building three different games

3. Add a lot of trendy features such as particles and tilemaps to your games to captivate your players

4. Full of illustrations, diagrams, and tips for building iPhone games, with clear step-by-step instructions and practical examples

Please check **www.PacktPub.com** for information on our titles

Printed in Great Britain
by Amazon.co.uk, Ltd.,
Marston Gate.